MANCHESTER AIRPORT

THROUGH TIME

Peter C. Brown

AMBERLEY

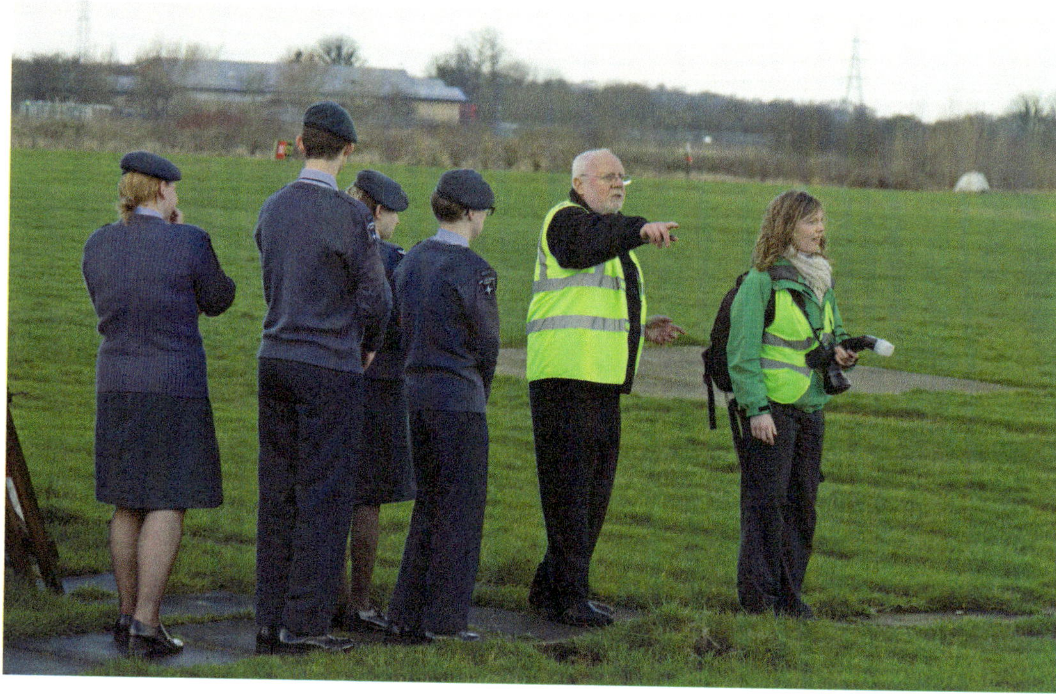

Eric Isaac directs air cadets on a helicopter landing on 3 March 2012 – the ninetieth anniversary of the Lancashire Aero Club's formation. (Chris Barham, Lancashire Aero Club)

In memory of Dr Eric Isaac, Vice Chairman, Lancashire Aero Club

First published 2017

Amberley Publishing
The Hill, Stroud, Gloucestershire, GL5 4EP
www.amberley-books.com

ISBN 978 1 4456 6390 6 (print)
ISBN 978 1 4456 6391 3 (ebook)

British Library Cataloguing in Publication Data.
A catalogue record for this book is available from the British Library.

Origination by Amberley Publishing.
Printed in Great Britain.

Glossary

ATR – Aerei da Trasporto Regionale is a French-Italian aircraft manufacturer
EGCB – ICAO code for Barton/City Airport
EGCC – ICAO code for Manchester/Ringway Airport
IATA – International Air Transport Association
ICAO – International Civil Aviation Organisation
Lorenz – C. Lorenz AG (1880–1958) was a German electrical and electronics firm primarily located in Berlin, which innovated, developed and marketed products for telephony, radar and radio
MAN – IATA code for Manchester Airport

The involvement of the city of Manchester with aviation dates back to James Sadler who, on 12 May 1785, became the first man to take to the air from the city in a balloon ascent from a field behind a garden on what is now Balloon Street. The first powered flight was made by the pioneering French aviator Isidore Auguste Marie Louis Paulhan (known as Louis Paulhan), who had won a race from London to Manchester against Claude Grahame-White to collect the £10,000 prize money offered by the *Daily Mail* to the first aviator to fly the 185-mile (298 km) distance (with no more than two stops) in under 24 hours. Paulhan landed his Farman III biplane in the early hours of 28 April 1910 at Barcicroft Fields at Pytha Fold Farm, on the borders of Withington, Burnage and Didsbury. A plaque at 25–27 Paulhan Road commemorates the flight.

Trafford Park

Manchester Aerodrome Ltd was formed in late 1910 to rent and prepare a surface for flying in a large part of the former deer park of Trafford Hall, just south of the Manchester ship canal between Trafford Park Road, Moseley Road and Ashburton Road. Subsequently, in the summer of 1911, the all-grass Trafford Park Aerodrome was opened. Henry Greg Melly, one of the north-west's pioneer aviators, is believed to be the first person to use the aerodrome, when on 7 July 1911, he flew his Gnome Blériot monoplane with fellow aviator Arthur Dukinfield-Jones as passenger on a non-stop flight from his base at Waterloo (just north of Liverpool) to meet aircraft pioneer and manufacturer Alliott Verdon Roe for lunch at Trafford Hall. The flight took only 40 minutes, and they returned non-stop to their Liverpool base later the same day in 63 minutes – at the same time becoming the first heavier-than-air flight to depart from Manchester. The centenary of Melly's flight was commemorated on 7 July 2011 by five light aircraft from the Liverpool Flying School: one Piper Cherokee (G-LFSG) and four Tomahawk (G-LFSA, G-LFSH, G-LFSM and G-LFSN) aircraft.

Around 8,000 people gathered at Trafford Park on 25 July 1911 to greet the remaining competitors in the five-day *Daily Mail* Circuit of Britain Air Race (which started at Brooklands, Surrey, with seventeen competitors on 22 July), who reached Trafford Park from Edinburgh via Carlisle – a distance of 103 miles. The French aviator Lieutenant Jean Louis Conneau (aka André Beaumont), in his Bleriot XI, was the first to arrive, winning the £10,000 prize money put up by the proprietors of the newspaper for the first to complete the circuit. He was followed by only three other flyers who completed the course: Jules Védrines in a Morane-Borel monoplane, James Valentine in a Deperdussin monoplane, and Samuel Franklin Cody in *Cathedral* – his own Cody III biplane.

The aerodrome was little used other than for trial flying after that event, although on 20 June 1914 it was the turning point for a Hendon–Birmingham–Manchester and Return Air Race, which drew a crowd of 100,000 people. Louis Strange was the first to arrive in his Bleriot monoplane – however, that was as far as he got after the Lord Mayor of Manchester stepped on a bracing wire to the landing gear upon greeting him. It subsequently broke upon take-off and smashed the Bleriot's propeller, putting Strange out of the race, which was won instead by Walter L. Brock in a Grahame-White-built Morane-Saulnier G monoplane. The aerodrome finally closed in 1918 and, today, Tenax Road (A576), which used to form part of the Manchester–York stagecoach route, runs north–south through the centre of the site of the old airfield, which was completely built over with what was to become the world's first industrial estate.

Alexandra Park

Taking its name from the nearby Alexandra Park railway station on the Great Central Railway branch line to Manchester, Alexandra Park Aerodrome was constructed and opened in May 1918 by the War Department, primarily for the assembly, test flying, and delivery of aeroplanes for the Royal Air Force (RAF). Two sets of large triple Belfast Truss hangars had been built to accommodate the aeroplanes, which were brought in major sections by rail and road to the aerodrome from A. V. Roe & Co. (Avro) at Newton Heath and the National Aircraft Factory (NAF) No. 2 at Heaton Chapel. A Relief Landing Ground was designated a mile away at Turn Moss, Stretford.

Civil flying in Britain returned on 1 May 1919 and, between 24 May and 30 September, the Avro Transport Company operated the UK's first scheduled air service, using (mainly) Avro 504 three-seat biplanes for the 45-minute flight from Alexandra Park via Birkdale Sands, Southport, to South Shore, Blackpool.

Daimler Airways operated a daily scheduled flight from Alexandra Park to Croydon Airport, London, from October 1922 until early 1924, and was the first company to use de Havilland DH.34 single-engine cabin biplanes.

John Fishwick Leeming, a businessman and early aviator, founded the Lancashire Aero Club (LAC) – the oldest established flying club in the country – in 1922. He was unstinting in his efforts to promote in the minds of businessmen and councillors that vision of growing success founded on readily available flights from a local airport. He had designed and built his own single-seat, high-wing monoplane glider, which he built with his friends and fellow glider builders Tom Prince and Clement Wood. It first flew on 24 May 1924 at Alexandra Park Aerodrome but, when the wartime lease ended in 1925, the land was scheduled for urban development, and the club moved to Woodford Aerodrome upon invitation from the Avro Aircraft Company (where there was also a good source of spares).

There, the club acquired its first two powered aircraft: de Havilland DH.60 Moths. LAC were requested to vacate Woodford at the start of the Second World War and moved to Barton, where all of their aircraft were impounded for the duration of the war. Post-war, the club started up again, initially using Auster Autocrat and de Havilland Tiger Moth aircraft. LAC moved to Kenyon Hall Farm (near Wigan) in 2007, which has a single 580 m by 30 m grass strip (23/05); it is where they currently operate flying seasons between March and late October.

The aerodrome was closed to air traffic on 24 August 1945. Under the terms of the land lease laid down by Maurice Egerton, the 4th Baron Egerton of Tatton, flying was to cease within five years of the end of the war. The ancillary buildings that had been erected for training RAF personnel were converted to provide accommodation for around 100 single constables of the Manchester City Police because of a desperate shortage of housing for families of men returning from the war. Avro moved to Woodford airfield, and the hangars were demolished. The site remained undeveloped until the Hough End playing fields were laid out in 1945. A plaque commemorating the aerodrome's existence hangs in the sports pavilion.

Wythenshawe

The famous aviator pioneer Sir Alan Cobham became famous for his exploits in the interwar years – one of his many contributions was the 'air-to-air' refuelling technique, while his development of the 'probe and drogue' is still used by air forces across the globe today. It was during the 1920s that he and Sir Sefton Brancker, the Director of Civil Aviation, set out together on a campaign to persuade councils to set up aerodromes to facilitate the potential benefits of air transport. Manchester's council, which was in desperate need of land to house the city's rapidly increasing population, began to realise that Manchester needed a permanent airport.

Manchester Corporation, which had been the recipient of a donation by the 1st Baron Simon of Wythenshawe Hall and 250 acres of land, purchased the rest of the estate, and what was once farmland was transformed into one of Britain's largest housing estates. Four fields located in the fork of Sale Road and Wythenshawe Road, west of the intersection with today's Princess Parkway and just north of Wythenshawe Park, were allocated for use as the Manchester (Wythenshawe) Aerodrome (although it was known locally as Rackhouse Aerodrome). Some ground had to be levelled and some hedges taken out, while a barn was converted to act as the hangar (which had space for only one aircraft) and a farmhouse fitted to serve as an office. It was very basic; there were no radio or lighting facilities, but it had the provision for fuel from temporary pumps that were installed. The airfield was identified from the air by the letters 'M/C' encircled on the ground.

The Lord Mayor of Manchester flew from the aerodrome with a civic party on 22 April 1929 to collect a temporary operating licence, with which it became the UK's first municipal airfield. An air pageant was held on 22 June, which attracted many aircraft and large crowds of spectators. Between April 1929 and early 1930, it was the base for the blue-and-silver two-seat de Havilland DH.60 Moths and Avro 504Ks of Northern Airlines (Manchester), which were used for charter work and private flying.

The last recorded flight from Wythenshawe took place on 19 June 1930 and, following a southward extension of Manchester's city boundaries in the same year, the site was developed for social housing.

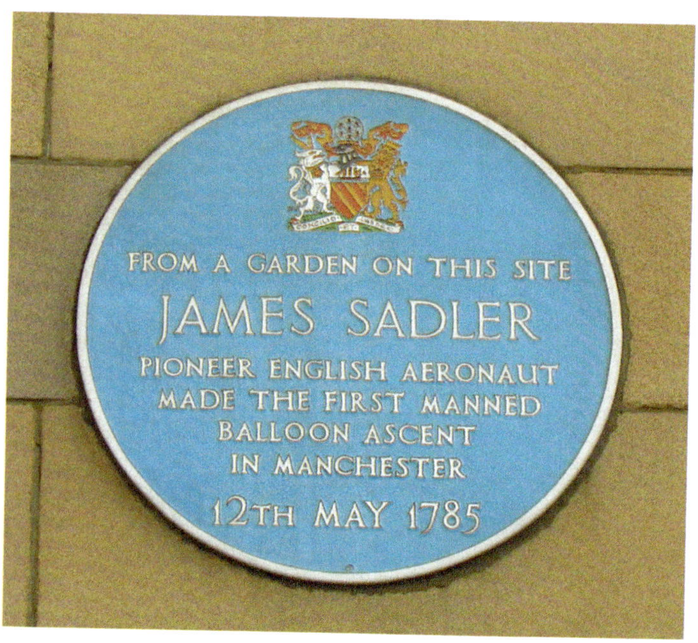

The blue plaque erected in Balloon Street in 1974, commemorating the first manned balloon ascent from Manchester by James Sadler. (Author's Collection)

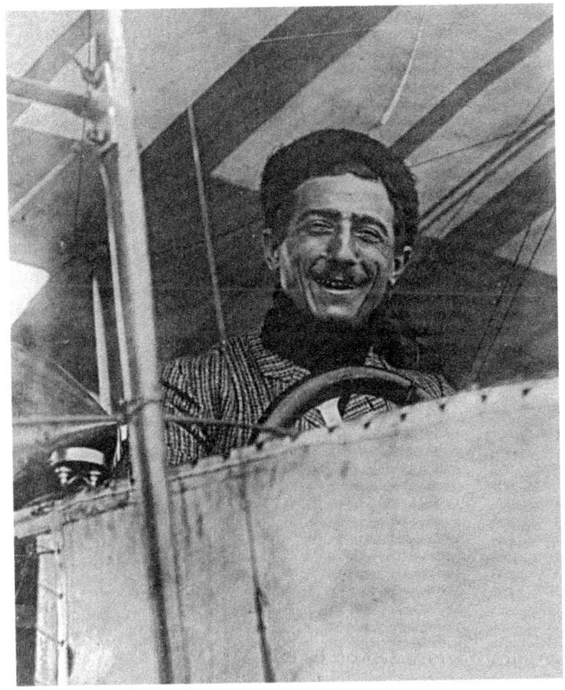

Right: Louis Paulhan (1883–1963) won several air races in 1910 (London–Manchester and the Dominguez International Air Meet in Los Angeles).

Below: Louis Paulhan flying with a passenger in his Henry Farman biplane in 1910.

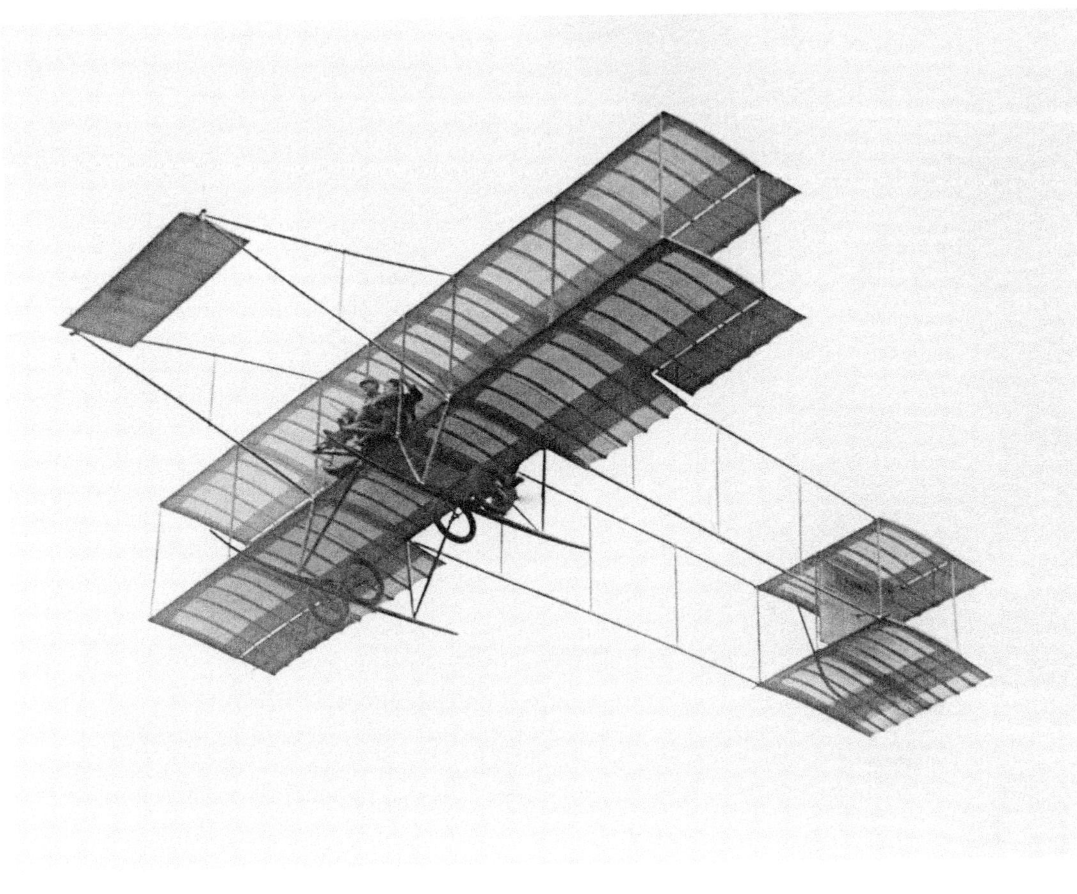

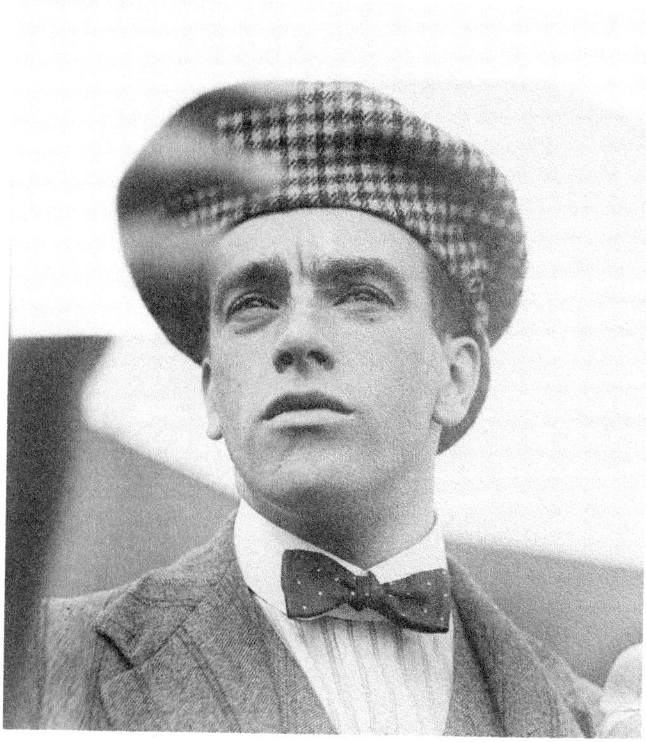

Left: Claude Grahame-White (1879–1959) was a pioneer of aviation, and the first to make a night flight during the *Daily Mail* London to Manchester race in 1910. (George Grantham Bain Collection)

Below: Alexandra Park Aerodrome hangars in 1923, looking west. (RingwayObserver)

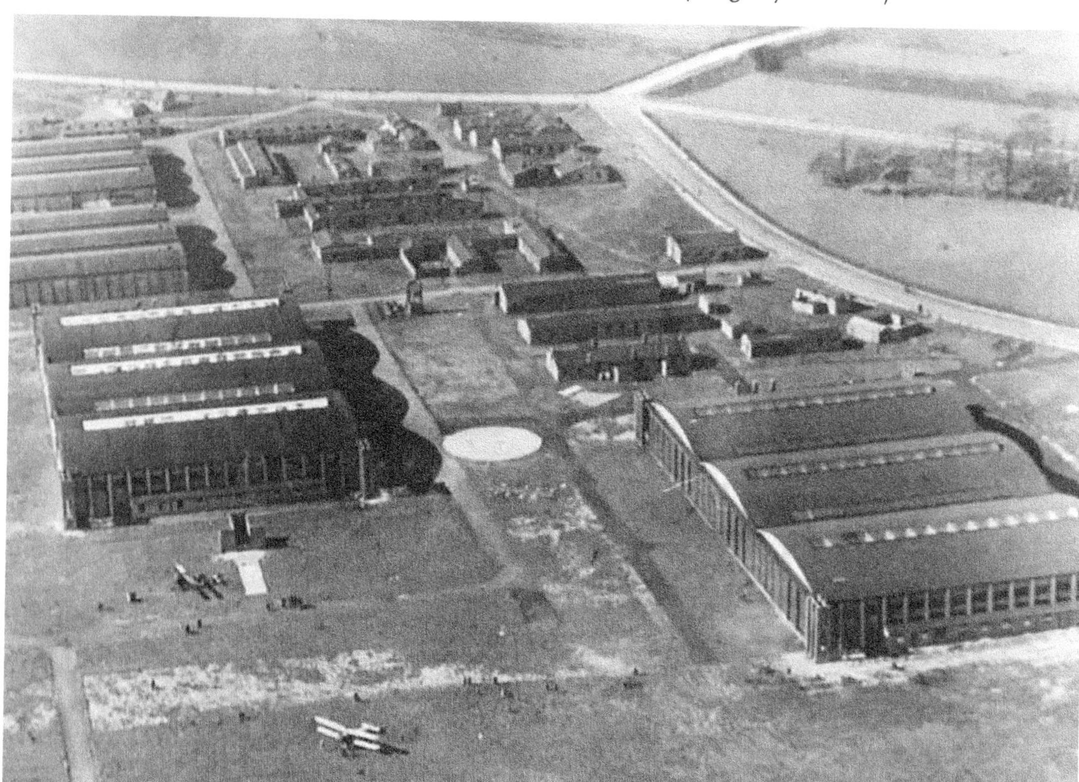

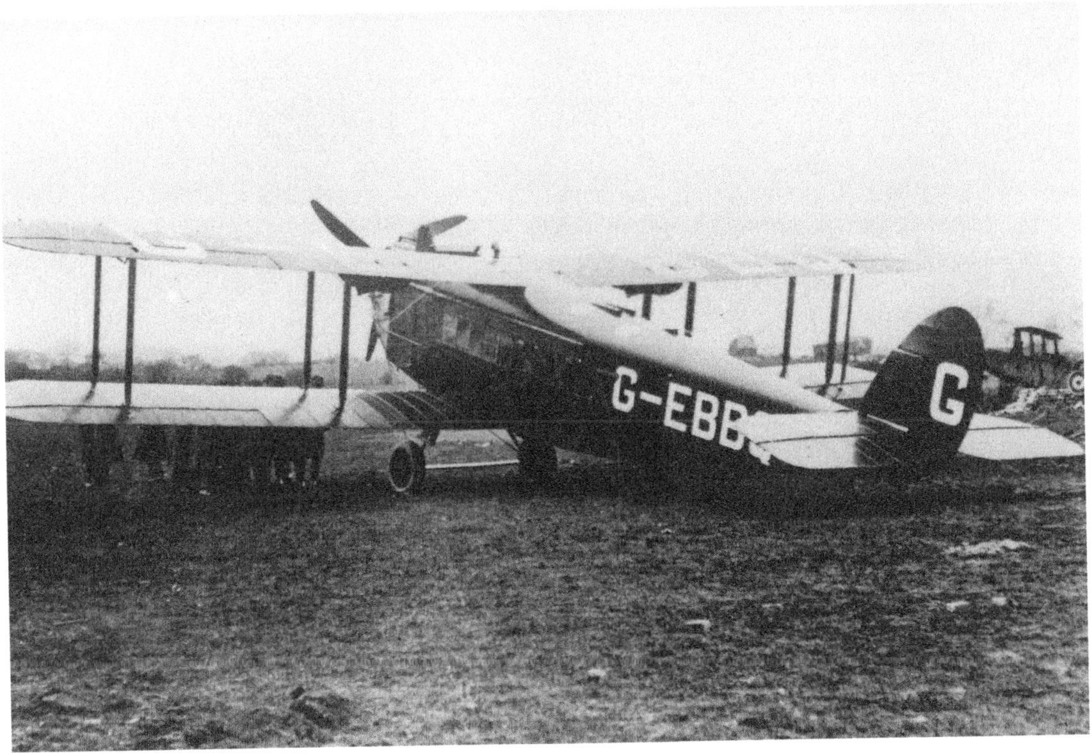

Above: The first prototype single-propeller de Havilland DH.34 (G-EBBQ) had a ten-passenger capacity and served with Daimler Airways. (Author's Collection)

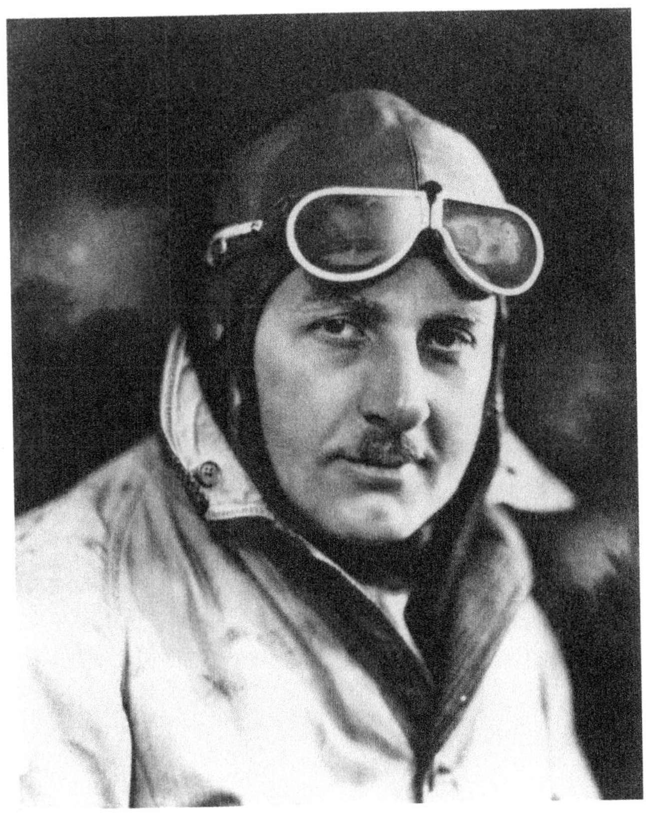

Right: Sir Alan John Cobham, KBE, AFC, explorer and pioneer of long-distance flight and aircraft technology.

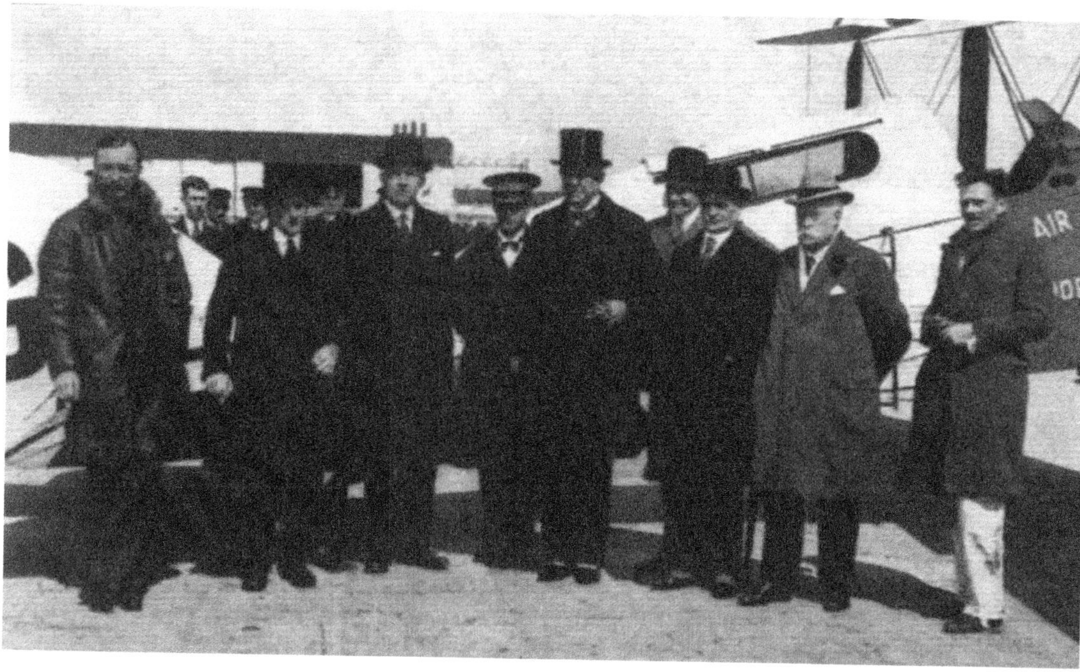

John F. Leeming, a director of Northern Air Lines Ltd (in the top hat), with a delegation of Manchester's civic officials at Croydon receiving the licence for Manchester's aerodrome from Sir Samuel Hoare on 22 April 1929. (*Flight*, 25 April 1929)

Barton/City Airport (ICAO: EGCB)

Manchester City Council has led the country since 1928 in resolving to have a municipal airport; Fox Hill Farm at Barton, alongside the present Liverpool Road (A57) just west of Eccles, was chosen as the site. The city's cleansing department already owned 2,600 acres of the land and, with additional persuasion by businessman and early aviator John Fishwick Leeming, an area of 80 acres east of the Fox Hill Glen area was selected, and construction began in March 1929.

The ground was actually quite unsuitable and required extensive drainage to cure a serious waterlogging problem. However, following the ground work, and the completion of a large brick-walled hangar and the control tower (designed by architect G. Noel Hill), Barton became the first municipal airport outside London that was able to communicate with aircraft in flight and give pilots bearings from the airfield. When it was officially opened on 1 June 1930, the aerodrome also became the first municipal airfield in the UK to be licensed by the Air Ministry. It was managed by Northern Air Lines (co-founded by John Leeming and Mr F. J. V. Holmes, acting as managers for the Manchester Corporation), who based several Avro 504 biplanes and other types for training, club, and charter flights there until 1933. The first use by a large aircraft at Barton was an Imperial Airways' three-engine Argosy on 23 May 1930, and the company operated a thrice-weekly scheduled service to London's Croydon Airport via Castle Bromwich Aerodrome, and Birmingham during the summer of 1930.

Barton was very quiet between 1931 and 1933 and, despite Railway Air Services (RAS) of Croydon starting a scheduled Croydon–Barton–Belfast–Glasgow route in August 1934 using a fleet of newly delivered de Havilland DH.89 Dragon Rapides, it was becoming clear to the council that the grass airfield was too small. It was inadequate when it came to handling the larger airliners such as the Douglas DC-2 and DC-3, which were then coming into service, and it was therefore not a viable location for a truly international airport. This view was endorsed by KLM (Royal Dutch Airlines) – who had been approached by the council about using the airport as a terminal for regular flights between Manchester and Holland – following a report by one of their pilots, Capt. Ivan Vasilyevich Smirnoff (the First World War Russian flying ace), who had been sent to the airport on 23 January 1934 using a Fokker F.XII three-engine high-winged monoplane airliner via Hull to Barton to test its facilities. He reported that Barton was totally unsuitable for the larger, heavier aircraft coming into service:

> The airfield is very small. Extensions would be very costly. From a meteorological standpoint (fog), this is the worst airfield in Europe known to me. Surrounding obstructions such as chimneys and pylons, etc., make approaches dangerous. Do not spend any more money on Barton, but find a more open ground.

This was a bad blow for the council, and the rejection led directly to the decision to seek another site for the airport. On 25 July 1934, following a report by aeronautical consultants, a site at Ringway, 8 miles south of Manchester city centre, was selected from several alternatives and approved, although only by one vote.

Barton was used for operations by the Air Ministry during the Second World War, after which it was returned to general aviation use. Ownership of the airfield was transferred to the Manchester Ship Canal Development Co., part of Peel Holdings in 2002, although it continued to be operated by the LAC until 2007, when the airport was renamed 'City Airport (Manchester)'. The operation of the airport was also transferred at this point to City Airport Manchester Ltd (and the name later changed to 'City Airport Ltd'), a subsidiary of Peel Airports. The management of the airport moved from Peel Airports to Peel Holdings in 2011; it is still a functioning airport, operating seven days a week for fixed-wing light aircraft, military, police, and air ambulance helicopters.

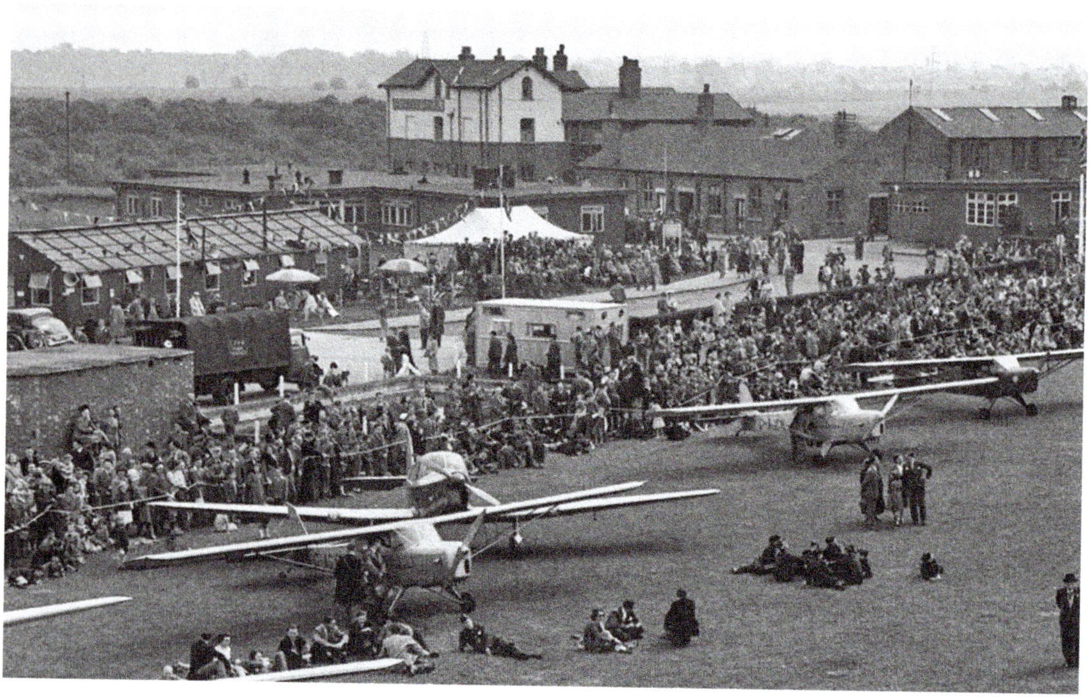

Barton Aerodrome in June 1951. Pictured is the pre-war Airport Hotel in Liverpool Road, with 1930s buildings converted to passenger facilities, behind a line-up that includes Auster J-1 Autocrat (G-AGYD). (RingwayObserver)

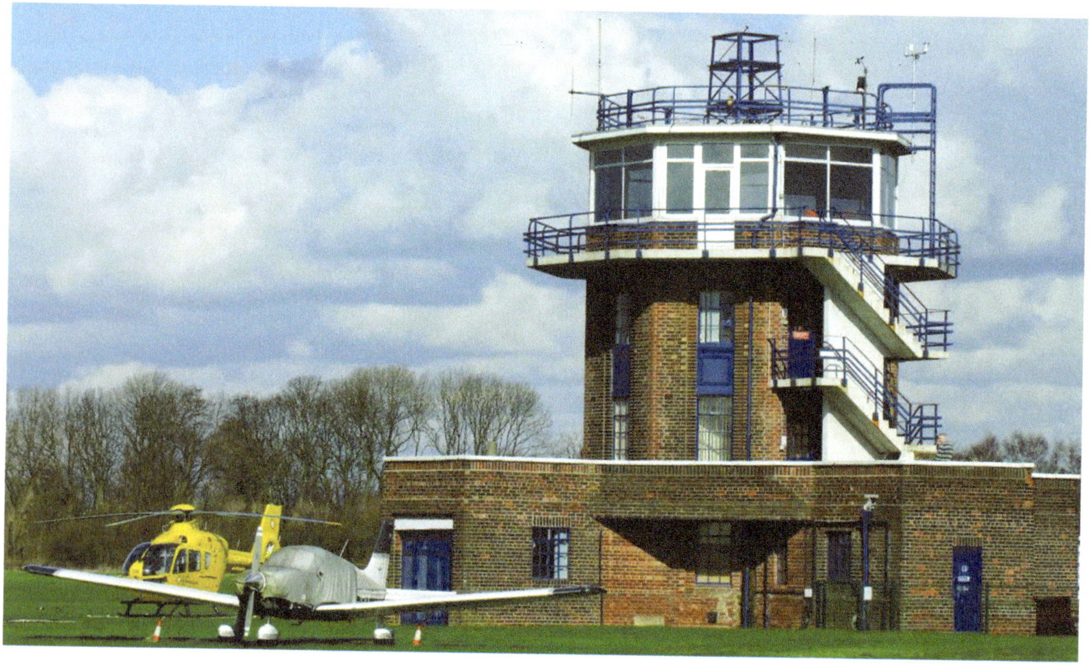

A view of the tower at City Airport Manchester, formerly known as Barton Aerodrome, on 18 March 2012. (Paul Atkinson)

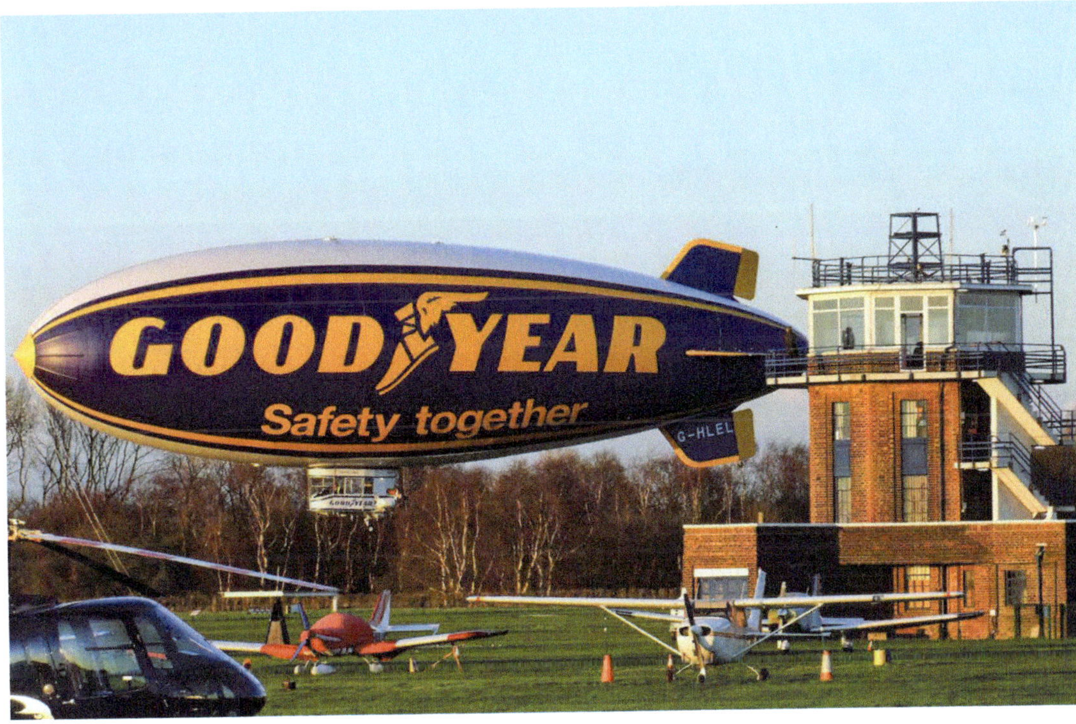

American Blimp Corporation A-60+ (G-HLEL), seen during its evening arrival at City Airport Manchester on 18 March 2012. (Paul Atkinson)

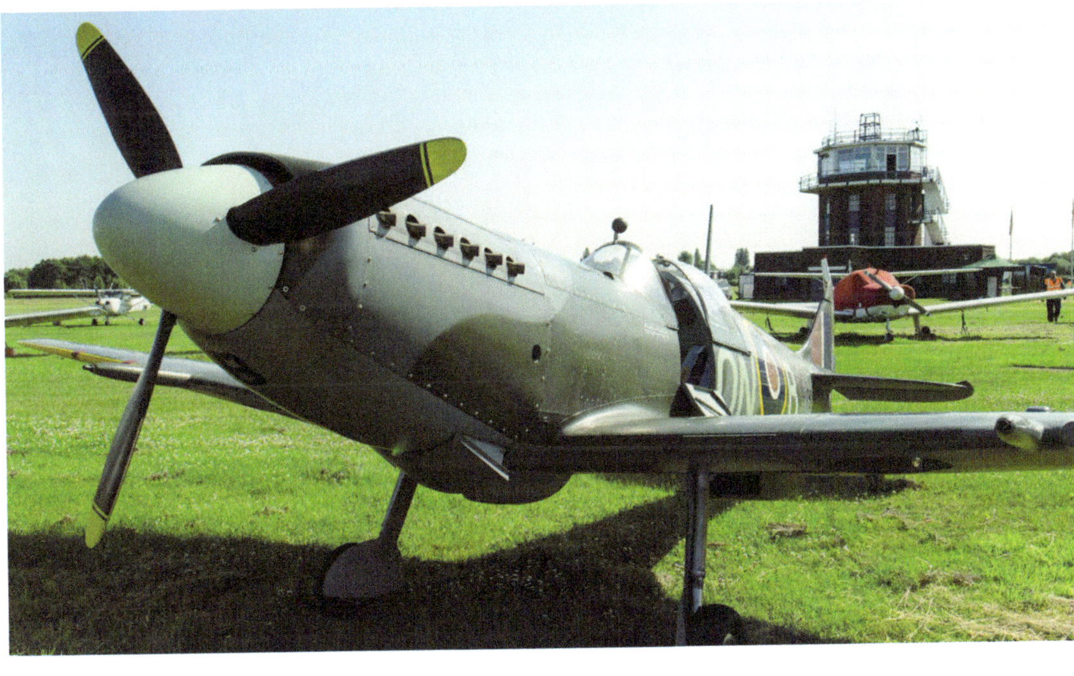

The replica Supermarine Spitfire Mk 26 (PV303) (G-CCJL), on display with Barton's historic tower in the background, on 7 July 2013. (Paul Atkinson)

Ringway (IATA: MAN, ICAO: EGCC)

Construction of the all-grass airfield at Ringway began after being ceremonially started by Alderman Joseph Toole on 28 November 1935. Its first use was on 17 May 1937, when a de Havilland Hornet Moth DH.87B (G-ADND), piloted by Duncan Menzies and bound for Barton airfield while en route from White Waltham in Berkshire, was forced by heavy rain to land at Ringway. This was a month before the first (westerly) portion was opened in June 1937 for use as a flight-testing facility by Fairey Aviation, who at the time were producing large numbers of the single-engine Fairey Battle light bombers for the RAF. On 17 May 2012, Duncan Menzies's son Peter returned to Manchester in G-ADND (W9385/YG-L), which was flown by its owner David Weston, to mark the airport's seventy-fifth birthday.

An assembly hangar was opened for Fairey Aviation from 8 June 1938, but was not officially opened for public use until 25 June. Two days later, Ringway handled its first scheduled flight: a KLM (Royal Dutch Airlines) operated a Douglas DC-2 – the first all-metal aircraft – to Amsterdam.

The first Runway Contact Light System outside the USA was installed in January 1939 to allow airport operators and ministry officials the opportunity to assess its performance in assisting the pilot from the ground in adverse weather conditions. The system of lighting was evolved for use in conjunction with the 'Lorenz' blind-landing radio navigation system, enabling the pilot to approach the airport down the beam to the last marker beacon, and then pick up the series of lights (known as Chance lights after the manufacturer of the system, Chance Brothers & Co. Ltd, of Smethwick, Staffordshire) with their coloured filters and illuminated cross-strips to gauge his position accurately in relation to the line down which he was landing.

The terminal building was the westernmost of the large buildings and incorporated the control tower, administration, restaurant, and the hangar, which was later called Hangar 1. It was adequate for the traffic of the day, which included services to UK destinations and Amsterdam. 7,600 passengers used the airport in the first fourteen months (which would account for a quiet hour in today's figures of over 61,000 passengers a day).

RAF Ringway

During the Second World War, Ringway became the main training centre for Britain's airborne forces; it was selected because it was far enough away from German raids, and the intense fighter and bomber activity over the eastern counties. Construction of a Royal Air Force station, which included two large hangars, workshops, barrack blocks and ancillary accommodation, had already started in the north-east corner of the airport during spring 1939, and was completed in March 1940.

RAF Ringway was initially used by No. 1 Operational Training Unit (OTU), RAF Coastal Command, and the Women's Auxiliary Air Force (WAAF) were set up in No. 6 hangar for parachute packing, where their teams worked eight-hour shifts around the clock.

Following a directive by Prime Minister Winston Churchill in mid-June that a force of 5,000 trained allied paratroopers (including male and female agents of the Special Operations Executive (SOE)) be created forthwith, a 'Central Landing School' (CLS – later to be known as the Parachute Training School (PTS)) was established. Squadron Leader Louis Strange, DSO MC DFC, arrived at Ringway to take command on the day of its official formation on 21 June. Other RAF personnel arrived over the next few days and, by 5 July, the first pilots were passed out on the unit's only aircraft – a converted Armstrong Whitworth Whitley bomber.

The airfield was bombed by the Luftwaffe during the Manchester Blitz on 28 November 1940 but, although no significant damage was caused, the all-grass runway, which always suffered badly in wet weather, froze solid during the winter of that year. The ruts caused damage to the undercarriage of taxiing aircraft. Between June and December 1941, two asphalt runways of 3,000 ft (910 m) length were laid down, designated 06/24 and 10/28. 06/24 was lengthened to 4,200 ft (1300 m) in January 1943 to accommodate four-engine aircraft, and a 3,300 ft (1,000 m) third runway (02/20) was also constructed. Three large permanent south-side hangars (numbered 521, 522, and 523) were built in 1941/2 to Ministry of Aircraft production designs; they were used for the assembly of Avro York military transport aircraft.

The landing ground at Ringway was soon deemed too busy for the trainee paratroopers, and an alternative location was found via Lord Maurice Egerton, who owned the large, secluded historic Tatton Park Estate, strategically located to the north of the town of Knutsford, just 5 miles south of Ringway. Initially only used as the main dropping zone, with the first drop taking place on 13 July, it was expanded as the intensity of parachuting activities increased. A 3,600 ft (1,090 m) emergency NE-SW landing strip was laid down, which was used by the Whitley and Vickers Wellington bombers, along with other aircraft that were placed for storage during 1942/3. Lord Egerton's co-operation contributed a great deal to the early success of the PTS. On 26 April 1941, Winston Churchill, accompanied by his wife, arrived to inspect the progress personally. As the initiator of the Allied Airborne Forces, he watched a combined exercise by the CLE and PTS; this involved a formation of six Whitleys dropping forty paratroopers and their equipment on Ringway, towing and formation landing of five single-seat gliders and a demonstration by the newly delivered eight-seat General Aircraft GAL.48 Hotspur troop-carrying assault glider. Churchill was said to have been 'reasonably satisfied with the progress made in difficult circumstances'.

'X Troop', which consisted of seven officers and twenty-eight other ranks selected from the 11th Special Air Service (SAS) Battalion in early 1941, trained for the first British parachute raid of the war against the Tragino Aqueduct in Italy, code named 'Operation Colossus'. A full-scale mock-up of part of the aqueduct was erected at the parachute training ground in Tatton Park for rehearsals ahead of the raid on 10 February, when six Whitleys flew 1,600 miles by night, some of it across occupied France, to reach their objective.

Squadron Leader (later Group Captain) Maurice Newnham, OBE, DFC, took over command of the PTS in July 1941 and, during his time there, British Army parachutists, trained by the PTS at Ringway and Tatton Park, were joined by Marine Commandos and RAF personnel. Many overseas troops were also trained, including American, Belgian, Canadian, Czech, Dutch, Norwegian and Polish soldiers. To increase the throughput of trainees, three large modified hydrogen-filled barrage balloons were used. These were fitted with a cage, with a hole through which the trainees would jump; each balloon was capable of dropping three times the number of trainees in an hour that a Whitley could. By May 1942, 250 men a week were passing through the rigorous training facility to gain their Para wings.

The radio and television comedian Frank Muir, CBE (1920–1998), who joined the RAF at the outbreak of the war, had spent several years at the school in the photographic technical section, taking slow-motion film of parachute jumps on a project intended to decrease the frequency of parachutes failing (sometimes called a 'Roman Candle'). He was also assigned to take pictures of the agents of the SOE training centre (which was housed in an Edwardian house on the outskirts of the airfield) for identity documents. By February 1943, 92,000 jumps had been made, almost all over Tatton Park. Twenty-six fatalities had occurred, with many of the deaths caused by twisted and tangled rigging lines. Improved equipment and training later reduced the fatality and injury rate.

In addition to the normal intake, many paratroopers returned to the PTS (which had by then Douglas DC-3 Dakota transport aircraft that could carry twenty fully equipped paratroopers to speed up the throughput) in early 1944 for refresher courses during the build-up to the large-scale invasion on D-Day, when thousands of Ringway- and Tatton Park-trained paratroopers jumped over the Normandy beachhead from a huge fleet of Dakotas in the early hours of 6 June. Other airborne troops were towed in hundreds of gliders, using techniques developed at Ringway. The 1st Parachute Brigade had been held in reserve and led the mass drop on Arnhem in September 1944.

The number of trainees was gradually reduced after VJ Day (Victory over Japan) on 15 August 1945 and, on 27 September, an RAF display with paratrooper drops made from Dakotas and balloons was provided for the public, along with their first and only chance to learn of the secret wartime activities that had taken place at Ringway and Tatton Park. The main PTS party departed from Heald Green railway station on 28 March 1946, en route to its new base at RAF Upper Heyford, Oxfordshire.

A large limestone memorial to the men and women of the Parachute Training School was erected on the edge of Tatton Park's dropping zone in 1976, alongside the four monuments in the Airport Memorial Garden, which is located on a traffic island opposite Olympic House at Ringway (adjacent to the ramp up to Terminal 1 departures). These are to the Parachute Regiment and Airborne Forces; the 6,000 Polish officers and soldiers of the 1st Independent Polish Parachute Brigade and members of the Special Operations Executive (SOE) who undertook parachute training together with nationals of Belgium, France, Holland and Norway; the Glider Pilot Regiment; Women's Auxiliary Air Force (WAAF), Air Transport Auxiliary; and 613 (City of Manchester) Squadron (Royal Auxiliary Air Force - RAAF).

Two of the hangars built in the north-west corner of the airfield during 1939/40 for use by Fairey Aviation remain in use today – one for aircraft maintenance and the other for ground operations. The two south-side hangars (Nos 6 & 7), used to store completed Fairey Battle aircraft, were demolished during the 1990s. Over 4,400 warplanes were built at Ringway by Fairey Aviation and Avro. Veteran aircrews of the No. 14 Ferry Pilot Pool of the Air Transport Auxiliary (which was based at Ringway in one of the Bellman hangars between 1940 and 1945) delivered many thousands of military aircraft to operational units, which had been built, modified or repaired at Ringway, Woodford, Barton and at other north-west aircraft factories and airfields.

Avro occupied one of the north-side hangars for an experimental department where they completed a series of 'firsts': the prototype Manchester bomber, which first flew on 24 July 1939; the prototype Lancaster bomber, which first flew on 9 January 1941; and the (last) prototype Lincoln bomber, which first flew from Ringway on 9 July 1944. Avro also built over 100 Avro York military aircraft in the three south-side hangars during 1942/3. 'Building 217' (the old Officers' Mess) along Ringway Road was the only surviving building from the wartime years and was last used as the Airport Archive until 2009, from when it remained disused until it was demolished in 2011 in order to make way for a further extension of car parking facilities.

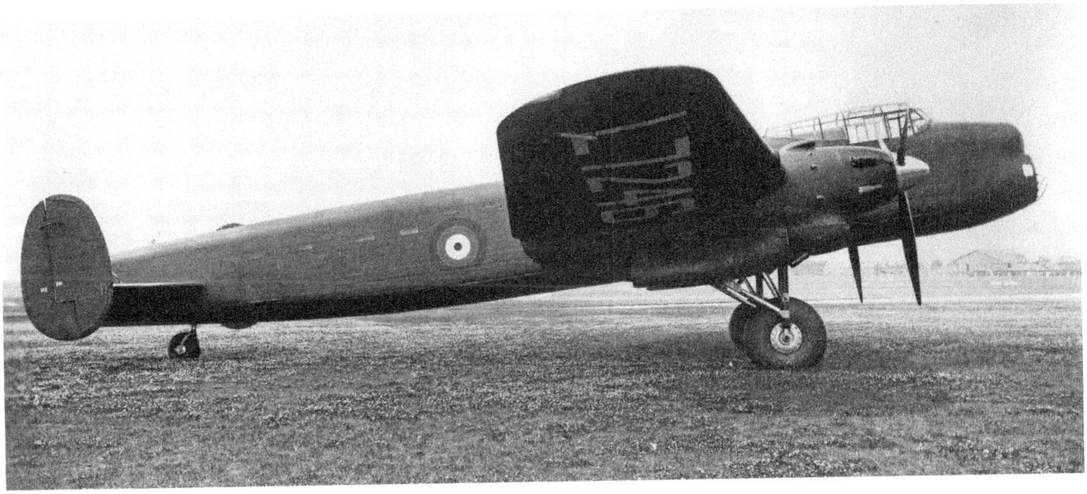

Avro's prototype Manchester (L7246) was assembled by their experimental department at Ringway and first flew on 25 July 1939. It is seen here in August. (Author's Collection)

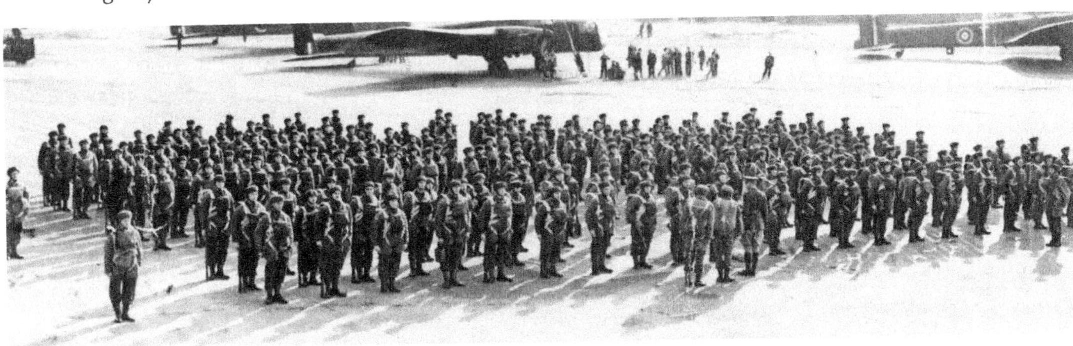

Brigadier Gale and Lt Col. Down inspect 1st Para Battalion, Ringway, 1941. (Airborne Assault, Duxford)

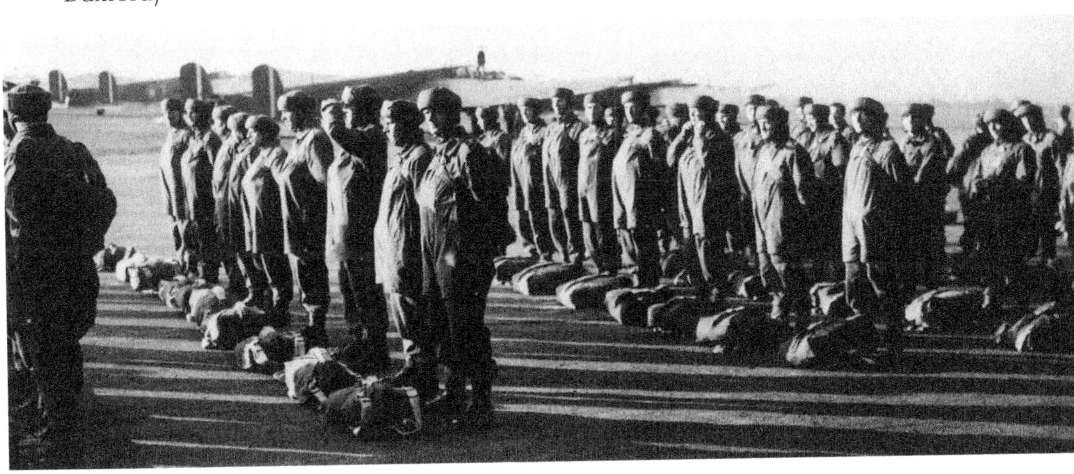

Members of 11 Special Air Service (SAS) Battalion at Ringway in 1941. (Airborne Assault, Duxford)

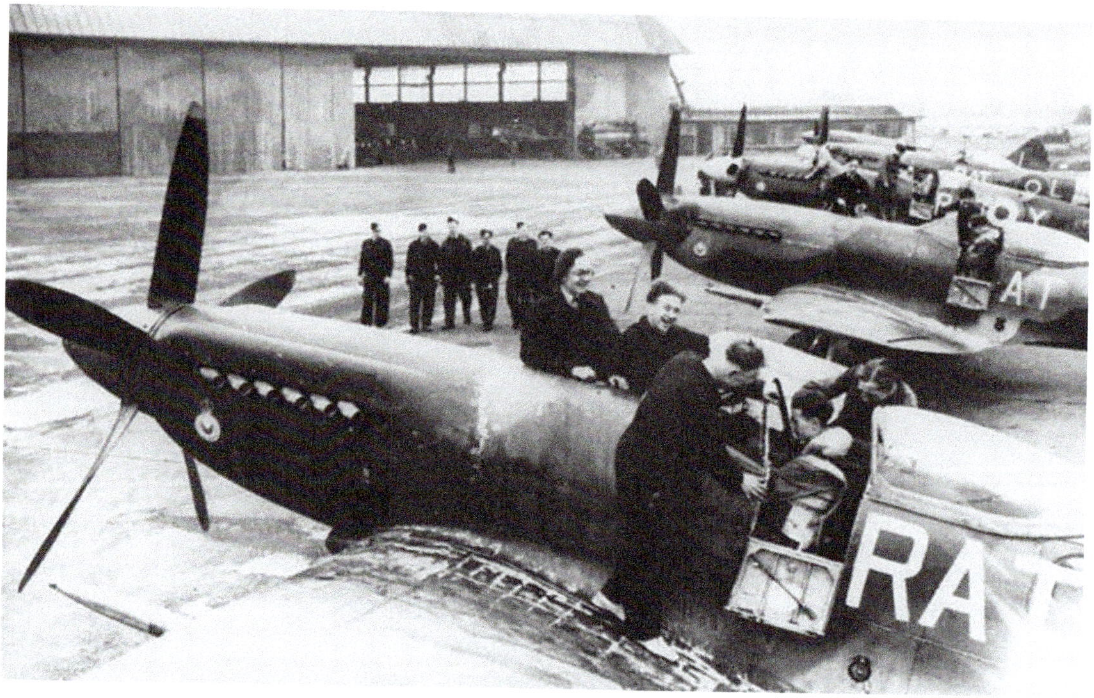

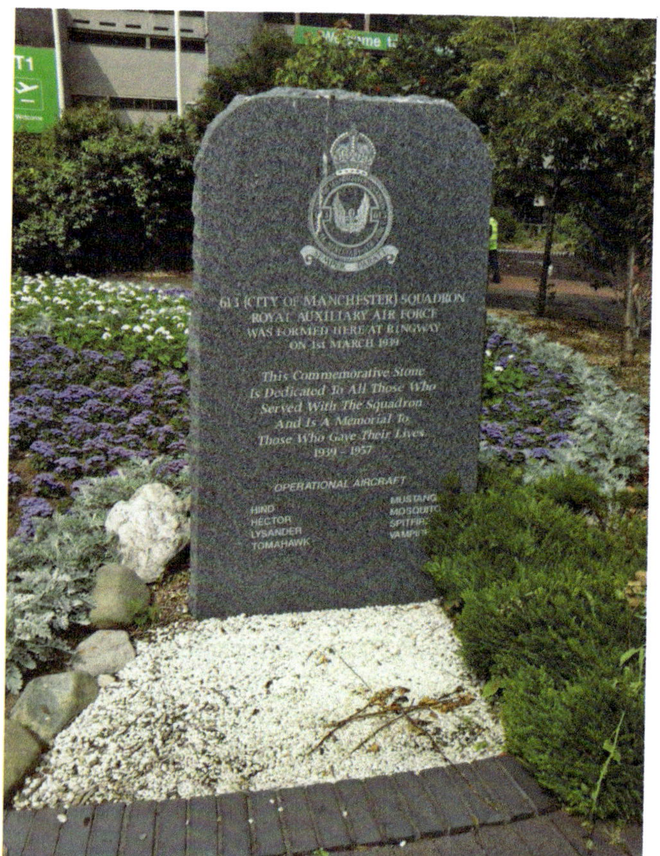

Above: 613 (City of Manchester) Squadron Spitfires at RAF Ringway in 1947. (RingwayObserver)

Left: Memorial to 613 (City of Manchester) Squadron, Royal Auxiliary Air Force. The Memorial Garden is situated between Terminals 1 and 3 (opposite Olympic House). (Callum Dodds)

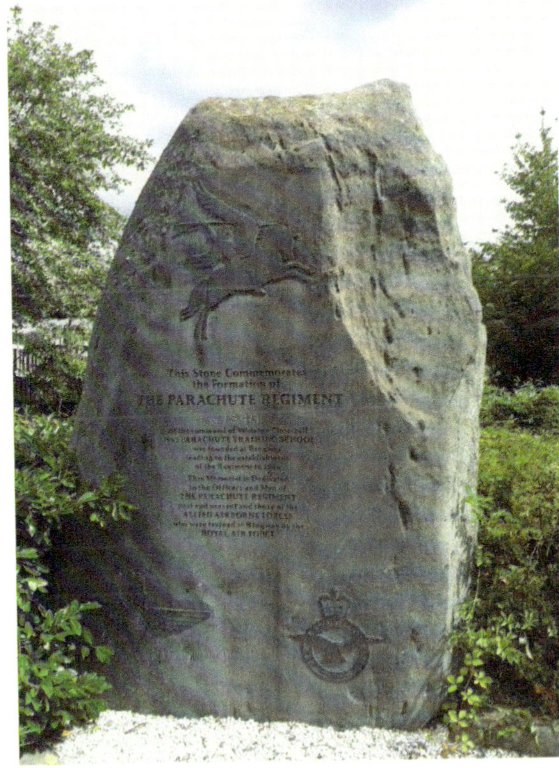

Memorial to the formation of the Parachute Regiment. (Callum Dodds)

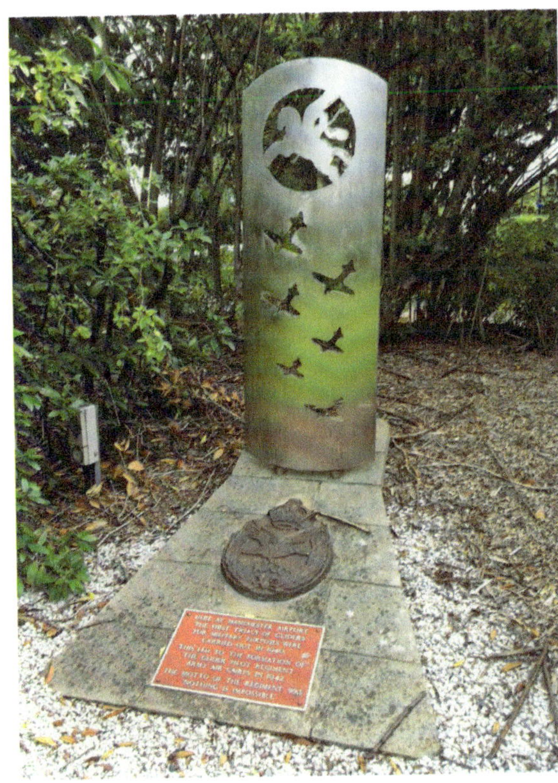

Memorial to the foundation of the Glider Pilot Regiment. (Callum Dodds)

Post-War

Railway Air Services began operating a twice-daily service in January 1946 between Belfast, Manchester, and London, using Avro Ansons. The Isle of Man route started again after a lapse of seven years, which signalled the reintroduction of scheduled services. Air France inaugurated the first post-war international airline service to Paris, using ex-RAF Douglas DC-3 Dakotas, on 16 June. KLM reintroduced their service to Amsterdam on 20 May 1947 and, on 1 July, the first Aer Lingus service (Dublin–Manchester–Amsterdam) began. By the end of the year, passenger numbers had tripled to more than 34,000 a year. Ringway staged its first air show on 24 April 1948, which recorded the first visit by jet aircraft (a Gloster Meteor F4 fighter), and, in August, a Douglas DC-4 of Transocean Airlines was the first large four-engine airliner to use the airport.

Part of the old PTS building was converted in 1949 as an extension to the terminal facilities to handle the increasing number of passengers flying from Manchester. The boom in air package travel continued to increase the demands upon airports throughout the country, and Manchester Airport was no exception. The check-in was in a converted hangar, and passengers were charged according to their standing weight on the big Avery scales; the large departure lounge (known as the Traffic Hall) had been converted from one of the big brick 'H' blocks. It was fitted with comfortable seating and a long bar, backed by a full-length, brightly coloured, three-dimensional collage. Outside, a small viewing area had been allocated adjacent to the west end of the terminal. Security was not the issue that it is today, and the BEA and Dan-Air DC-3 Dakotas would regularly cause the chain-link fences to be blown over (no push-back then) because they had no steerable nose wheels – just full throttle and a hard right rudder.

During the 1950s, the USAF Sabre jets were a big draw at Ringway. They were based on the Styal Road side of the field and, along with de Havilland Vampires and, now and again, a Gloster Meteor, were used for pilot training exercises. These involved circuits and bumps, steep climbs with various loops, rolls and steep dives – which wouldn't be allowed over a populated area today.

The main runway was extended in 1951 from 4,199 ft (1,280 m) to 5,900 ft (1,798 m), and the first Ground Controlled Approach radar was installed. In an agreement reached in 1952 with the then Ministry of Civil Aviation, Ringway was accepted as a major international airport. The ownership remained with Manchester Corporation and the name Ringway was changed to Manchester Airport.

Passenger levels had risen to 163,000 by 1952, and 24-hour operations commenced as Manchester became 'the airport of choice' for northern travellers wishing to avoid long journeys south to either Gatwick or Heathrow. An Avro York operated by Skyways Ltd made the first transatlantic flight in 1952, and Ringway became an intercontinental airport in 1953 when Sabena Belgian World Airlines introduced their first scheduled transatlantic service from the north of England with its Brussels–Manchester–New York (Idlewild Airport – now JFK Airport) service on 28 October. A report submitted to the Airport Committee in the same month recommended the building of a new terminal that allowed for future expansions in light of the envisaged increase in passenger numbers.

By 1954, the 1949 terminal was no longer able to cope when passenger numbers had reached 265,000. The airport had recorded its millionth passenger since the Second World War, and Hangar No. 5 was demolished to facilitate a westerly extension of the main apron, along with other modifications. The runway/threshold lighting was upgraded as new services appeared using turbine-powered airliners operated by BEA and Aer Lingus.

Hunting-Clan Air Transport operated a Douglas DC-3 Dakota on a service to Newcastle in 1954, and inaugurated Britain's first scheduled Avro York ('Africargo') all-cargo twice-weekly service from Manchester and London to Africa on 23 July 1955. Five years later, the company merged with the Airwork Group to form British United Airways (BUA).

The British Overseas Airways Corporation (BOAC) initially operated their Boeing 377 Stratocruiser (G-ALSC) *RMA Centaurus* on the New York flights from Manchester (the inaugural flight took place on 7 May 1954), but had reservations about using the runway in bad weather and diverted to Burtonwood (2 miles north-west of Warrington, Cheshire). The diversion quickly became a permanent feature until the runway at Manchester was extended, by which time the Stratocruisers were being replaced by the new Douglas DC-7Cs. However, BOAC had been overcautious; Sabena was already flying DC-7Cs Manchester to and from New York via Shannon (but flew direct when the winds allowed).

Upon the disbandment of 613 (City of Manchester) Squadron in March 1957, RAF Ringway was closed and its hangars and other buildings handed over for civil airline operations, including cargo and maintenance. Ground clearance and piling work began in October 1957 in advance of an extension to runway of 7,000 ft (2,133 m), which opened on 23 April 1958, permitting regular non-stop scheduled flights to North America. Temporary traffic lights and level-crossing-style gates were installed across the A538 road (which ran across the threshold) for about six months afterwards, while the new route for the A538 was being built. These were closed whenever an aeroplane crossed the road.

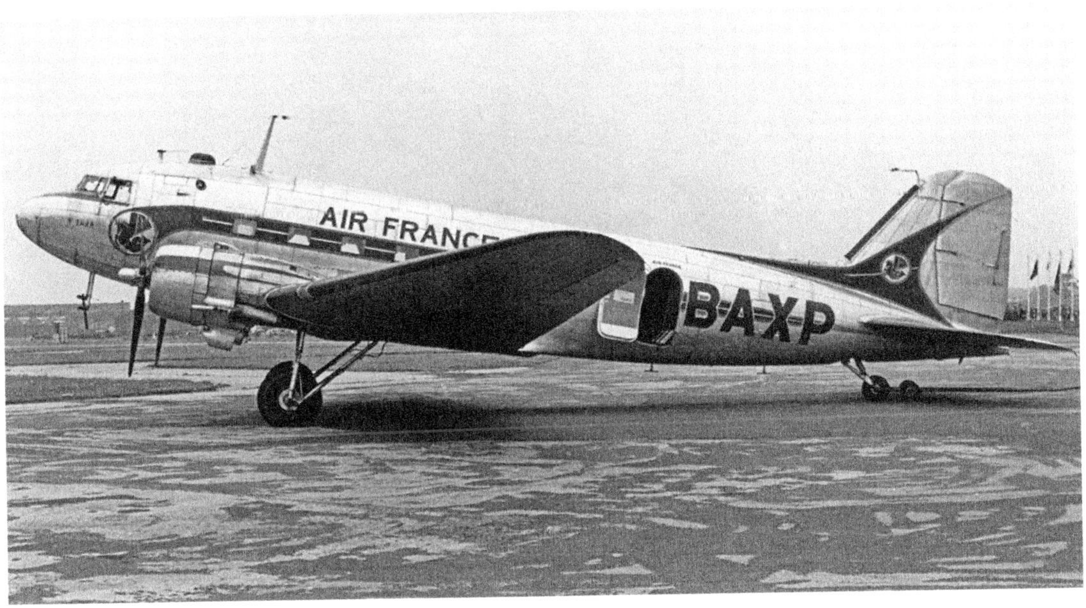

An Air France Douglas C-47A (DC-3) (F-BAXP) at Ringway on 6 July 1952. (RuthAS)

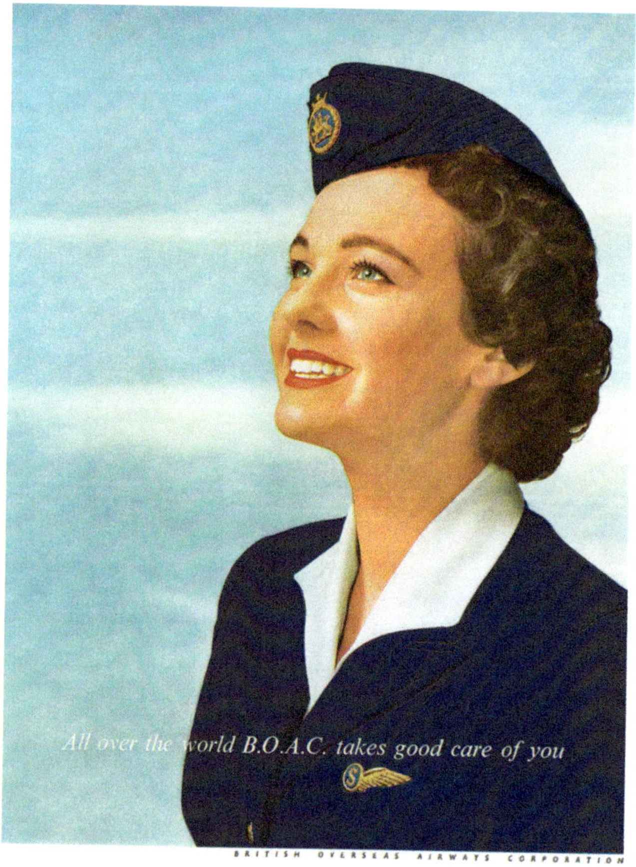

Left: BOAC 1956 advert. (Author's Collection)

Below: USAF Canadair Sabre (FU-484) at Ringway in June 1956. (RuthAS)

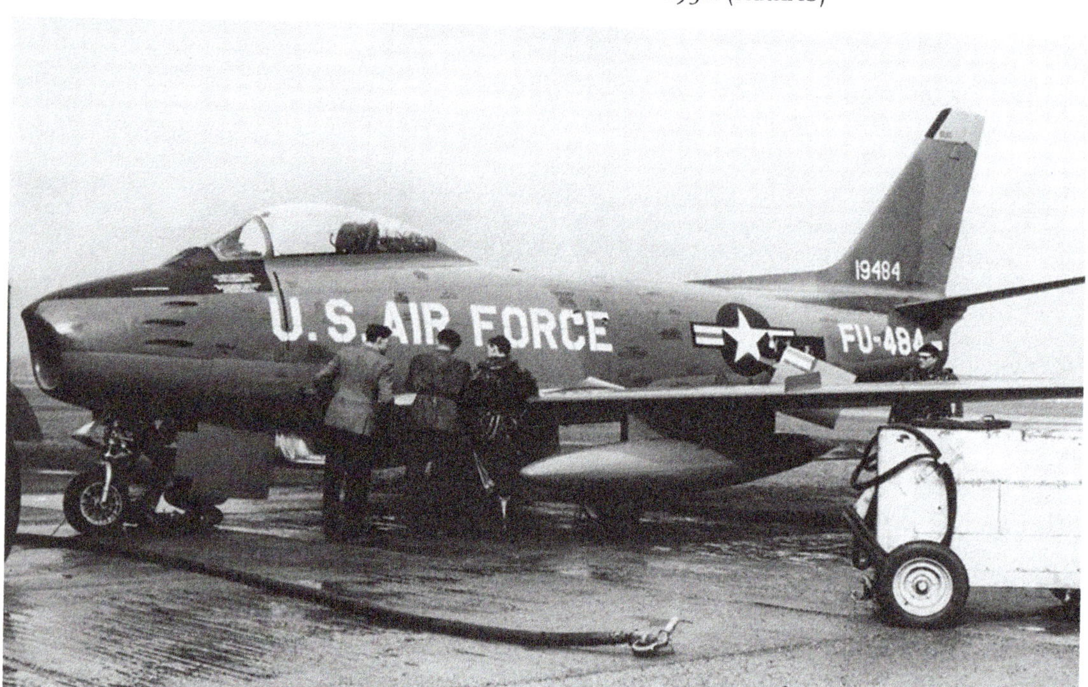

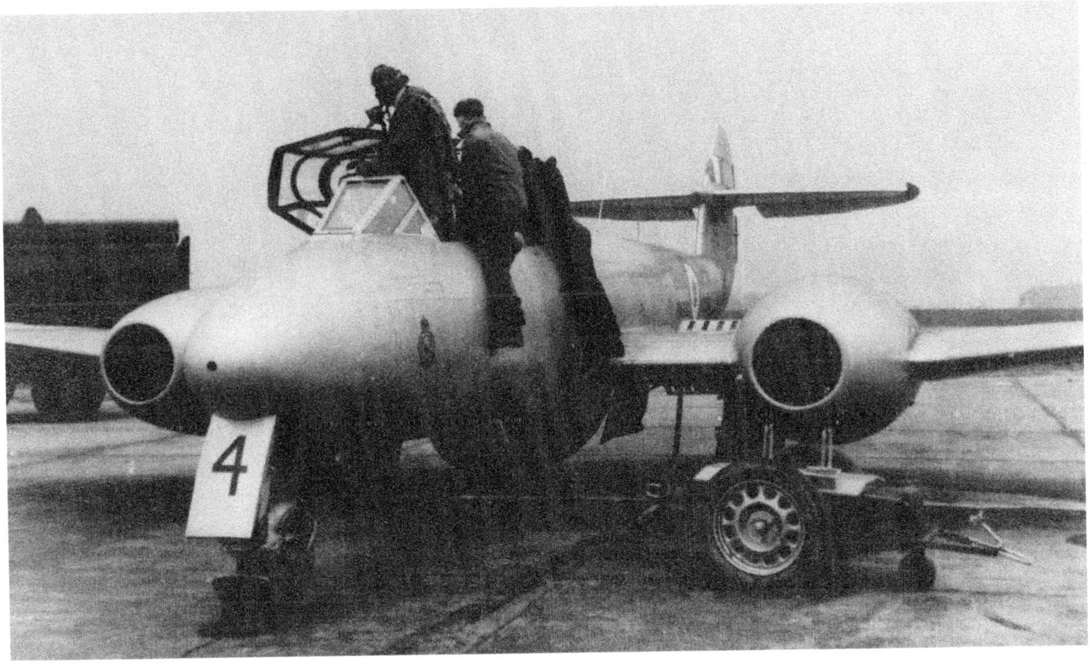

A pilot and ground crew with a Gloster Meteor at Ringway in 1956. (Author's Collection)

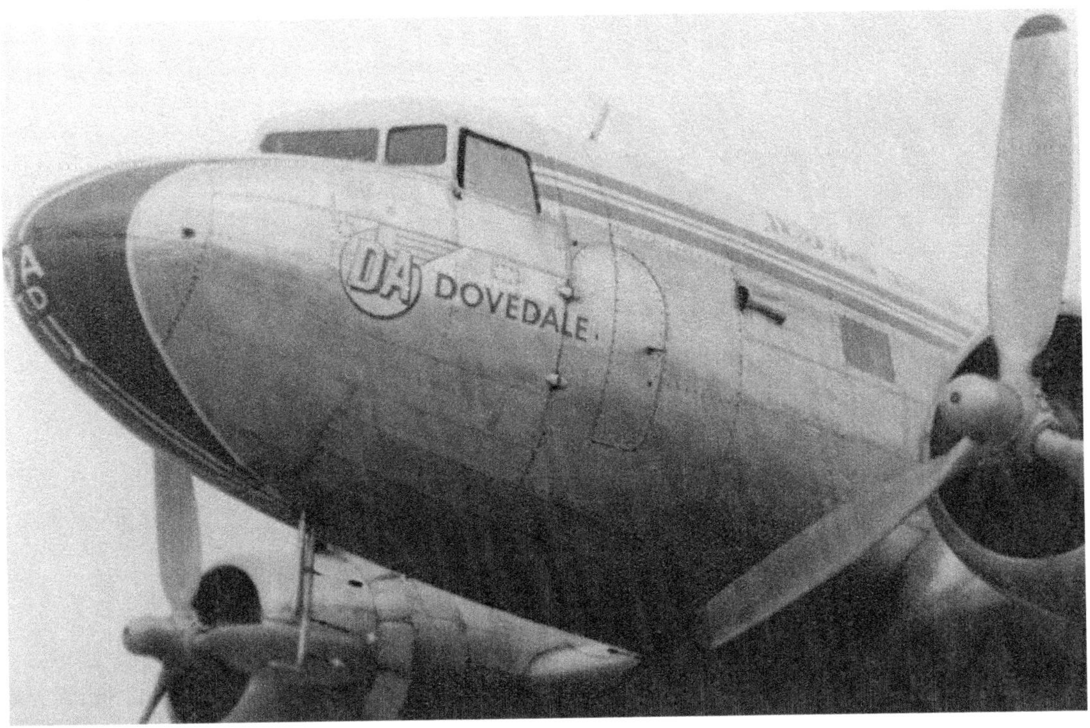

Derby Aviation Ltd Dakota DC-3 *Dovedale* at Ringway in 1957. The airline was later renamed Derby Airways and, in 1964, moved to East Midlands Airport and became British Midland Airways. (Author's Collection)

Into the Jet Age

The airport saw continuing growth in flying training, private aircraft and air-taxi work, as well as cargo services and inclusive tours (better known as charter flights), which had been on the increase from Manchester since the first Transair flights to Ostend in 1955. These became significant factors in the traffic mix, as the number of piston-powered propliners on scheduled transatlantic flights gradually declined after jet airliners entered civilian service in 1952. BOAC still introduced the turbo-prop engine Bristol Britannia 312 into the fleet for its New York schedules, but in late 1958, a French Sud Aviation SE-210 Caravelle demonstrator jet airliner arrived at Manchester on a VIP trip in late 1958, pointing the way to a new generation of transatlantic aircraft. The next to appear at Manchester was Sabena's long-range four turbojet engine Boeing 707, which began its first scheduled New York flights on 10 April 1960.

The runway was extended by a further 500 ft between February and April 1961 in time for the first European jet service to Paris on 1 June, which was operated by Air France with a Sud Aviation SE-210 Caravelle 1. On 12 July, three months to the day after he completed a 108-minute orbit of the Earth and became the first human in space, Russian Cosmonaut Yuri Gagarin landed at Manchester, en route to receive honorary membership (he had been a foundryman before training as a pilot) of the Amalgamated Union of Foundry Workers at their headquarters in the city.

The wartime Bellman hangars were cleared away in 1962 to increase apron space as part of site redevelopment, and the old terminal building, which had been adequate in 1938, was replaced at the cost of £2.7 million – an astronomical figure at the time. It was the first to incorporate the 'pier' system, providing cover for travelling passengers, who prior to this would have had to brave the elements when boarding or upon their return. Terminal 1 was officially opened by Prince Phillip, the Duke of Edinburgh, on 22 October, and was in full operation from 3 December. The development heralded two decades of burgeoning traffic and successive improvements being made to other buildings, which included a ten-storey control tower, a third pier, a new departure hall and a longer runway to keep pace with the rising numbers of passengers. Built-in hydrant refuelling points were installed on the aprons, and an open-air park for 1,300 cars was provided.

Sabena withdrew their services to New York in March 1964, following the loss of its 'Fifth Freedom Traffic Rights' through Manchester after sustained pressure from BOAC and the British government, which capped their operations to just two services a week. BOAC introduced a daily service to New York with Boeing 707s in May. (Fifth Freedom Traffic Rights allow an airline to carry revenue traffic between foreign countries as a part of an airline's long haul routes, but tend to be viewed by local airlines and governments as potentially unfair competition.)

Aer Lingus began their Frankfurt service on 7 June 1965 with BAC 1-11s and, a year later, in July 1965, BEA introduced jet Tridents into their Paris service. The first visit to Manchester by a BOAC Super VC-10 (G-ASGC) was on a flight from New York on 26 October 1965 as a weather diversion from Heathrow. The new jets with full payloads that were coming into service had to be better accommodated, and work was under way in September 1968 on a further runway extension to 9,200 ft (2,804 m). 143 acres of land had been purchased, and the Altrincham–Wilmslow Road (A538) was diverted beneath the runway. The new bridge required four tunnels – two for pedestrians and two for road traffic – and was officially opened on 7 January 1969. The first non-stop scheduled flight to New York began on 29 April 1969 with BOAC Super VC10s.

Growth and Investment in the 1970s

British Airways had been operating a transatlantic all 'cargo service' since 1966 with their Boeing 707-336C and, by the start of the 1970s, Manchester could boast links with Canada, USA, South America, most major European cities, and connections worldwide. BOAC's Boeing 747-100 'Jumbo Jet' (G-AWNC) made a pivotal and historic occasion as the first wide-body airliner to arrive at the airport on 17 August 1970 in order to test Manchester's facilities, and familiarise ground crews and staff for the aircraft type that would revolutionise world travel for the average person.

Hawker Siddeley Aviation built complete wings (including the leading and trailing flaps) at Chester for the Airbus A300B, which were transported by road from the final assembly unit to Manchester. They were then airlifted to the Airbus Assembly Unit at Toulouse by the Boeing 377 Stratocruiser and C-97J Turbo Stratofreighter-derived Aero Spacelines Super Guppy – the first flight of which was on 23 November 1971.

Laker Airways (Freddie Laker's third and most prominent airline venture) operated the first transatlantic Advanced Booking Charter (ABC) flight from 2 April 1973 on any route with a 345-seat McDonnell Douglas DC-10 to Toronto. The system greatly simplified the charter business and ushered in the concept of cheaper fares and shorter booking periods; by the mid-1970s, it had become the undisputed, global ABC flight market leader.

Wardair Canada commenced the first regular 747 operations from Manchester on 12 June 1974, and the holiday charter airline Court Line Aviation was the first operator to bring the medium-to-long-range, wide-body Lockheed TriStar onto the British Register when they operated their two long-term lease L-1011s (G-BAAA and G-BAAB) from early 1973 until August 1974. The aircraft were distinctive in their corporate livery; the hostesses wore multi-coloured uniforms designed by Mary Quant.

A new departure hall was opened in 1973, featuring numerous innovations including travellators, waiting lounges, air conditioning, and, for the first time, 'air bridges', which connected passengers directly to the aircraft. The airport, which had been in the hands of the Greater Manchester Council, was redesignated as an International Gateway airport in 1974, following local government reorganisation. A joint governing body was set up, which took the title 'Manchester International Airport Authority', and the new managers were quick to take advantage of its new status. Direct long-haul flights operated to and from Manchester; further terminal extensions were made; the Intercontinental Pier 'C' (capable of handling Boeing 747s) was opened; and a 20,000-space multistorey car park was built to cope with the additional traffic.

Runway 24 was showing severe problems by the mid-1970s. No proper foundations or drainage had been laid when it was constructed during the war, and it was cracking and flexing under the weight of the heavier modern aircraft. It was determined that major repairs would need to be carried out by the early 1980s. The Airport Committee drew up plans for a second runway, 10,500 ft (3,200 m) long and 1,500 ft (457 m) wide, to the south-east of the existing Runway 24; however, these were shelved after objections by concerned homeowners in the village of Styal (on the River Bollin) because of the threat of disruption and additional noise it would cause.

In July 1975, the airport was formally renamed 'Manchester International Airport' by the Manchester Airport Joint Committee, in recognition of it being designated a major international gateway, although many locals still referred to it as 'Ringway'.

British Airways' Aérospatiale-BAC Concorde 102 (G-BOAA) made its first (unscheduled) landing at Manchester on 14 November 1976, after being diverted from London Heathrow due to fog on its flight from Washington. When it took off again, the A538 was blocked off and it was watched by thousands of people; it registered a lower decibel reading than the Boeing 747 that had taken off five minutes earlier.

A revised plan for a second runway was put to the planning authorities in May 1976. It illustrated not only a second tunnel for the A538, but that the runway would cross the Bollin Valley, which was designated by Cheshire County Council as a country park. The idea was shelved again, although a compromise was reached between the Airport Committee and the Greater Manchester Transport Action Group for the necessary repair work to be carried out on Runway 24. Subsequently, the massive engineering job was carried out at night between 11 p.m. and 7 a.m. from March until the end of October 1979, which enabled the airport to operate normally for the remaining sixteen hours. Heavy earthworks had to be carried out in the Bollin River Valley to provide the level ground for the extension, and the A538 road had to be diverted further south to a tunnel under the runway; the cut ends of its old course became the back gates to the airport. The runway was also extended by 800 ft (243 m) to its current length of 10,000 ft (3,048 m) and opened on 17 August 1982; the new taxiway was opened a year later.

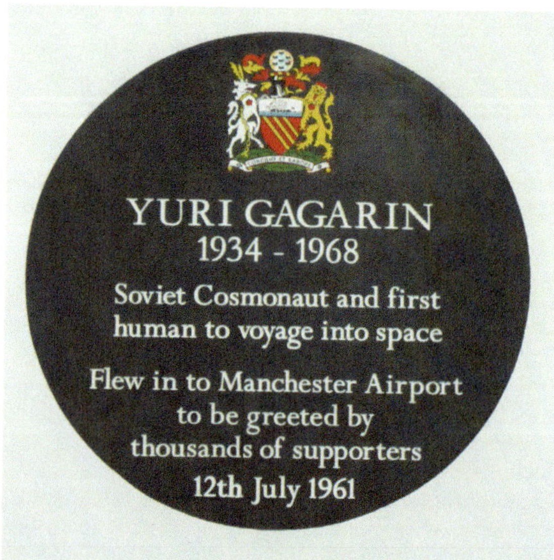

Left: Plaque inside Terminal 3, commemorating the visit to Manchester Airport of Russian Cosmonaut Yuri Gagarin on 12 July 1961. (Author's Collection)

Below: The four glass chandeliers in the Terminal 1 Departure Hall were unveiled by the Duke of Edinburgh in 1963. Designed by royal architect Stefan Buzas, they were 17 feet long and weighed almost 2 tons each; they cost £3,000 to make. They were removed in 2003 as part of the redevelopment of the terminal and placed into storage. (Swellmap@flickr Collection)

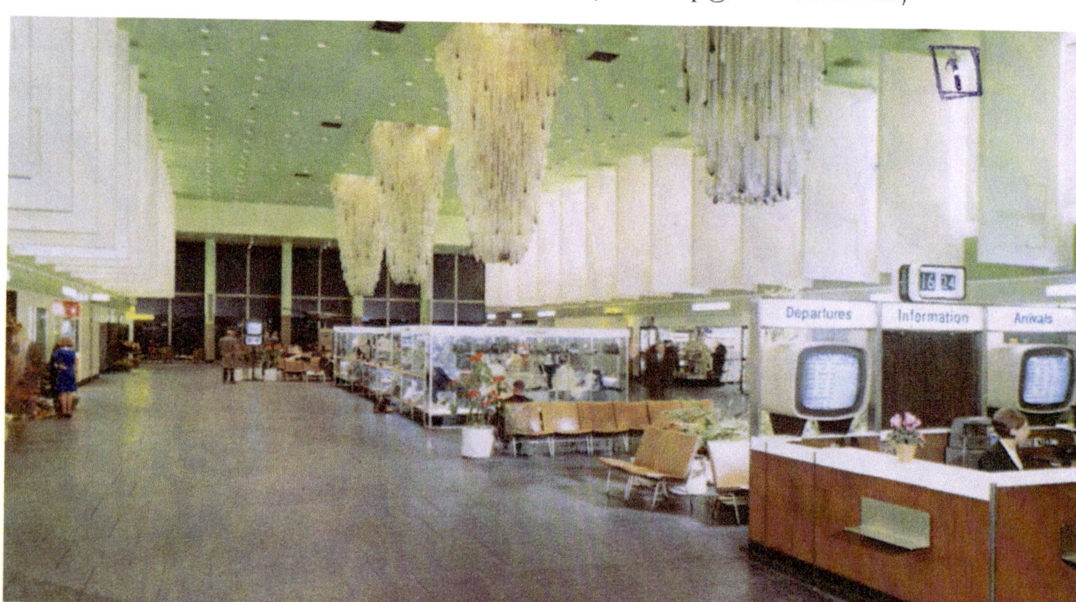

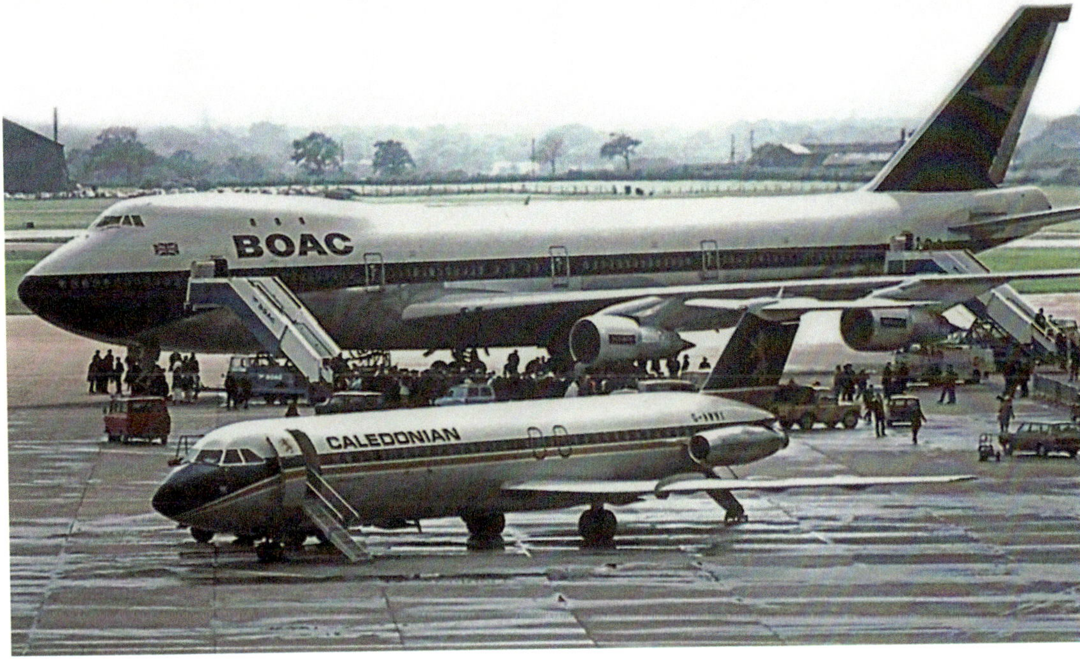

First visit of a BOAC Boeing 747-136 (G-AWNC) on 17 August 1970. British Caledonian BAC 1-11 (G-AWWX) is in the foreground. (RingwayEnthusiast)

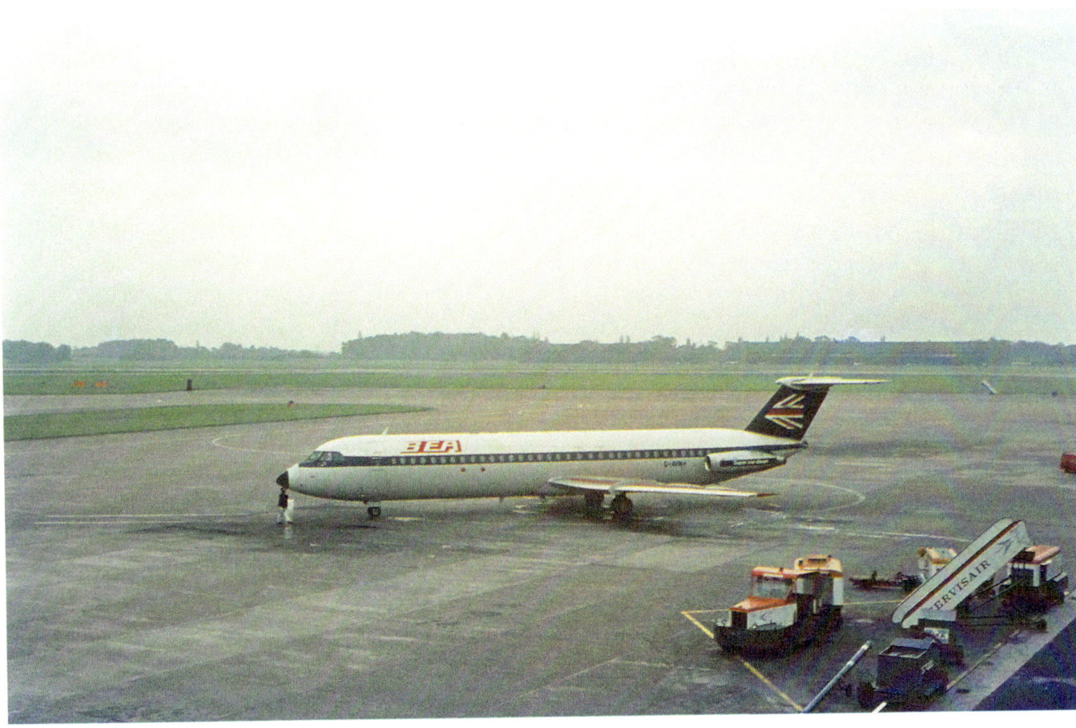

BEA (G-AVMU) the thirteenth BAC 1-11 510ED-derivation aircraft on 27 October 1972. (Keith Long)

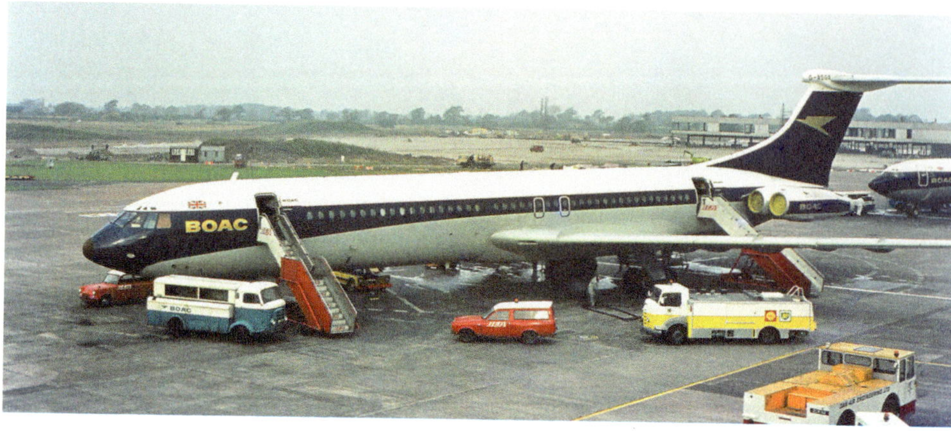

BOAC Vickers VC10 (G-ASGA) at Manchester with Flight BA537 Heathrow to New York, Barbados and Trinidad on 27 October 1972. This aircraft is now preserved at Duxford. (Keith Long)

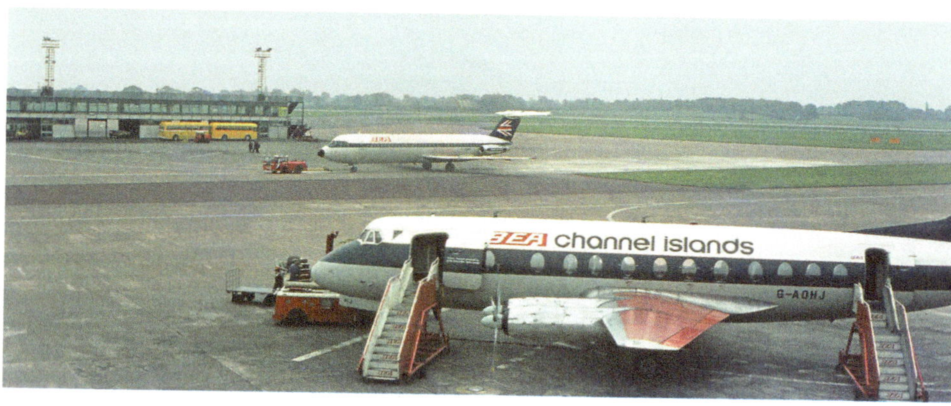

BEA BAC1-11-510ED (G-AVMU) and a BEA Channel Islands V.802 series Vickers Viscount (G-AOHJ) on 27 October 1972. (Keith Long)

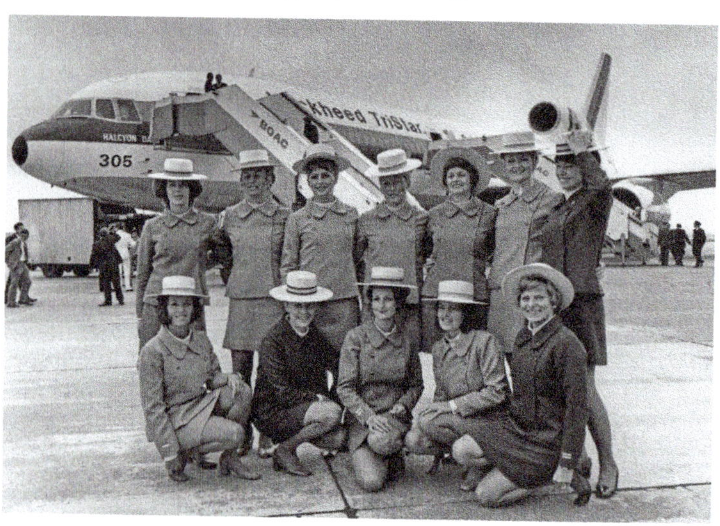

Some of the airline's hostesses, wearing their multicoloured uniforms, in front of the Court Line/Eastern TriStar L1-011 Demonstrator (N305EA), which was leased from Lockheed on 15 September 1972. (RuthAs)

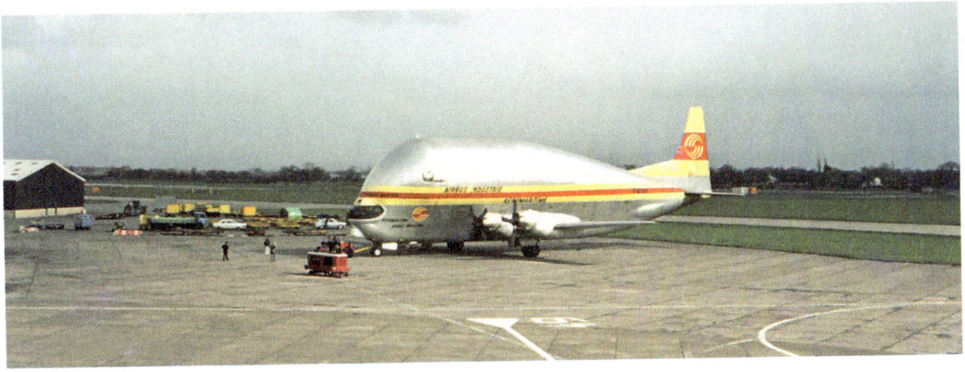

Aero Spacelines Super Guppy 201 (F-BTGV, Ex N211AS), 17 March 1974. (Keith Long)

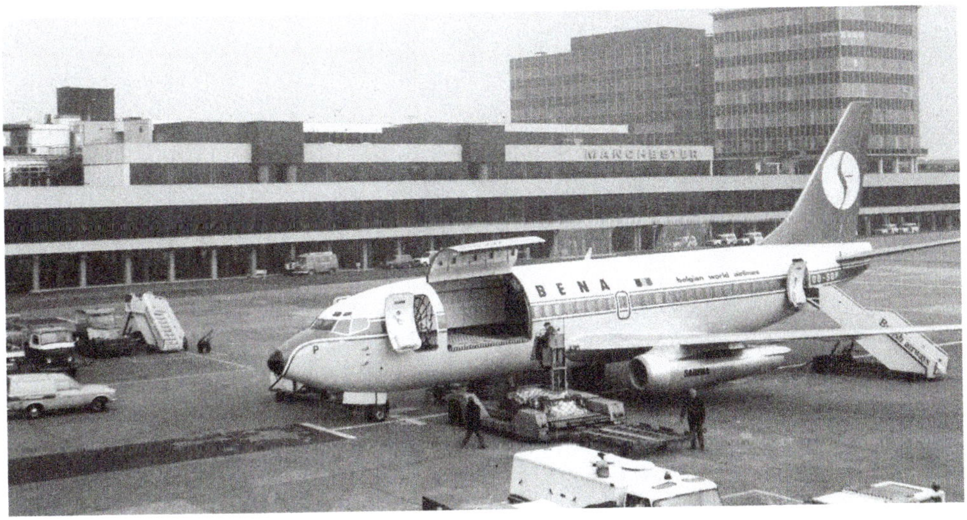

Sabena (Belgian World Airlines) Boeing 737-229C(A) (OO-SDP) in 1975. (Howard Litherland)

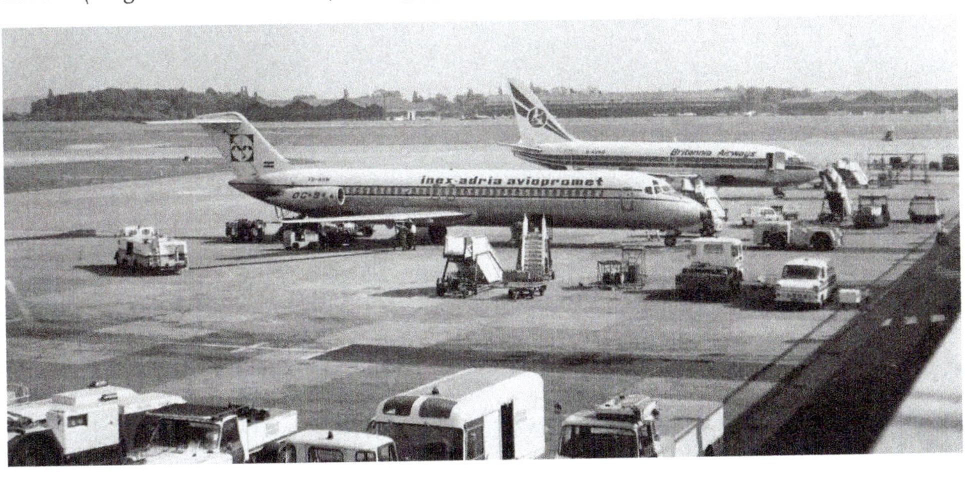

Inex-Adria McDonnell Douglas DC-9-33RC (YU-AHW) with Britannia Boeing B737-204 (G-AVRO), *c.* 1975. (Howard Litherland)

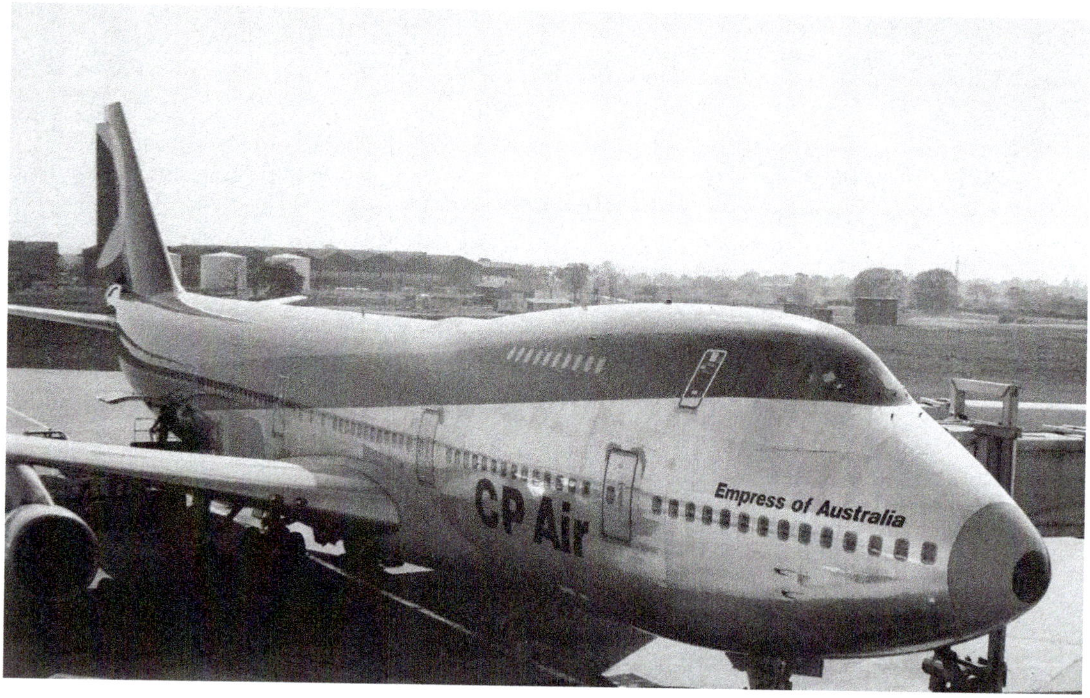

CP Air Boeing 747-217B (C-FCRD) *Empress of Australia* in the mid-1970s. (Howard Litherland)

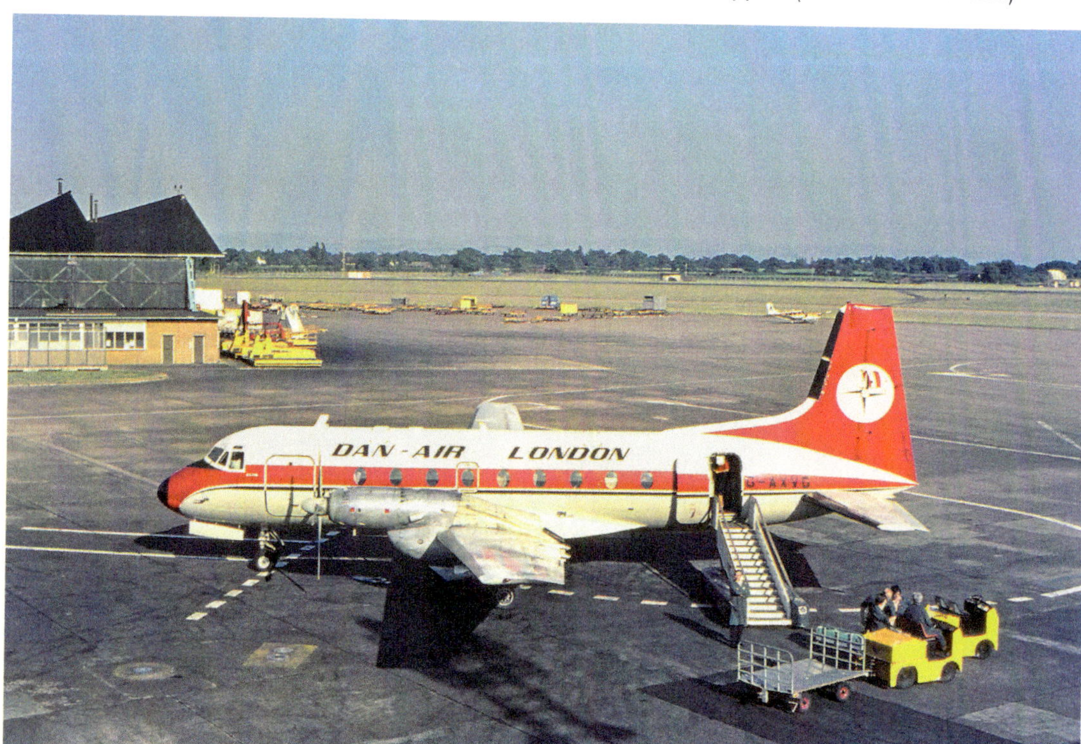

Dan-Air Hawker Siddeley HS-748 (G-AXVG) on 25 June 1975. (Keith Long)

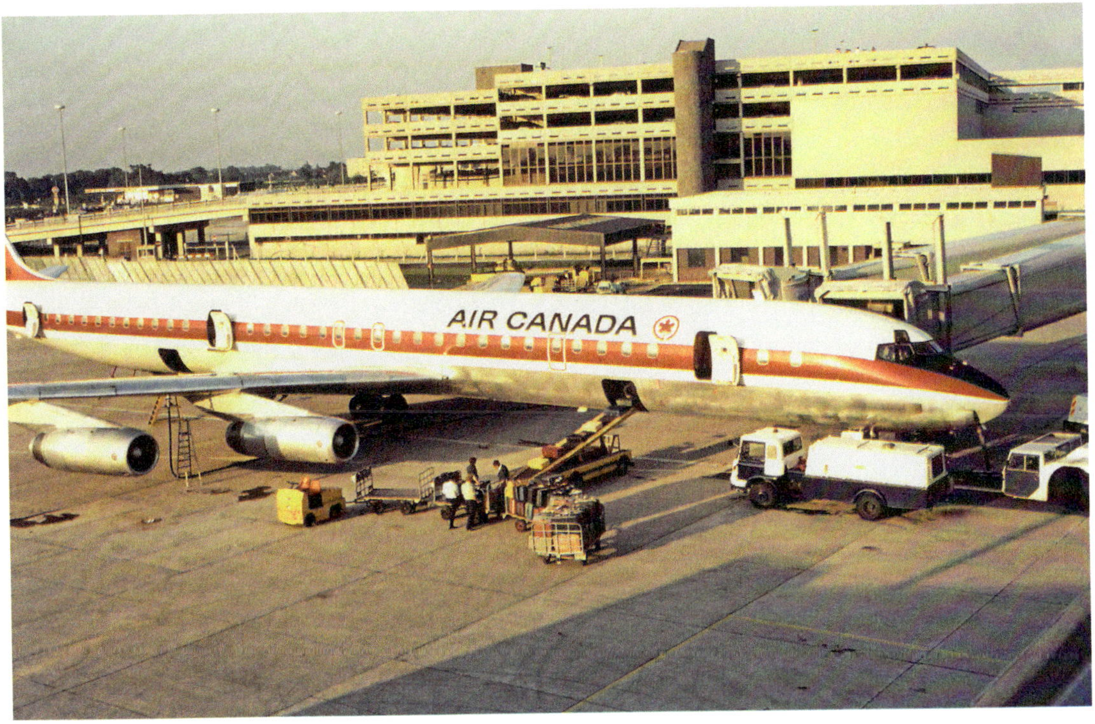

Air Canada McDonnell Douglas DC8-63 Turbofan (CF-TIM) being loaded on 25 June 1975. (Keith Long)

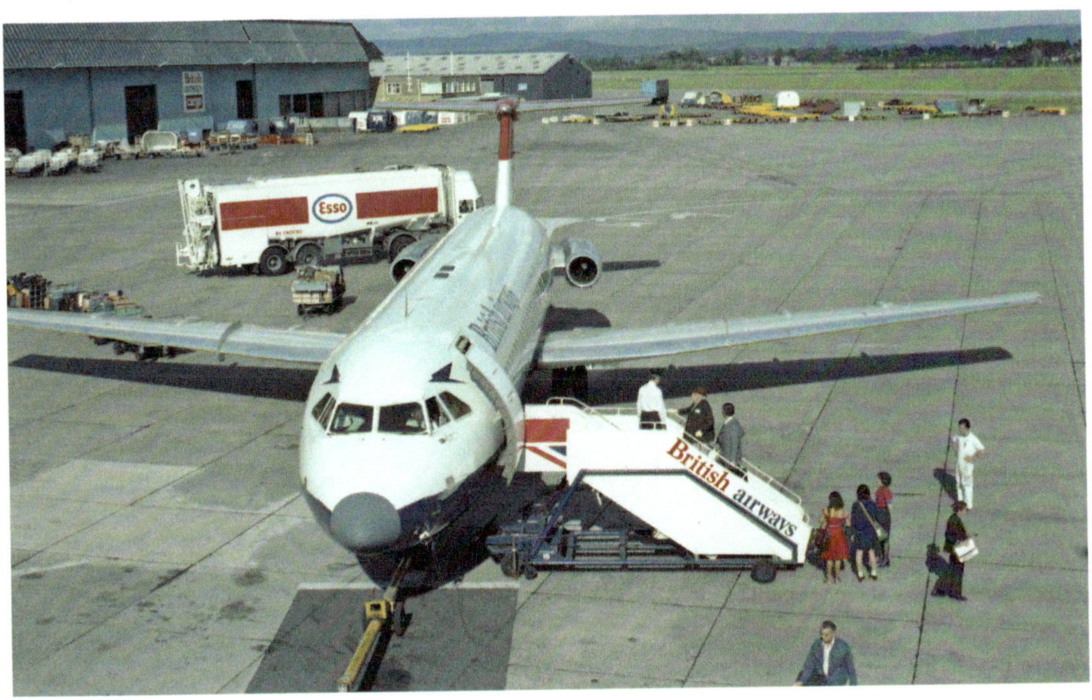

British Airways BAC 1-11 in July 1977. (Nigel Musgrove)

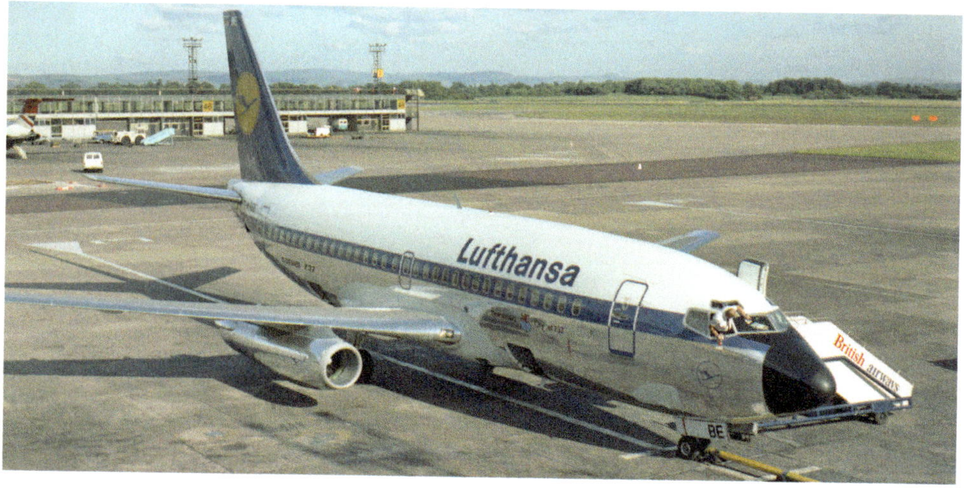

Cleaning the windshield on a Lufthansa Boeing City Jet 737 in July 1977. (Nigel Musgrove)

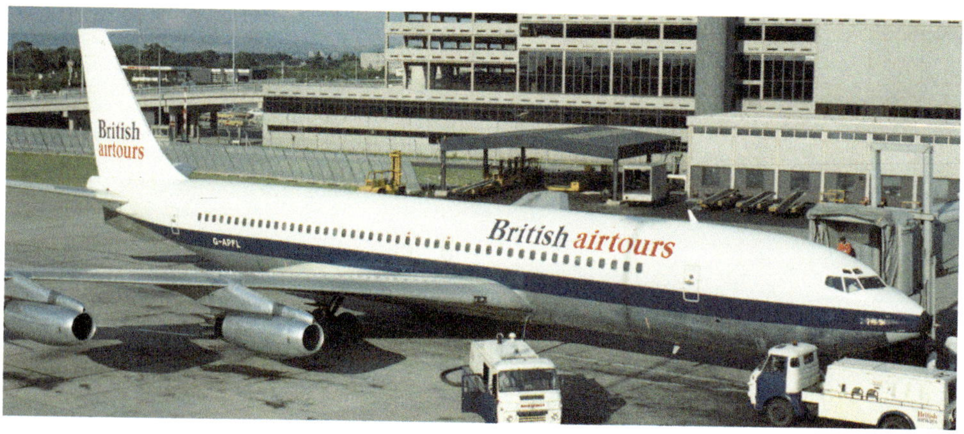

British Airtours Boeing 707-400 (G-APFL) in July 1977. (Nigel Musgrove)

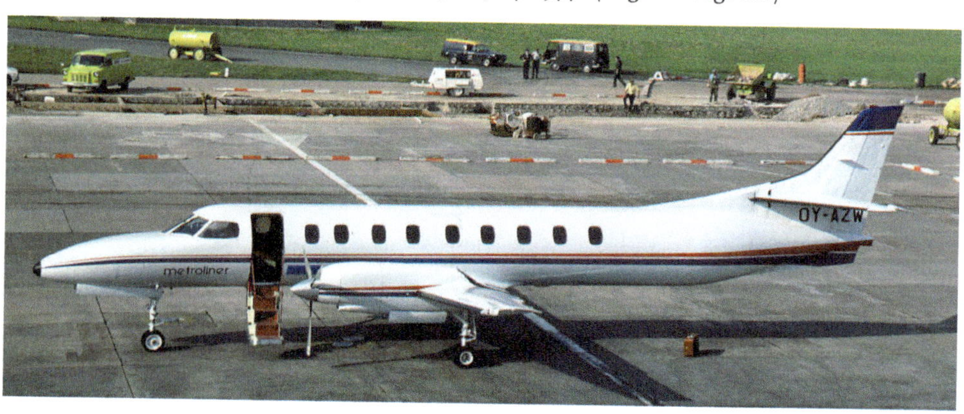

View from the old south-side sheds of Fairchild Swearingen Metroliner SA226-TC (OY-AZW) in 1978. The ground work is in progress for the TCX hangar in the background. (Author's Collection)

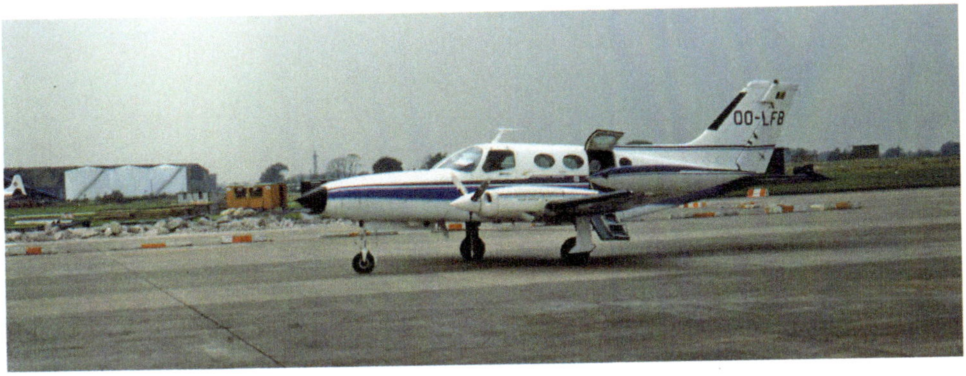

Abelag Aviation (Belgium) air charter Cessna 402 (OO-LFB) on 6 September 1978. (Author's Collection)

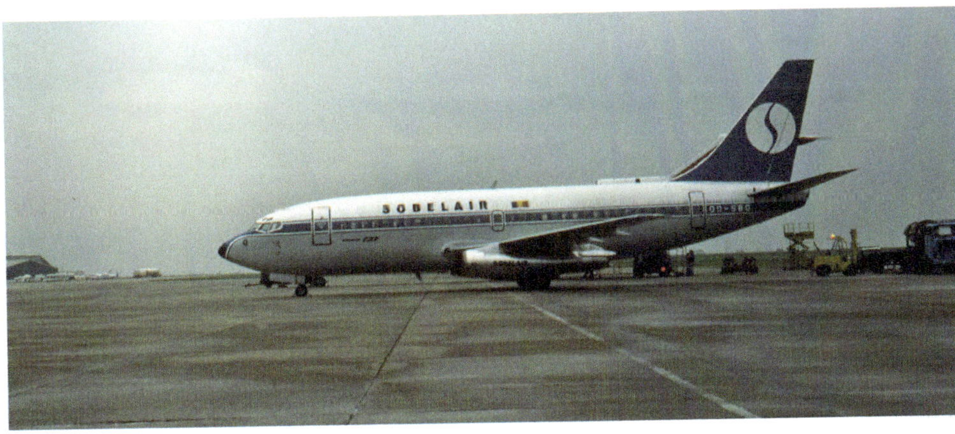

Sobelair (Belgium) Boeing 737-229(A) (OO-SBQ) on 17 October 1978. (Author's Collection)

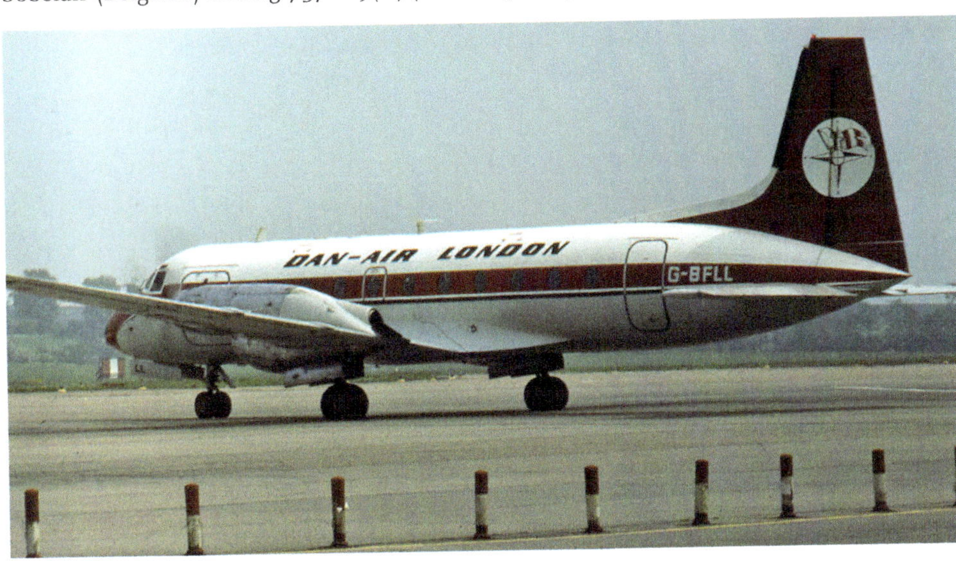

Dan-Air Hawker Siddley HS.748 (G-BFLL) in 1979. (Author's Collection)

An International Gateway

Gilbert Williamson Thompson, who had been a general manager for British Airways at Ringway in the mid-1970s, began his twelve-year tenure as Chief Executive at Manchester Airport in 1981. His bold vision and flamboyant style made an early impact by leading negotiations that allowed global carriers such as Singapore and American Airlines to fly direct to Manchester. He also oversaw the addition of a second major terminal, and many other improvements to the airport's infrastructure and ground transport connections.

British Airways Concorde (G-BOAB) (208) enjoyed her first trip between Manchester and New York on 18 July 1983 when she carried the cream of the US golf world – pro-golf's Pantheon – Jack Nicklaus, Arnold Palmer, Tom Watson, Floyd, Lee Trevino, Ben Crenshaw, Tom Kite, Curtis Strange, Gary Player, Hale Irwin – and their wives back home on a charter flight after performing at The Open at Royal Birkdale in Southport.

Manchester became the first airport with automatic docking in early 1984, and the Greater Manchester County Council (GMCC) approved a further £13-million expansion on a 50/50 basis to cope with the anticipated 9 million passengers by 1987.

The World Freight Terminal is the airport's dedicated 24/7 cargo gateway, which opened in 1986 to meet the needs of industries and shippers in the air cargo and logistics supply chain. Comprising 645,834 sq. ft (60,000 sq. m) of logistics space, it currently handles around 100,000 tonnes of import freight, export freight and mail a year (as of June 2016), carried in both passenger aircraft and freight-only aircraft.

Manchester City Council and the GMCC owned 50 per cent each of the airport until March 1986, when the County Council was abolished after local government reorganisation. The shares of the company were held as 55 per cent by the City Council and the remainder equally by Bury, Bolton, Oldham, Rochdale, Salford, Stockport, Tameside, Trafford and Wigan District Councils between them. Manchester Airport plc was formed and was subsequently granted a 125-year lease on the land. On 1 April, the airport name was changed to Manchester Airport.

In April 1986, American Airlines became the first US carrier to operate direct flights to Chicago O'Hare International Airport from Manchester with the Boeing 767-200 – Boeing's first wide-body twinjet and its first airliner with a two-crew glass cockpit – which at the time was the most modern aircraft in the world. The £10.5-million World Freight Terminal opened in September 1986; its construction expanded the airport westwards, which took up land around the Grange Lane junction and obliterated most of the west remnant of Yewtree Lane and the north part of Pinfold Lane.

Gilbert Thompson, who had been appointed OBE in 1985, had created a shining example of an internationally competitive business under public-sector ownership after control of the airport passed to 'Manchester Airport plc' in 1986 (although it was designated as an International Gateway, and the word 'International' was dropped from its name). Thompson's response to this investment saw passenger figures rise to 1 million per month in 1987.

The airport celebrated its Golden Jubilee in 1988 and, since operating under the guidance of Thompson, was able to list record-breaking results: cargo traffic increased by 51 per cent; around 100 airlines were operating to 168 destinations around the world; and passenger numbers had risen to more than 11 million (a rise of 20 per cent), pushing the turnover up to £92 million, with pre-tax profits rising by 50 per cent to £30.5 million. HRH the Princess of Wales opened the new 'Terminal A' (now a part of Terminal 3), which included dedicated check-in and car-parking facilities, in 1989.

Etrop Green Farm, in Hasty Lane, was demolished in 1989, along with a road junction, trees and a pond, to create the western long-term car parking area. An eastwards expansion took up the land of Heyhead (a group of old houses, a shop and a chapel) that didn't fall into the catchment of preservation orders.

With Manchester becoming one of the leading airports in Europe, a new 'Development Strategy' was published in 1991, which included plans for a twenty-first-century airport designed to handle 30 million passengers a year by 2005 – complete with proposals for a second runway, at an estimated cost of £36 million, to keep up with the growth in air traffic.

An official Aviation Viewing Park was created just off Wilmslow Old Road on the south-western side of the airfield, replacing the unofficial plane-spotting area at Oversley Ford, where the Altrincham road crosses the River Bollin. The park was developed to provide a wider range of attractions for the airport's visitors and spectators. It includes several static aircraft exhibits, the highlight of which is one of British Airways' Concorde aircraft.

Terminal 2, which was opened by the Duke of Edinburgh on 5 March 1993, doubled the airport's capacity to around 20 million passengers a year. In May, the new railway station was opened as part of a £26-million investment in the central transport hub to provide direct connections to many towns and cities in the north of England. It is linked to the airport's three terminals and is connected to each by an escalator, ramps and an elevated covered walkway (known as the 'Sky Link'). Gilbert Thompson took his leave of the airport in 1993 (and was knighted at Buckingham Palace on 3 December) after twelve years to become the chair of the British Airports Group; Development Director Geoff Muirhead, who had joined in 1988, had been promoted to Chief Executive in 1992 in order to replace him.

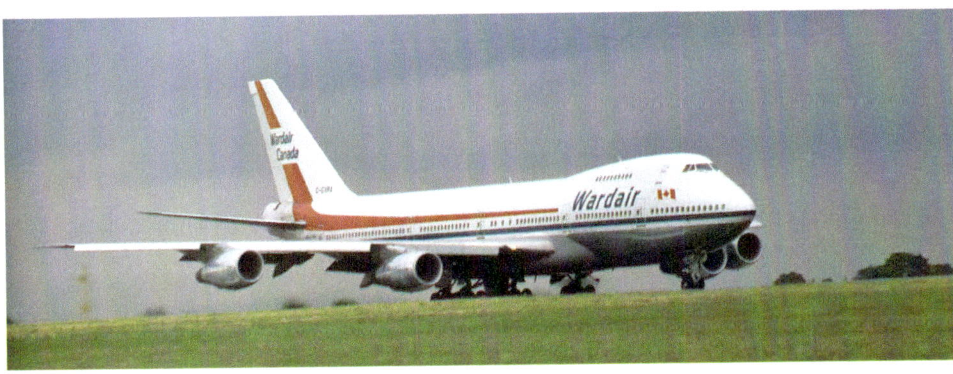

Wardair Canada Boeing 747-211B (C-GXRA) at the start of its take-off run at Manchester in the early 1980s. (Author's Collection)

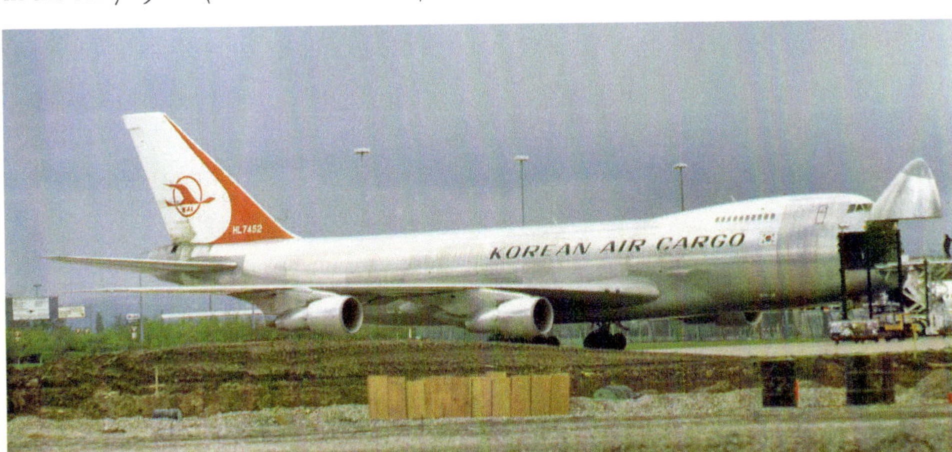

Korean Air Cargo Boeing 747-2B5F (HL7452), being loaded on 4 May 1981. (Author's Collection)

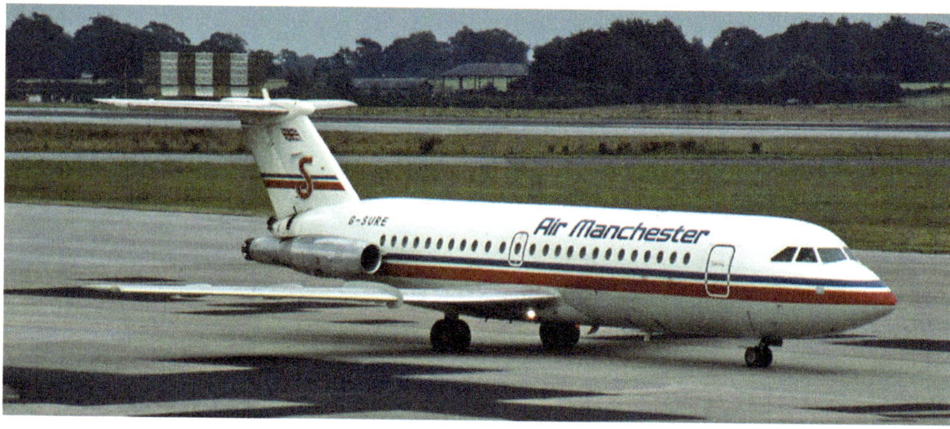

The short-lived charter airline Air Manchester's BAC 1-11-416 (G-SURE, previously G-AVOE with British Airways) in July 1982. (Author's Collection)

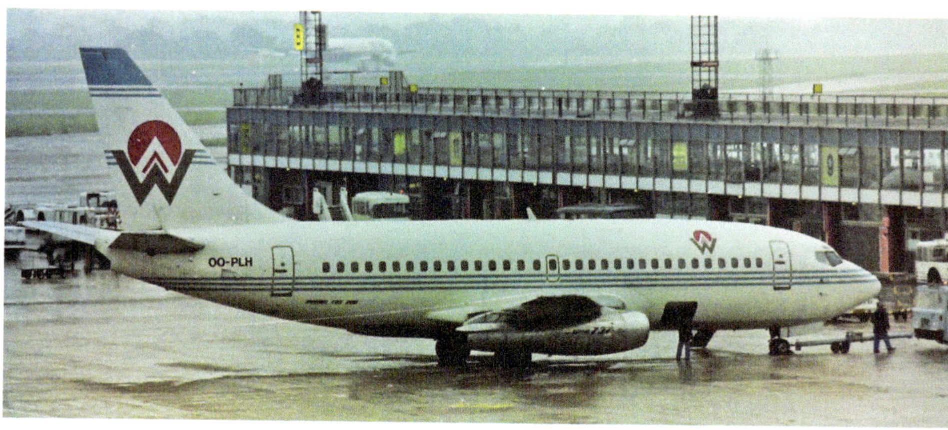

Britannia Airways Boeing 737-247 (OO-PLH) (on lease from Air Belgium) on 21 July 1986. (Mike Illien)

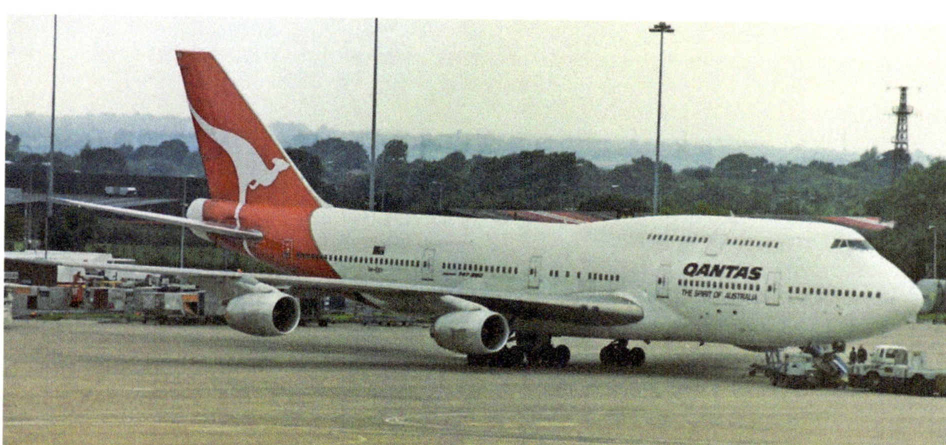

Qantas Boeing 747-338 *The Spirit of Australia* (VH-EBY) on 14 August 1988. (Mike Illien)

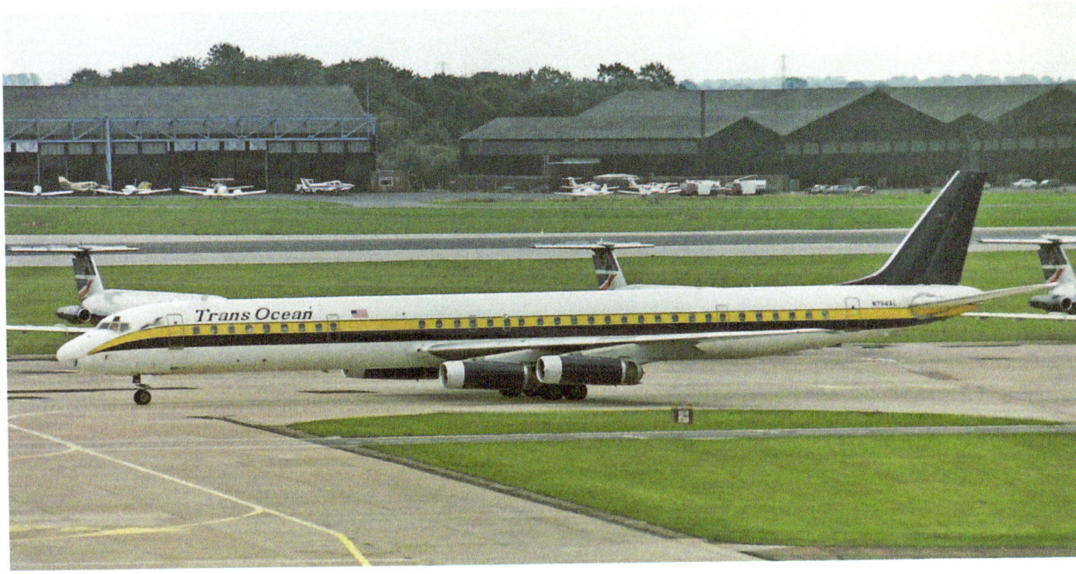

Trans Ocean Airways Douglas DC-8 (N794AL), leased from Aerolease, on 20 August 1989. (Mike Illien)

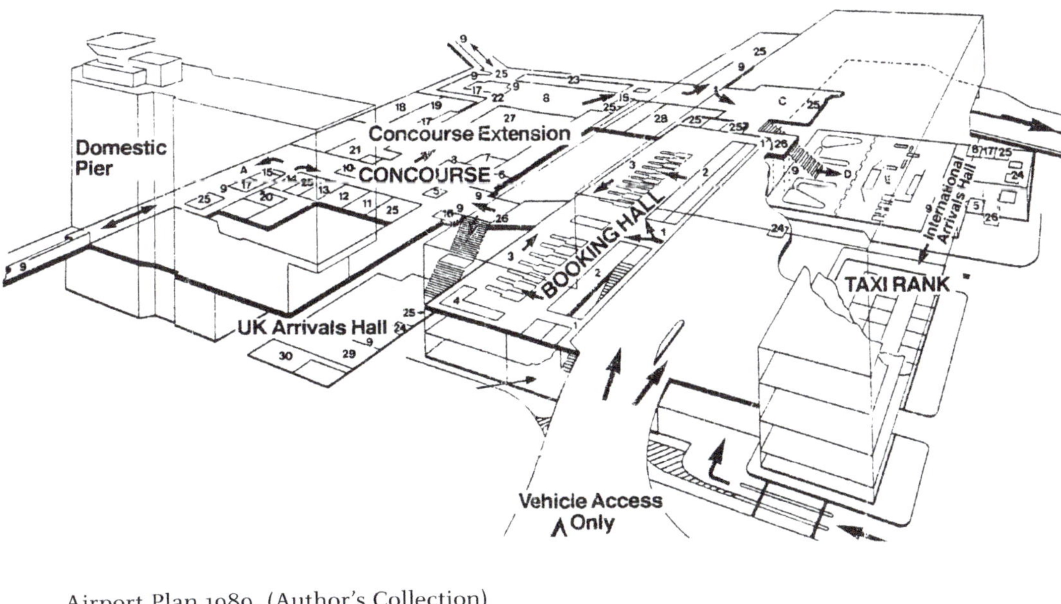

Airport Plan 1989. (Author's Collection)

Key: **A.** Domestic (Buffet) Lounge. **B.** International Departure Lounge **C.** Immigration & Passport Control **D.** International Baggage Re-claim. **E.** Customs Hall **1.** Main Flight Departure Entrances. **2.** Airline Offices. **3.** Check-in Desks. **4.** Tour Operators' Desks. **5.** Information Desks. **6.** Post Office. **7.** Book Shop. **8.** Bank & Bureau de Change. **9.** Telephones. **10.** Gift Shop. **11.** Record Shop. **12.** Florist. **13.** Chemist. **14.** Gents Hairdressers. **15.** British Airways Transfer Desk. **16.** Nursery. **17.** Buffets. **18.** Lancaster Restaurant. **19.** Grill Room. **20.** Grill Bar. **21.** Cocktail Bar. **22.** International Departure Lounge. **23.** Duty Free Shop. **24.** Car Hire Desks. **25.** Toilets. **26.** Lifts. **27.** Customs & Passport Control (Out). **28.** Health Control. **29.** Police Offices. **30.** Airport Security Offices. **31.** Spectators' Entrance.

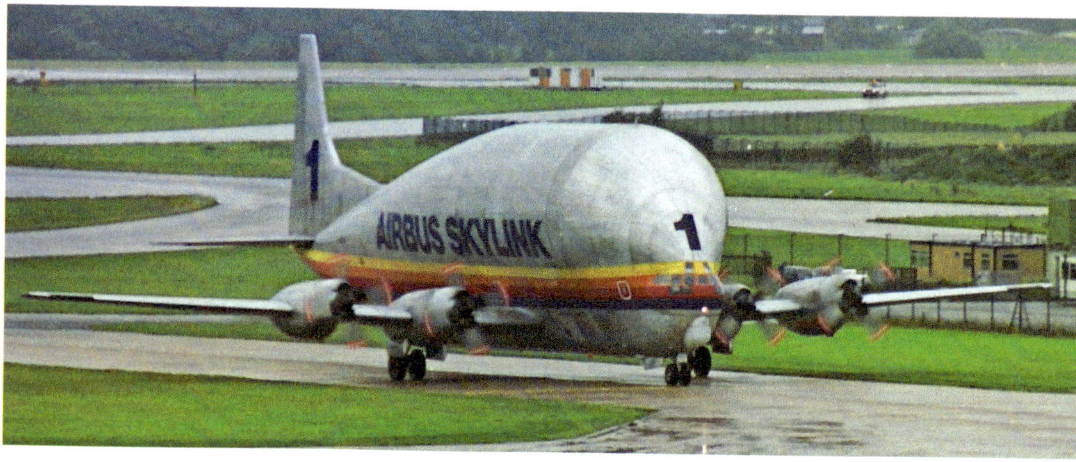

Airbus Skylink Aero Spacelines 377SGT Super Guppy (F-BTGV) on 27 August 1992. (Mike Illien)

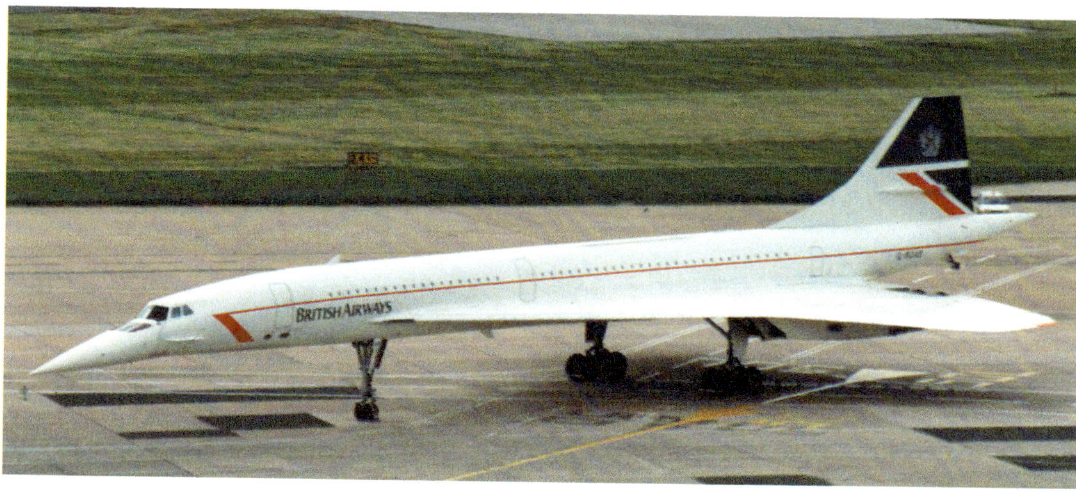

British Airways Concorde (208) (G-BOAB) rounding Pier 'A', *c.* 1992. (Alan Lord)

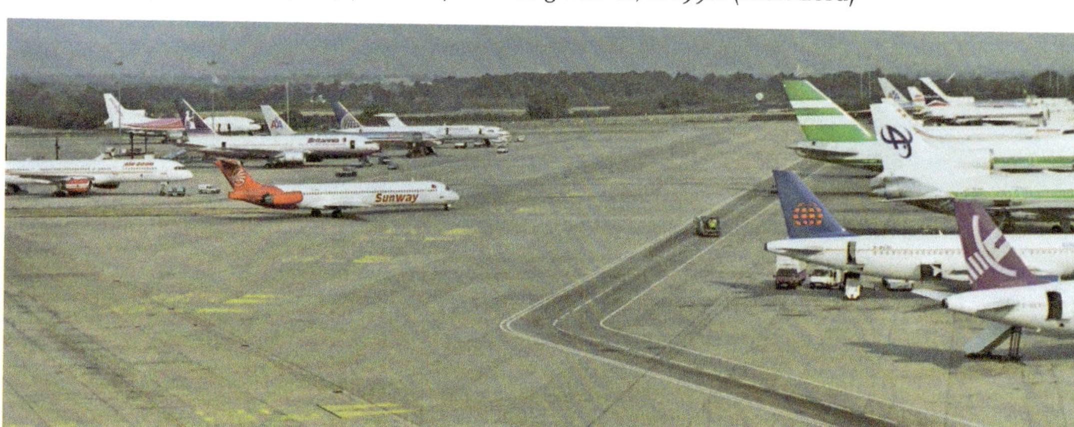

Monday morning traffic at Manchester Airport on 21 August 1995. (Mike Illien)

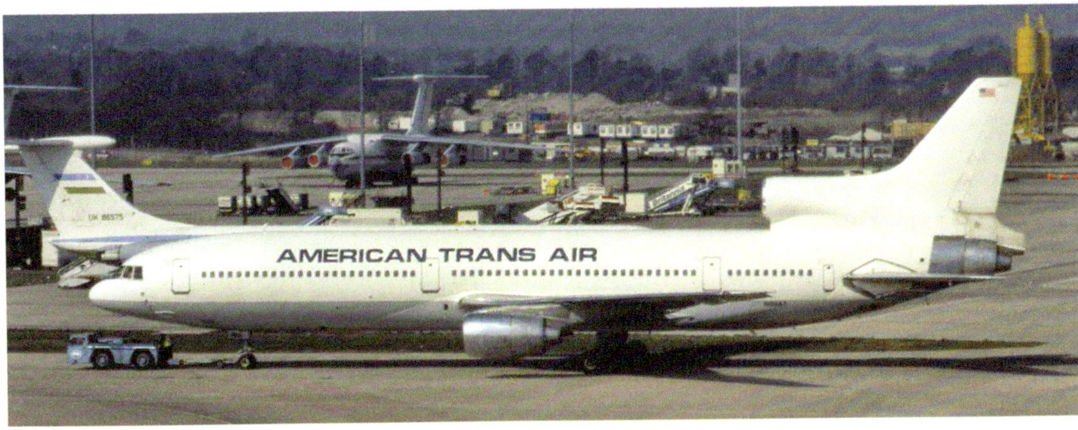

American Trans Air Lockheed L-1011-385-1 Tristar 50 (N188AT) in April 1996. (Paul Atkinson)

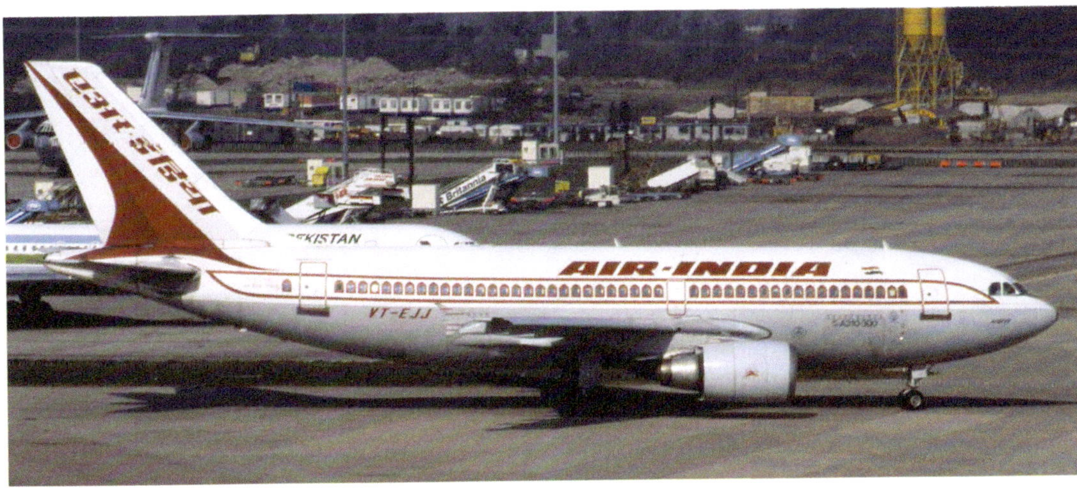

Air India Airbus A-310-304 (VT-EJJ) in April 1996. (Paul Atkinson)

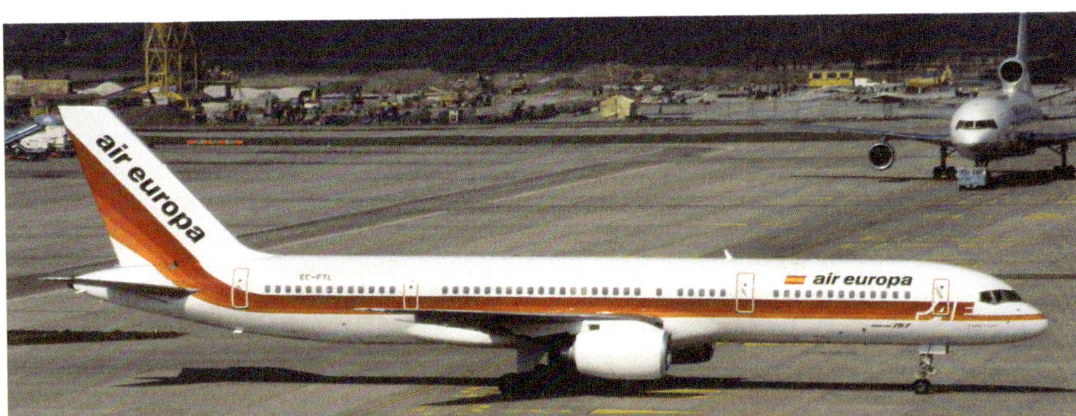

Air Europa Boeing 757-236 (EC-FTL), with work under way in the background for the west apron extension at the far end of Terminal 2, in April 1996. (Paul Atkinson)

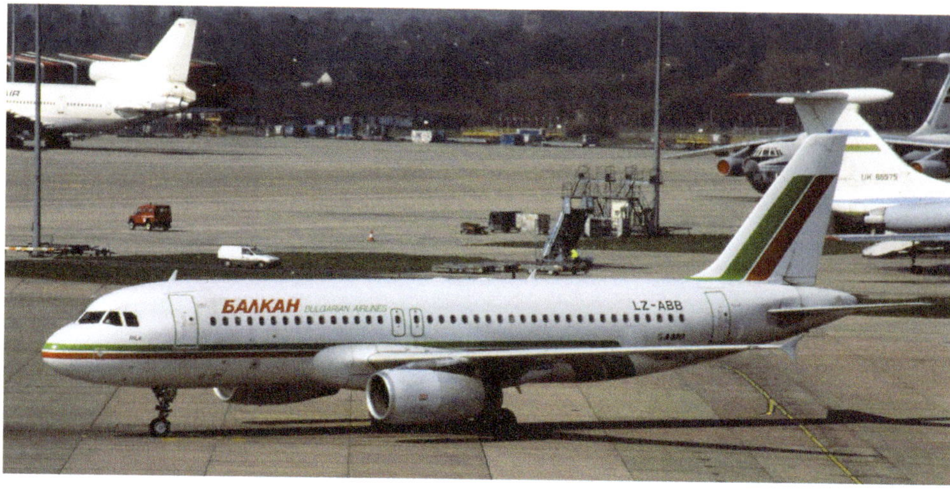

Balkan Bulgarian Airlines Airbus A-320-231 (LZ-ABB) in April 1996. (Paul Atkinson)

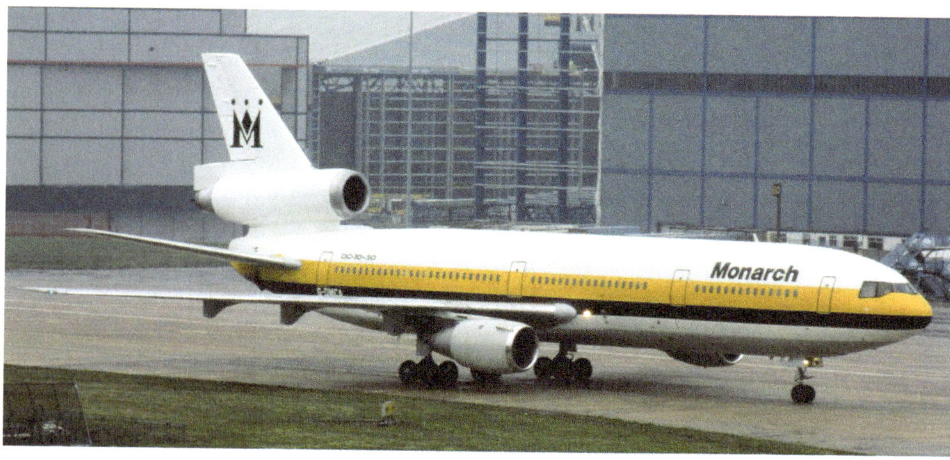

Monarch Airlines McDonnell Douglas DC-10-30 (G-DMCA) in May 1996. (The nose section of this aircraft is preserved in the Aviation Viewing Park, Manchester Airport.) (Paul Atkinson)

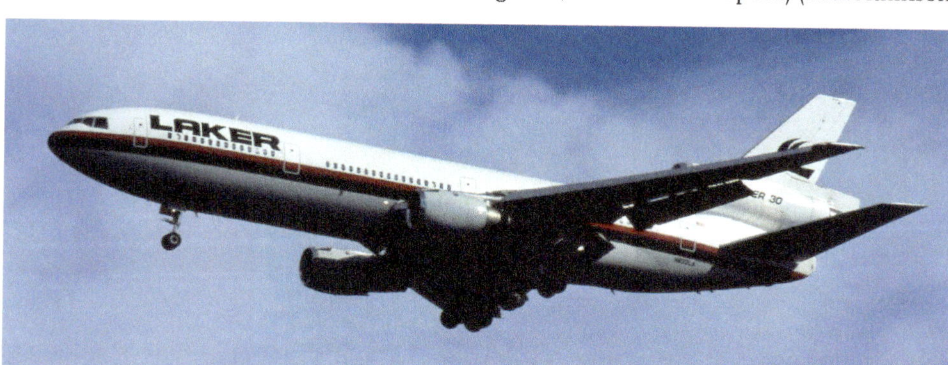

Laker Airways McDonnell Douglas DC-10-30 (N833LA), approaching runway 24 (now 23R). (Paul Atkinson)

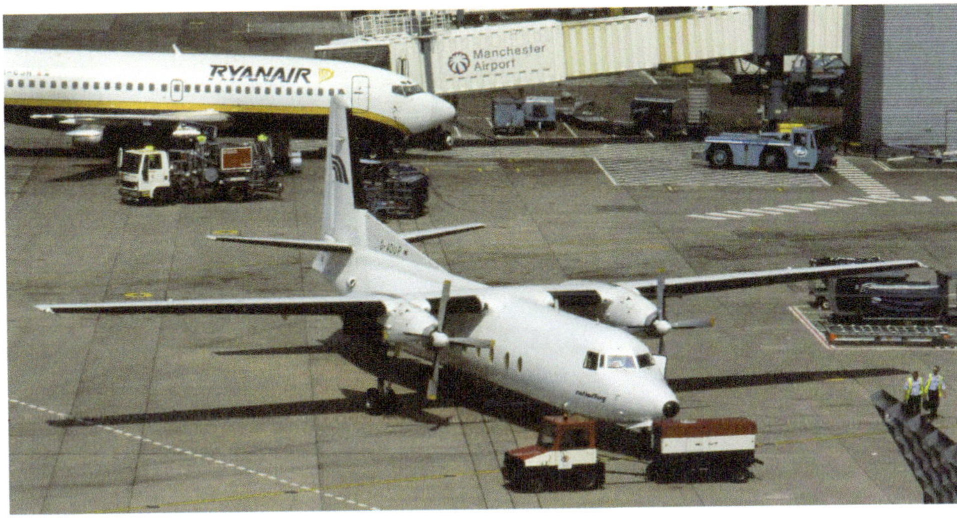

Ratioflug Fokker F-27-500 Friendship (D-ADUP) in June 1996. (Paul Atkinson)

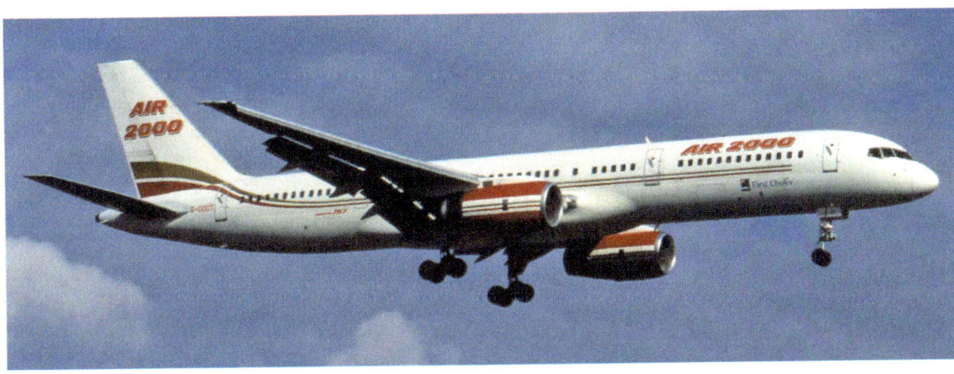

Air 2000 Boeing 757-236 (G-OOOT), approaching runway 24 (now 23R) in June 1996. (Paul Atkinson)

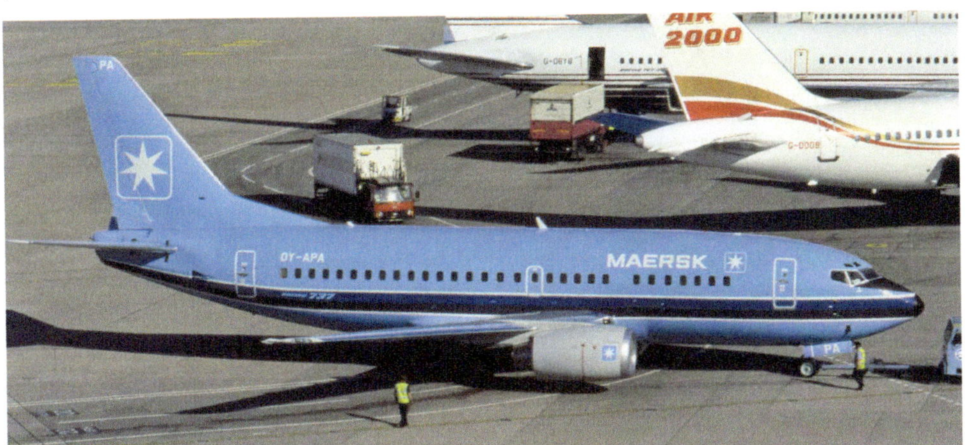

Maersk Air Boeing 737-5L9 (OY-APA) in June 1996. (Paul Atkinson)

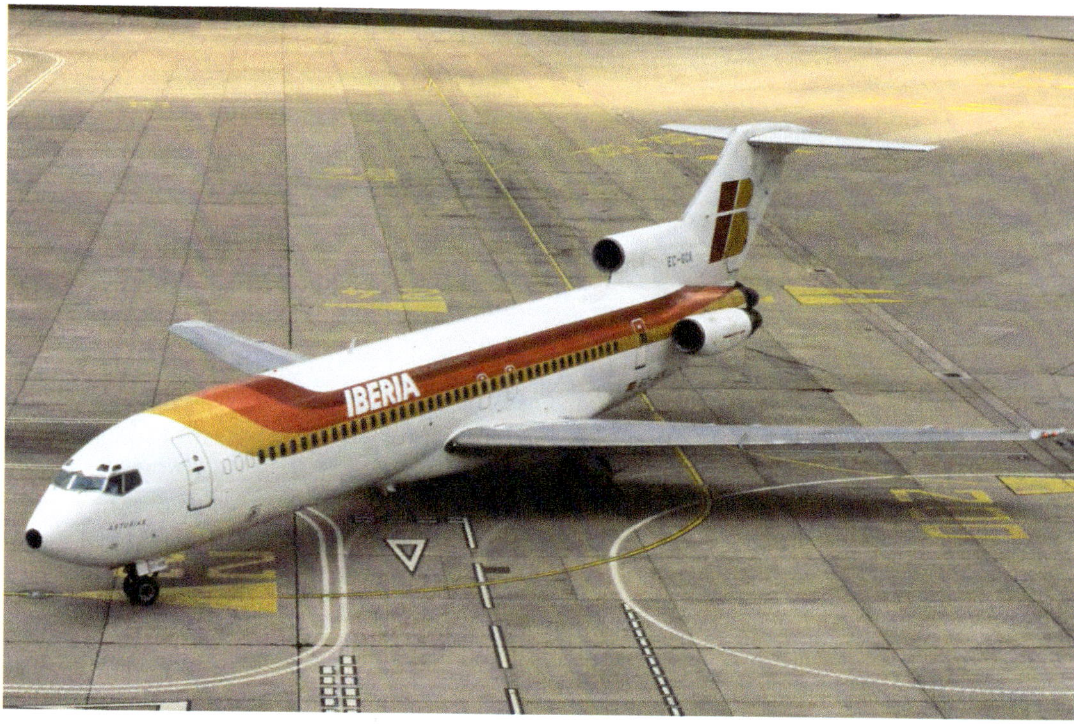

Iberia Boeing 727-256 (Adv) (EC-GCK) *Asturias* in July 1996. (Paul Atkinson)

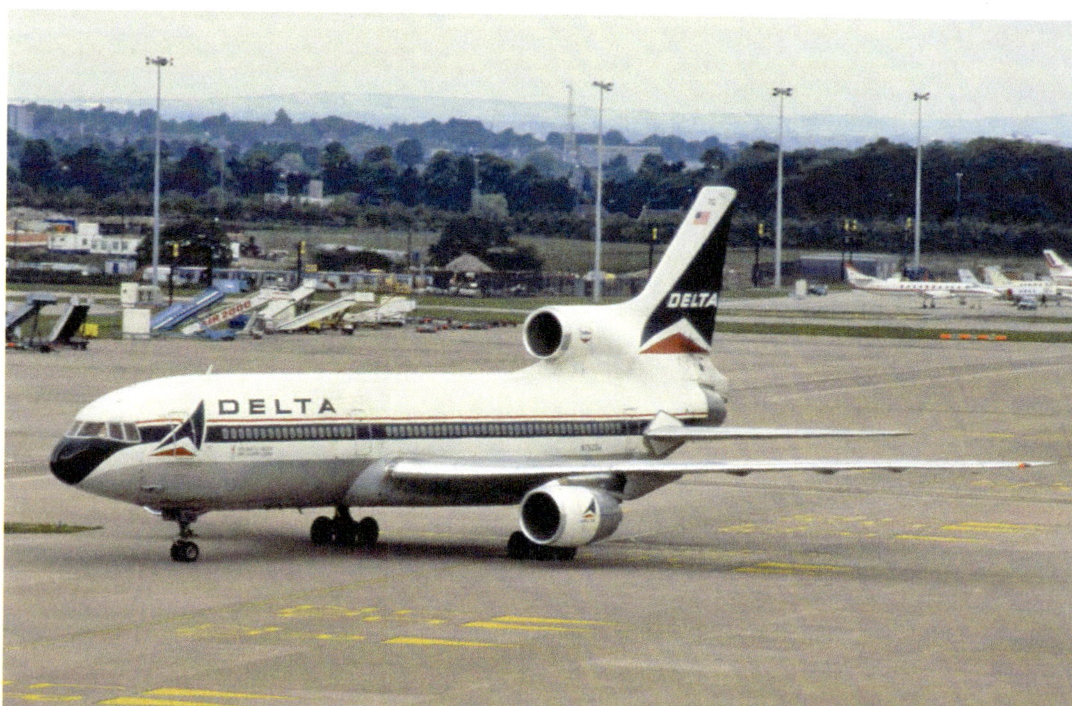

Delta Airlines Lockheed L-1011-385-3 Tristar 500 (N752DA) in July 1996. (Paul Atkinson)

A Decade of Redevelopment

With passenger numbers reaching 15 million in 1995, the two 1939/40-built hangars were demolished to make way for the construction of the new Terminal 3, of which British Airways paid part of the building costs. BA then made a further investment of £75 million to open their own facility and extension to the terminal for primary use by themselves and their partner airlines in June 1998.

Almost ten years after the plan for a second runway was lobbied, approval was finally granted on 15 January 1997, and construction began on Runway 2 (designated 06R/24L) in the same year. Negative public reaction over the intrusion into woodland in the Styal area of the £172-million project resulted in protest camps being set up. Heavy earthworks were required to embank the new runway over the A538 (which now runs through tunnels under both runways) and were extended further into land in the Oversley Ford area. The runway was officially opened by Prime Minister Tony Blair and became operational on 5 February 2001.

Manchester Airport bought a majority shareholding in Humberside International Airport in 1999, and just two years into the new millennium had completed the purchase of the East Midlands and Bournemouth airports so that it could expand and operate efficiently in a changing market place. In doing so, it became the second largest airport operator in the UK. The company was restructured and became Manchester Airports Group plc (MAG) as the holding company owned by the ten metropolitan borough councils of Greater Manchester.

Construction work began in 2000 on the £60-million Integrated Public Transport Interchange – a four-year project that would create a hub for easy connections for bus, coach, and rail passengers to several other large cities in the UK. The government gave the go-ahead for a £289-million Metrolink extension to the airport.

A £5.5-million retail upgrade of Terminal 1 was under way in 2002, and extensive development work of Terminal 2 got under way in the following year. Manchester was also successful in its bid to house one of the retired Concorde fleet: G-BOAC, British Airways' first Concorde and the flagship of their fleet, arrived on 31 October 2013 and was placed on display in the Runway Viewing Park.

In 2004, Manchester was chosen as one of a select few airports worldwide capable of accepting the 517-seat double-decker Airbus A380 aircraft – the world's largest commercial airliner, designed to meet air transport needs in the twenty-first century – and £10 million was spent in making the necessary adaptions. These included strengthening the runways, moving ground signs back, and purchasing new Scania fire engines as part of the larger expansion at the airport. Hundreds of staff joined thousands of people to see the Emirates A380 (Flight EK017) from Dubai land for the first time on 1 September 2010, making Manchester the first regional airport in the world to have a daily A380 service.

The budget airline Jet2 (which had opened a base at Manchester in 2004) began early advertising of its daily summer service flights to Nice for 2006 in August 2005, following BA's announcement that it was to withdraw from the route. Jet2 also added Ibiza as its sixteenth route from Manchester later the same month.

Manchester Airport handled over 22 million passengers a year for the first time in 2005, according to Civil Aviation Authority (CAA) statistics and, in 2007, a Land Use Plan was published as part of the Manchester Airport Master Plan. This set out the long-term development strategy to 2030, by which time the Department of Transport has projected that around 50 million people a year will be using the airport.

At 1 a.m. (BST) on 7 June 2007, the runway markings were changed because of their location and compass heading changed from 06L-24R and 06R-24L to 05L-23R and 05R-23L respectively to account for changes in the Earth's magnetic field. This geological phenomenon is due to changes in the flow of the Earth's molten iron core, where the Earth's magnetic field is generated, causing the slow movement of magnetic north. All airports were affected and made the necessary changes to their runway location numbers. The next change is not expected until around 2063.

The British low-cost airline carrier easyJet purchased the entire share capital of the UK airline GB Airways from the Bland Group on 25 October 2007. The deal was worth £103.5 million and was used by the airline to expand operations at Gatwick, and also to establish a base at Manchester Airport.

A major refurbishment of Terminal 1 began in 2007 to improve the flow of passengers and create one of the UK's largest airside shopping and catering facilities. A £14-million, fourteen-lane security area was installed to reduce queuing times, and retailers invested almost £15 million on an overhaul and improvement of the shop outlets (which covered around 4,000 sq. m).

Around twenty former Concorde pilots and engineers were joined by dignitaries and guests on 25 February 2009 for the opening of the new £1m Concorde hangar and visitor centre at the airport's Aviation Viewing Park, which will protect Concorde, safeguarding her for future generations. Concorde (G-BOAC) had been on display in the open air since October 2003.

The airport began to trial imaging technology in October 2009 as a replacement for the pat-down security check, in order to optimize check-in throughput in Terminal 2. The technology, called Rapiscan Secure 1000 SP (Single Pose), uses high-definition X-rays to check passengers' front and back for concealed objects. The new imaging technology was permanently introduced in Terminals 1 and 2 in February 2010 as part of a new government-mandated legislation as a measured response to the bomb plot on Northwest Airlines Flight 253 to Detroit on 25 December 2009. The layout was also altered in Departures of Terminal 1 so that the only part that is accessible is the passage at the front close to the airline ticket offices. The former hall was divided into lounges and passages on two levels; the huge chandeliers were removed and are now in a museum in Manchester.

In March 2010, the Dubai-based airline Emirates announced that it will bring the double-deck Airbus A380 to Manchester, the first regional airport to host the aircraft. Etihad Airways (the second-largest airline of the United Arab Emirates) also announced an increase in capacity and the construction of a new lounge for Manchester, its third outside of Abu Dhabi. Manchester became a Category 10 airport as it could handle the A380 and Code F aircraft (wingspans of 65 m up to but not including 80 m, and an outer main gear wheel span of 14 m up to but not including 16 m), which meant having extensive rescue and firefighting cover, as determined by the Civil Aviation Authority (CAA). This includes being capable of reaching any incident within the airport (including the predetermined boundaries outside of the airport) within a set time of three minutes.

In an announcement by the Chancellor of the Exchequer in the March 2011 Budget, Manchester Airport was confirmed as the location within Greater Manchester of one of the government's twenty-one UK 'Enterprise Zones'. As part of an investment of £800 million by the Beijing Construction Engineering Group, an 'Airport City' – in which the airport, its terminals, apron, and runways, and on-airport businesses such as air cargo, logistics, offices, retail, hotels, and leisure facilities are all 'inside the perimeter fence' – will be created by 2020.

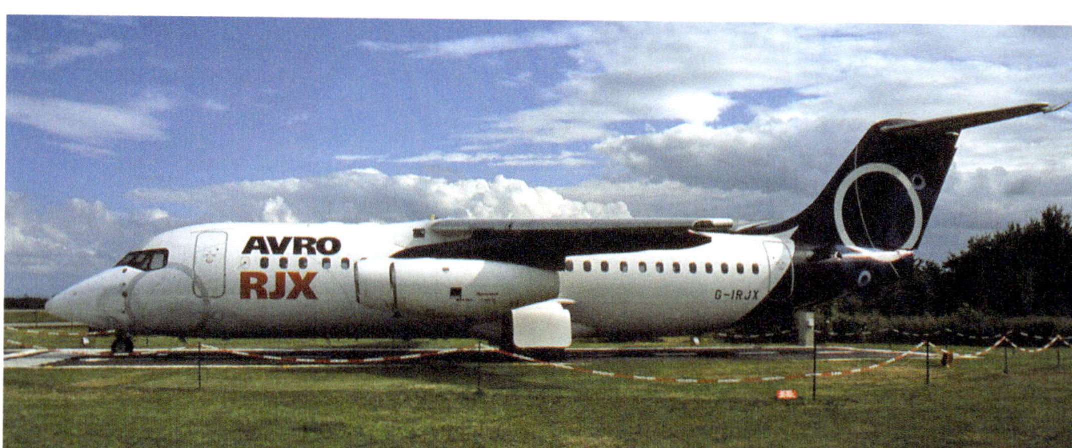

BAe 146/Avro RJX-100 Whisperjet (G-IRJX) in 2003. (Author's Collection)

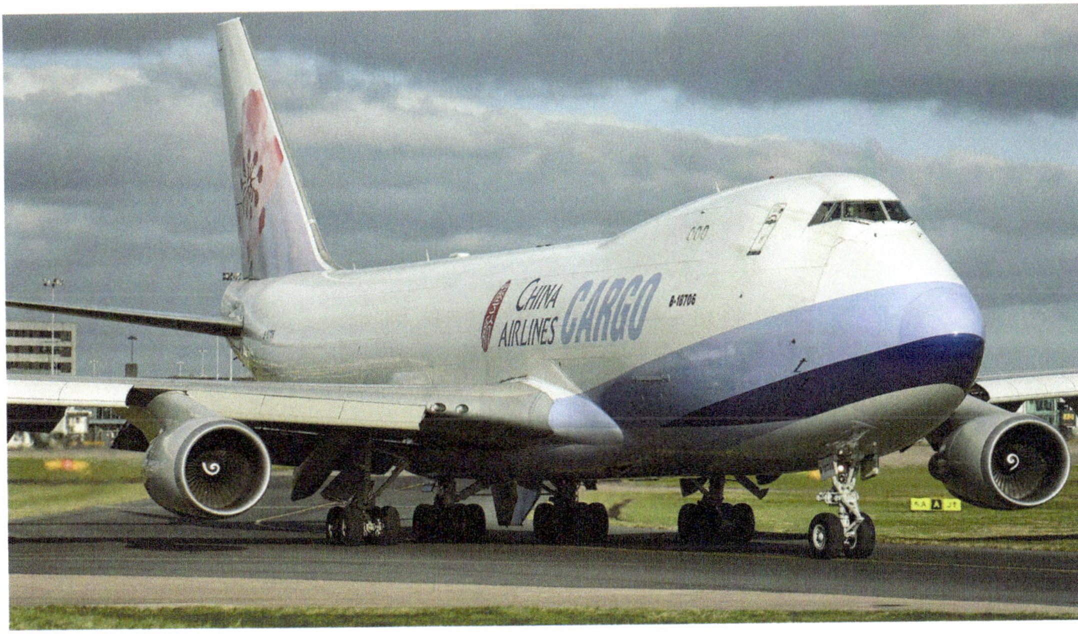

China Airlines Boeing Cargo 747-400F (B-18706) on 21 February 2004. (Enda Burke)

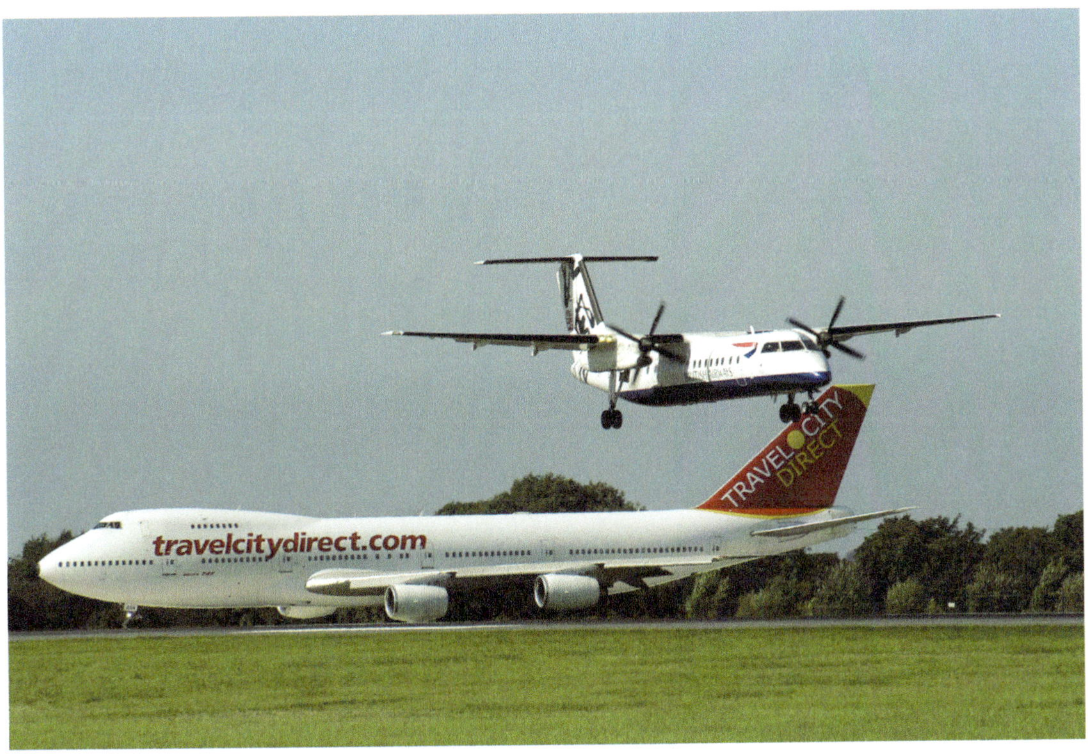

TF-ABA Travel City Direct Boeing 747-200. Manchester's runway 05R is not usually used for take-offs. Here the aircraft has backtracked and is awaiting its slot, while a British Airways Dash 8 crosses the threshold on 9 September 2004. (Alan Lord)

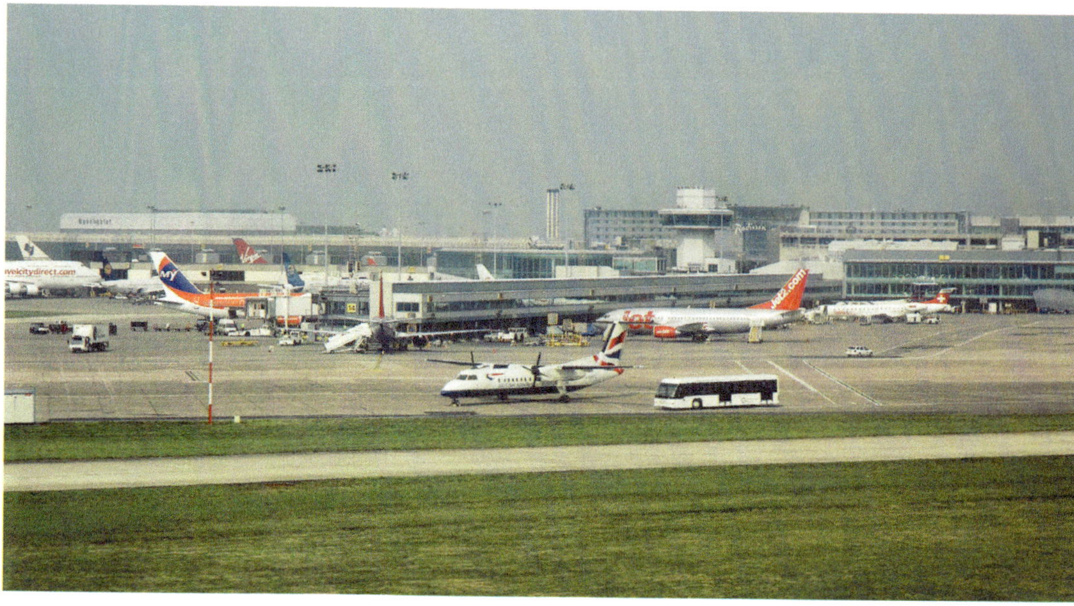

Rotating left to right off runway 06L: Travel City Direct (Air Atlanta Icelandic) Boeing 747-312, Pakistan International Airlines (PIA) Boeing 747-367, Lufthansa Airbus A319-114, MyTravel Airways Boeing 757-225 (G-RJGR), Virgin Atlantic Airways Boeing 747-219B, Thomas Cook Airlines Airbus A330-243, Jet2 (Channel Express) Boeing 737-330 (G-CELX), British Airways (G-BRYZ), de Havilland Canada DHC-8-311Q Dash 8, Jet2 (Channel Express) Boeing 737-330 (G-CELJ) and Swiss International Air Lines HB-JAV Embraer EMB-145LU (ERJ-145LU). Pictured on 2 April 2005. (Robert Frola)

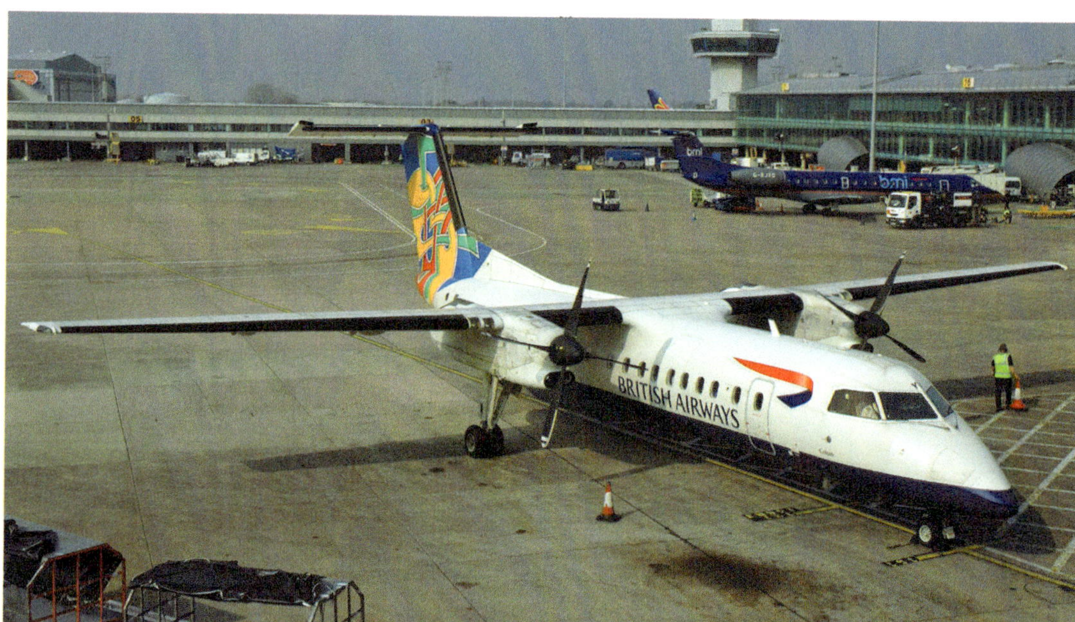

British Airways Bombardier Dash 8-Q311 (G-BRYV) *Colum* (meaning 'dove'), sporting the World (Utopia) Tail, Ireland, on 2 April 2005. (Robert Frola)

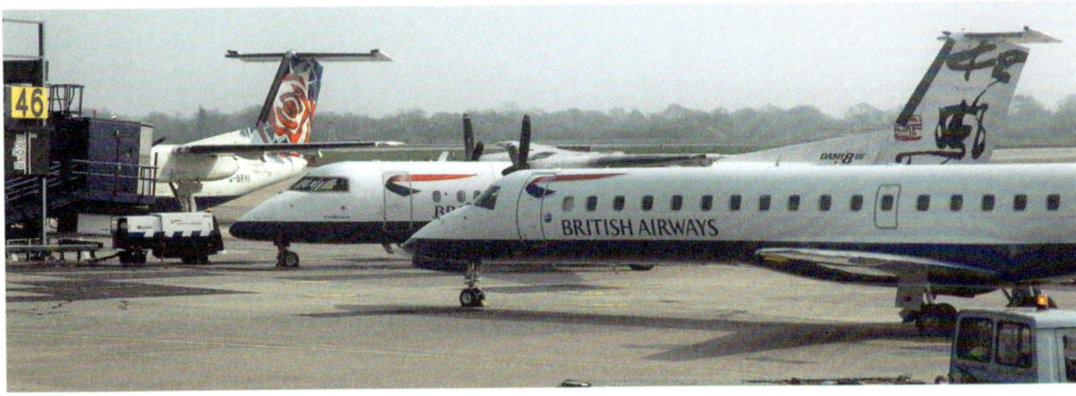

British Airways Bombardier Dash 8-Q311 *Chelsea Rose* (G-BRYI), sporting the World (Utopia) Tail, England; Bombardier Dash 8-Q311 *Rendezvous* (G-BRYY) sporting the World (Utopia) Tail, China; and Embraer EMB-145EU (ERJ-145EU) (G-EMBI). Pictured 2 April 2005. (Robert Frola)

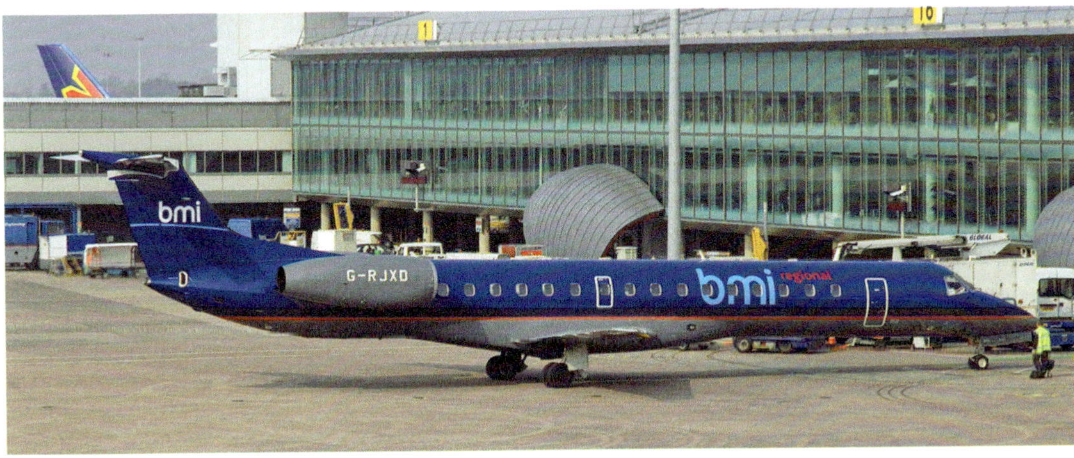

bmi Regional Embraer ERJ-145EP (G-RJXD) on 2 April 2005. (Robert Frola)

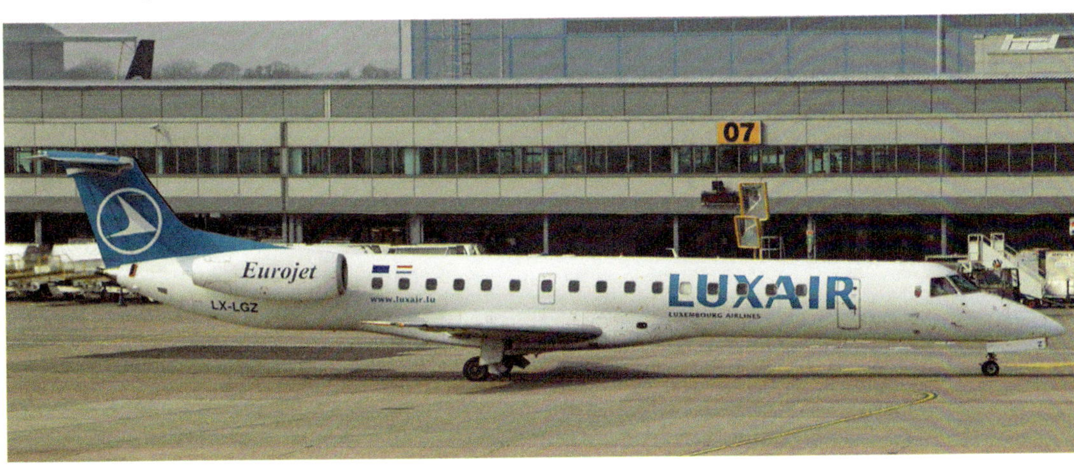

Luxair Embraer ERJ-145LU (LX-LGZ) on 2 April 2005. (Robert Frola)

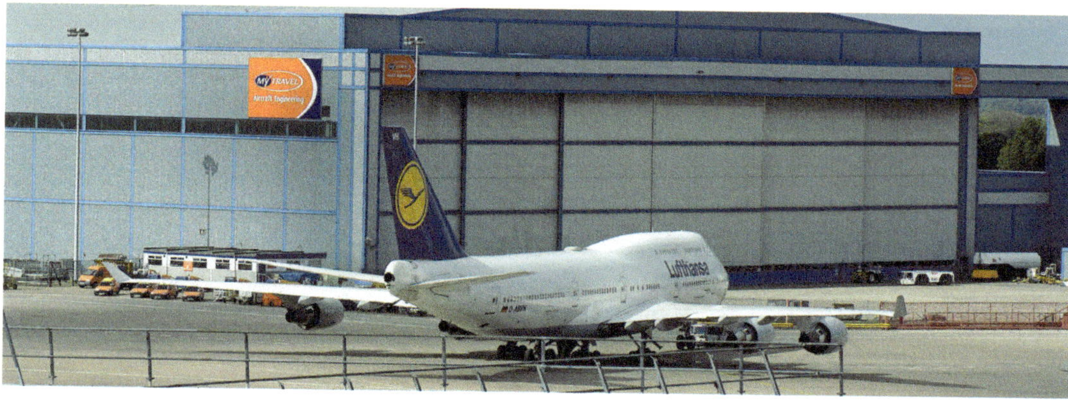

Lufthansa Boeing 747-400 (D-ABVH), paying an unexpected visit to Manchester on 22 May 2005. (Alan Lord)

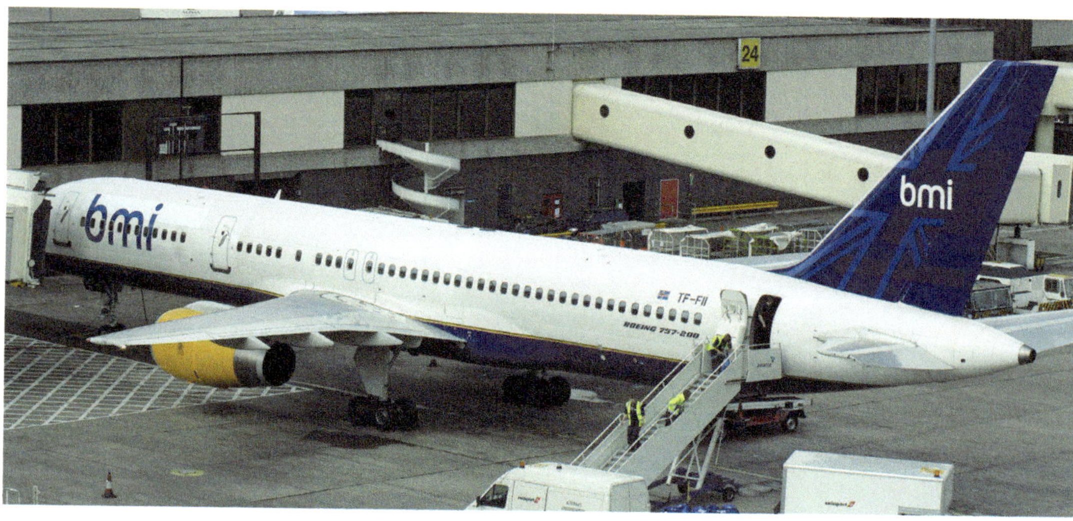

bmi British Midland Boeing 757-208 (TF-FII), on lease from Icelandair, being cleaned before its next flight on 22 May 2005. (Alan Lord)

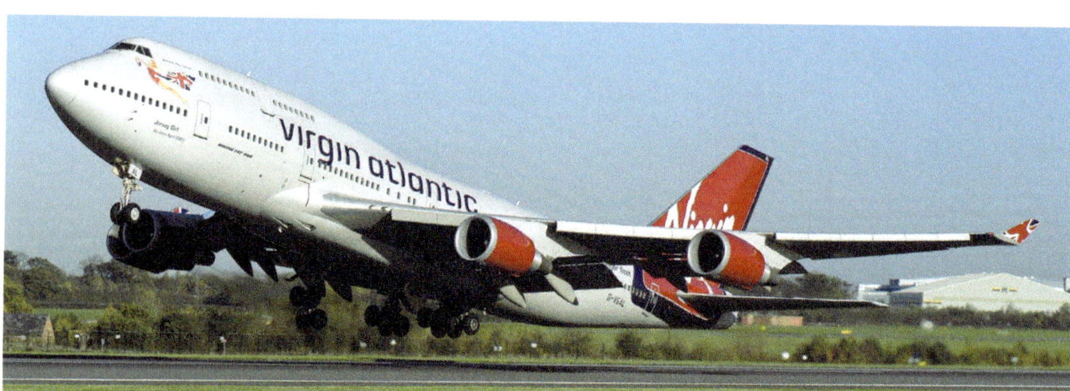

Virgin Atlantic Boeing 747-400 (G-VGAL) on 13 November 2005. (Alan Lord)

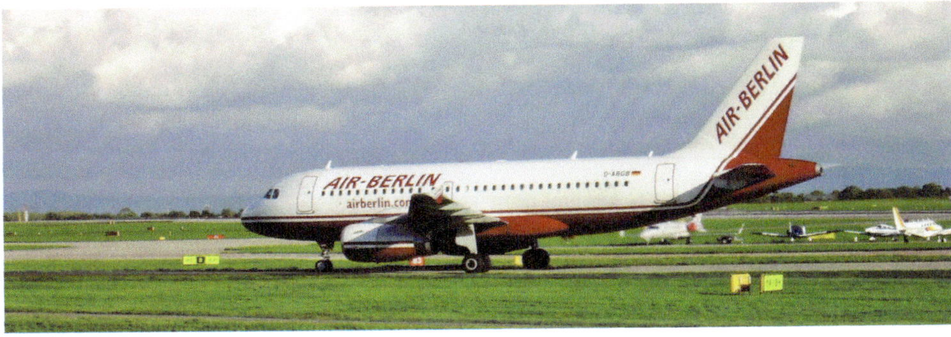

Air Berlin A319-132 (G-ABGB) on 24 October 2006. (Martin Jones)

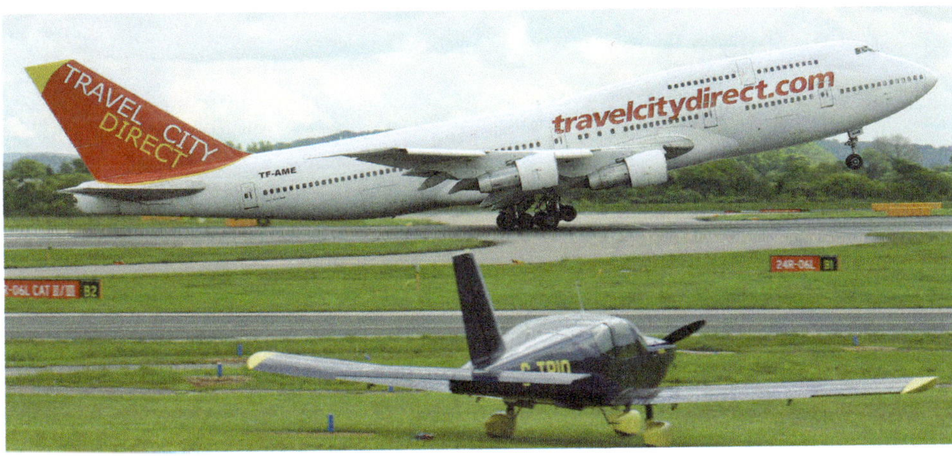

Travel City Direct Boeing 747-312 (TF-AME), departing 23R on 22 May 2006. (Enda Burke)

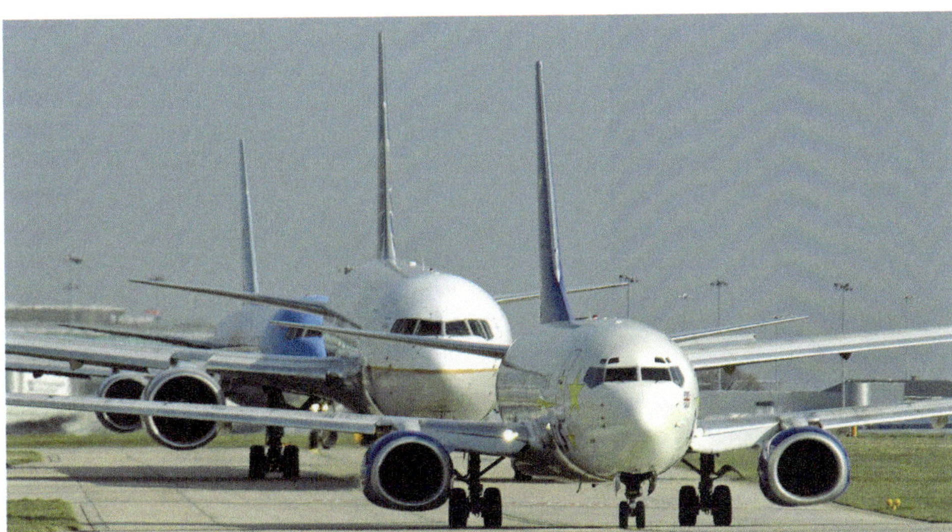

Manchester Airport morning departures line up, as a series of aircraft proceed to the runway on 23 March 2006. (Alan Lord)

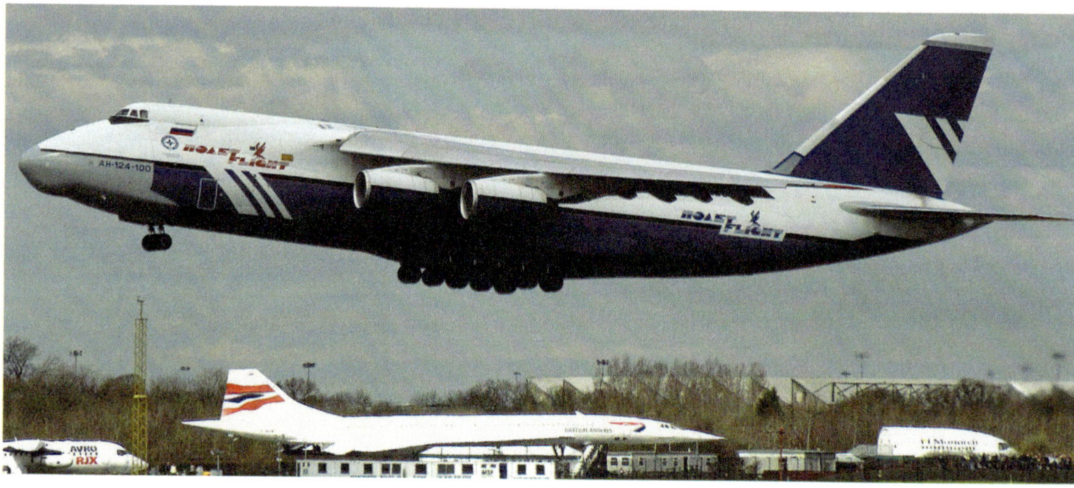

Polet Airlines Antonov An-124-100 Ruslan (RA-82080), climbing away with Manchester's Concorde (G-BOAC) in the background on 10 April 2006. (Alan Lord)

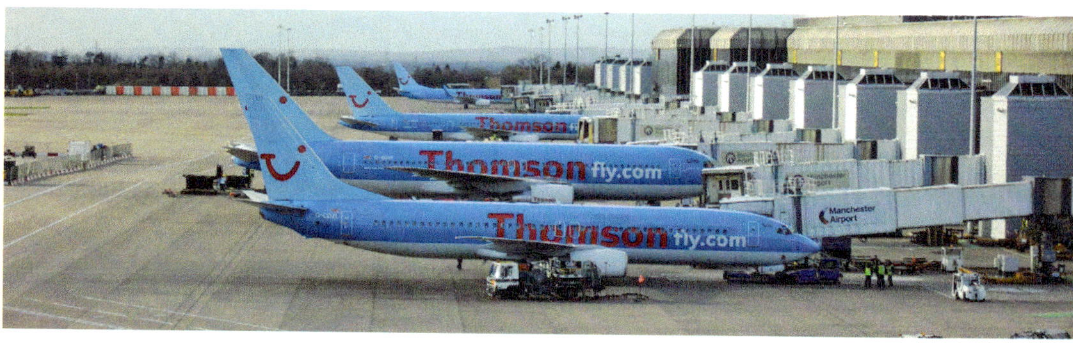

A row of Thomsonfly Boeings, fronted by 737-804 (G-CDZL) and 767-200 (G-BRIF), on 3 March 2007. (Martin Jones)

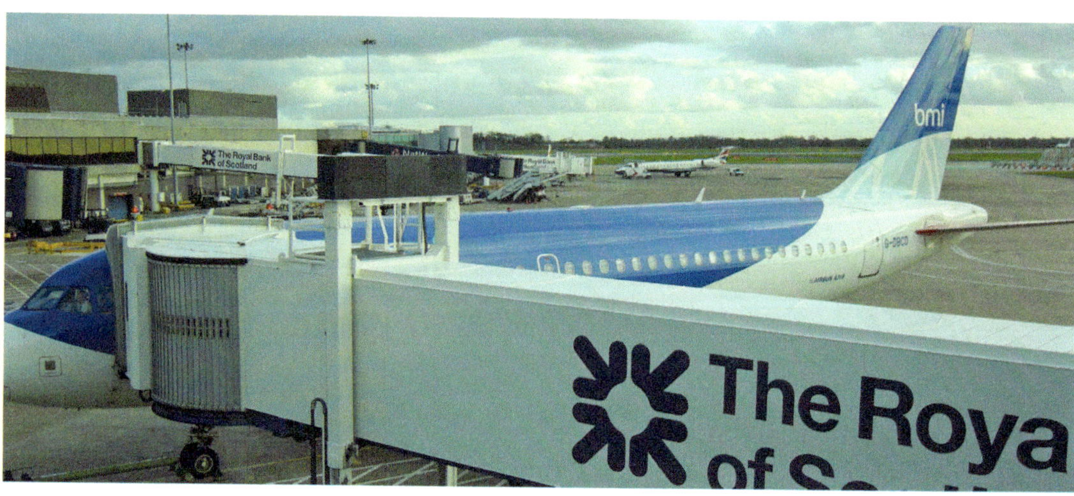

bmi British Midland Airbus A319-131 (G-DBCD), finishing up on 3 March 2007. (Martin Jones)

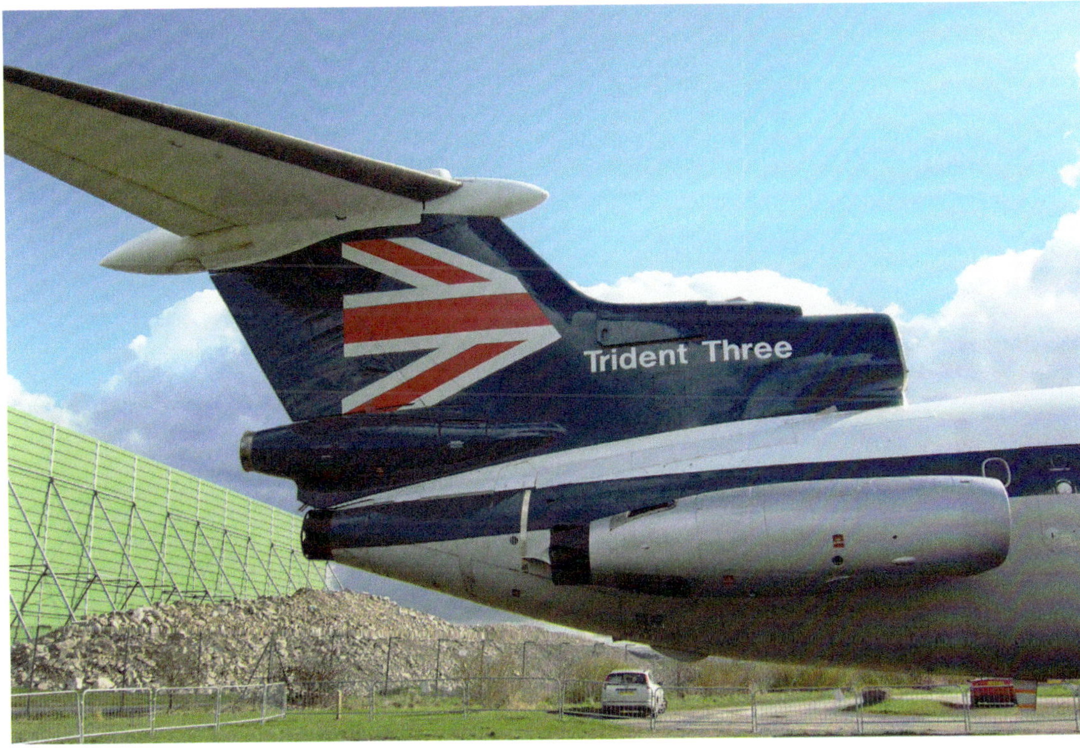

Trident 3 tail, 3 March 2007. (Martin Jones)

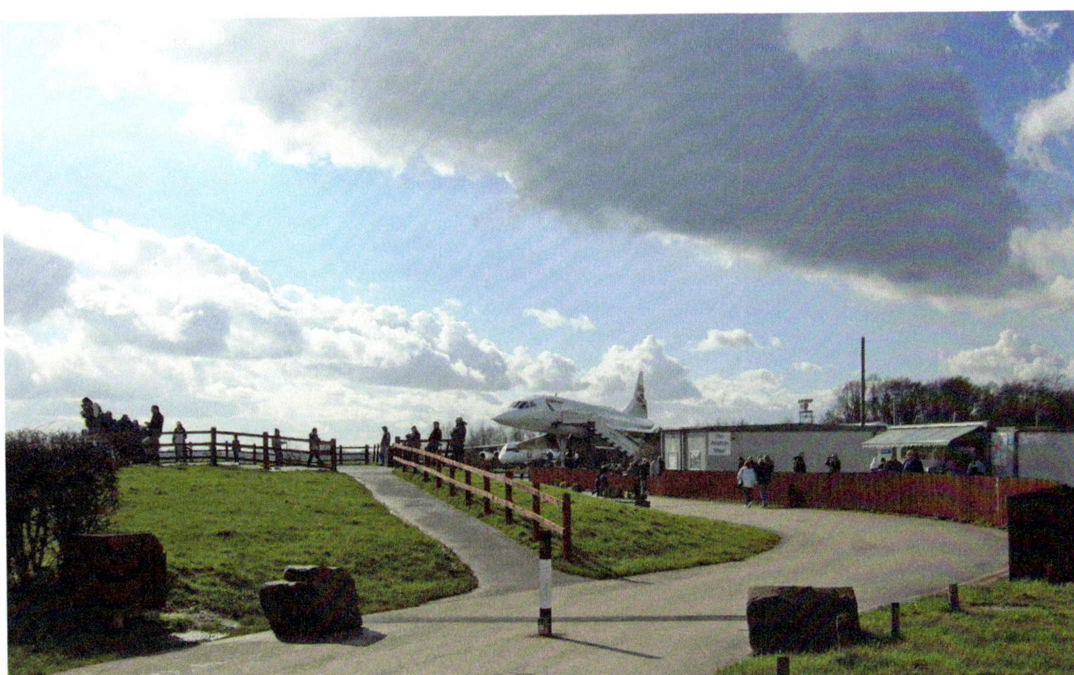
What Manchester Airport Viewing Park used to look like; 3 March 2007. (Martin Jones)

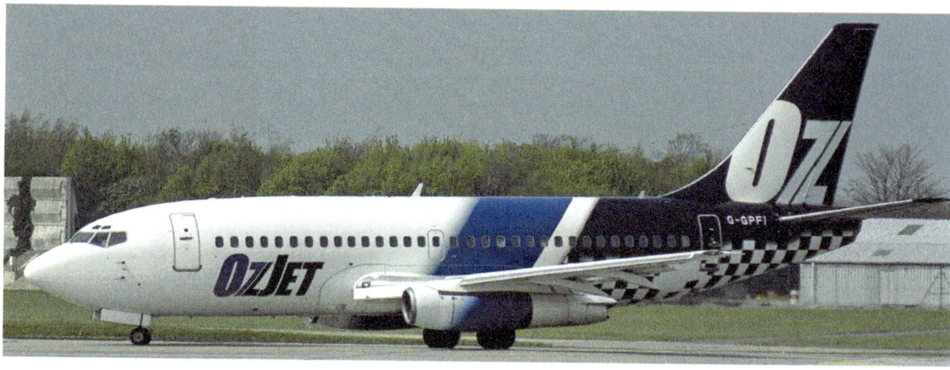

Boeing 737-200 (G-GPFI) in scheduled and charter airline OzJet Airlines colours. It should have still been flying as VH-OZQ for OzJet in Australia, but was in the UK on 15 April 2007. (Alan Lord)

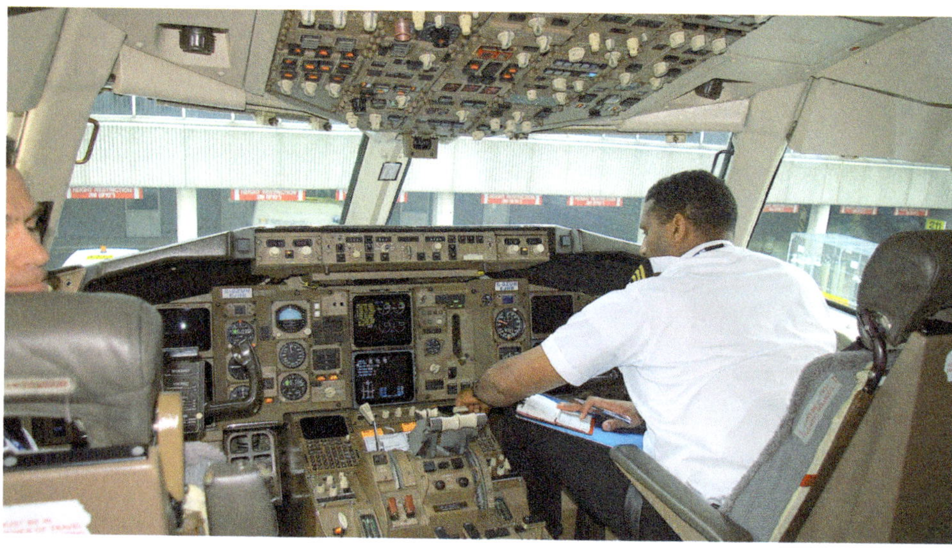

Cockpit of Zoom Airlines B767-300 (C-GZUM) on 16 December 2007. (David Hinsley)

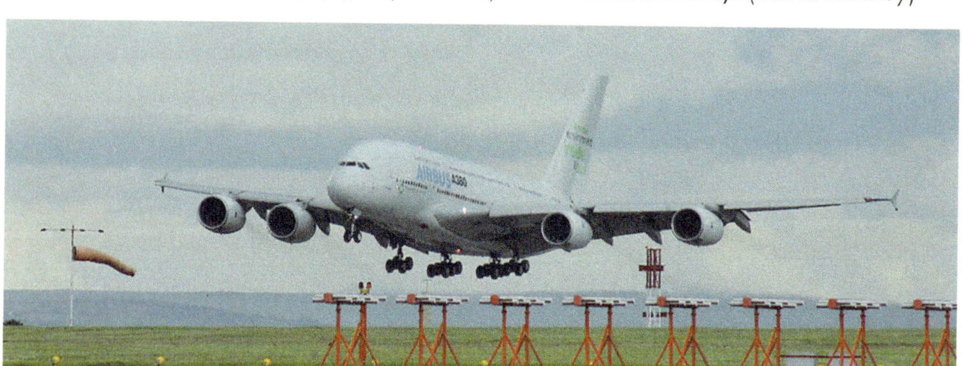

The first ever visit of an Airbus A380-861 (F-WWDD) to Manchester, on 12 July 2008. (Enda Burke)

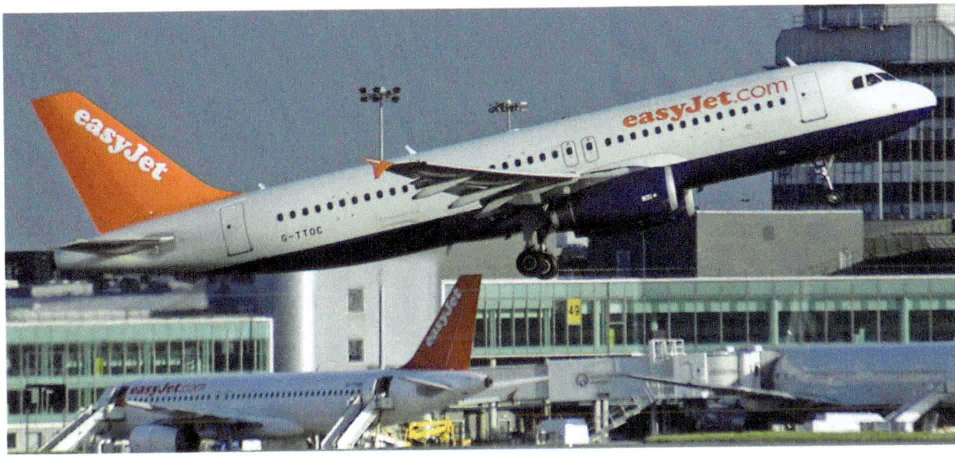

Having acquired GB Airways in March 2008, Airbus A320-232 (G-TTOC) was flown in this colour scheme for easyJet, but now flies for Meridiana Airlines as I-EEZN. 21 May 2008. (Alan Lord)

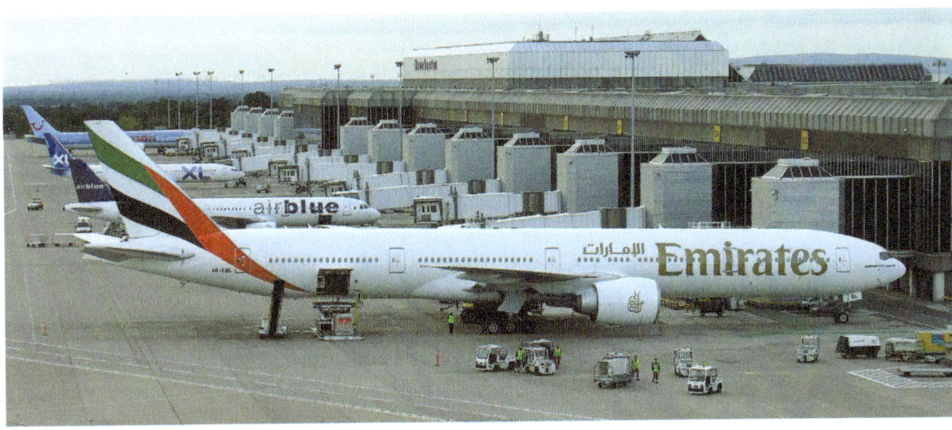

Overview of Terminal 2 on Sunday evening, 13 July 2008. (Paul Atkinson)

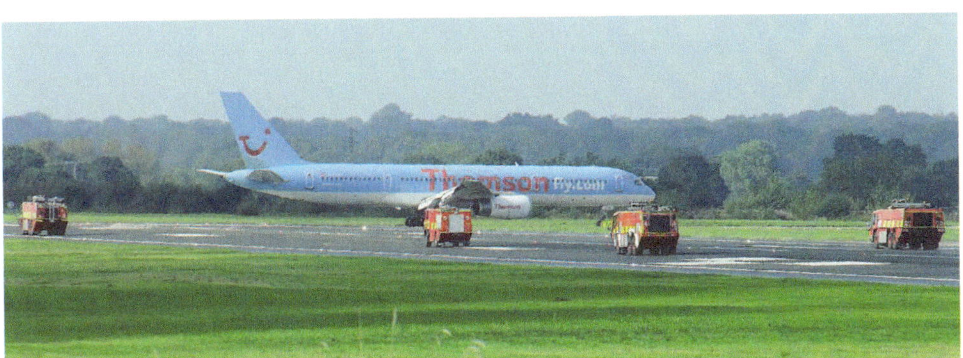

Manchester Fire Service vehicles on their way to attend Thomsonfly Boeing 757-204 (G-BYAK), which aborted take-off after problems with its hydraulics on 13 September 2008. (Paul Atkinson)

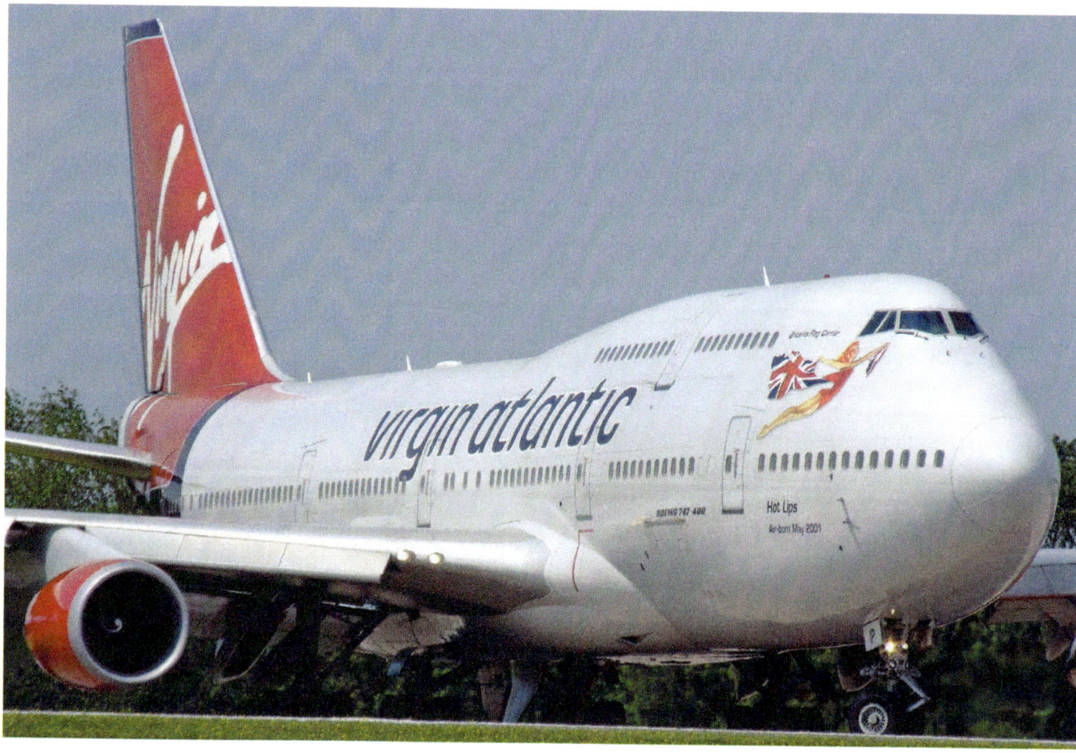

Virgin Atlantic Airways Boeing 747-443 (G-VLIP) on 24 May 2008. (Paul Atkinson)

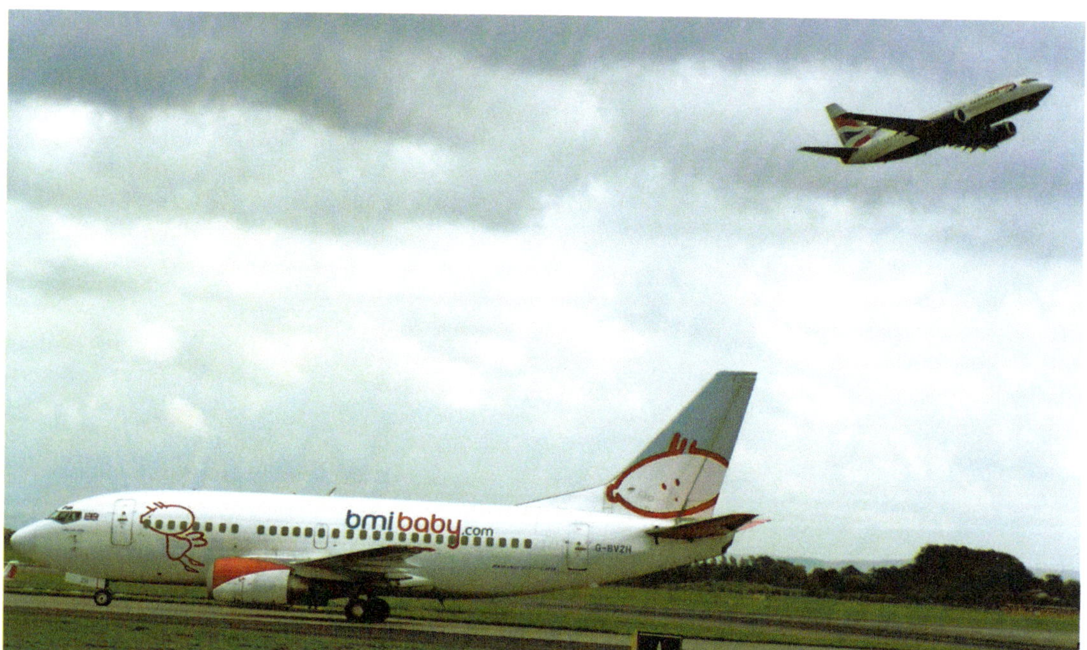

bmibaby Boeing 737-500 (G-BVZH) – an example of the world's best-selling airliner in 2008. (Martin Jones)

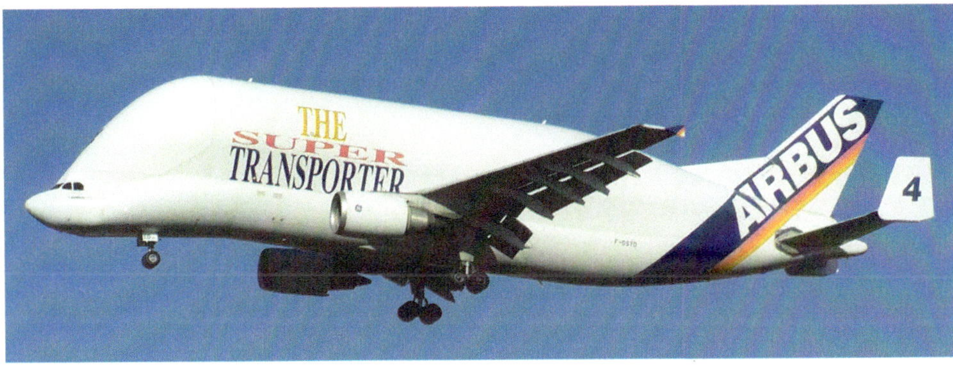

Airbus Transport International Beluga A300B4-608ST (F-GSTD) on 19 February 2008. (Paul Atkinson)

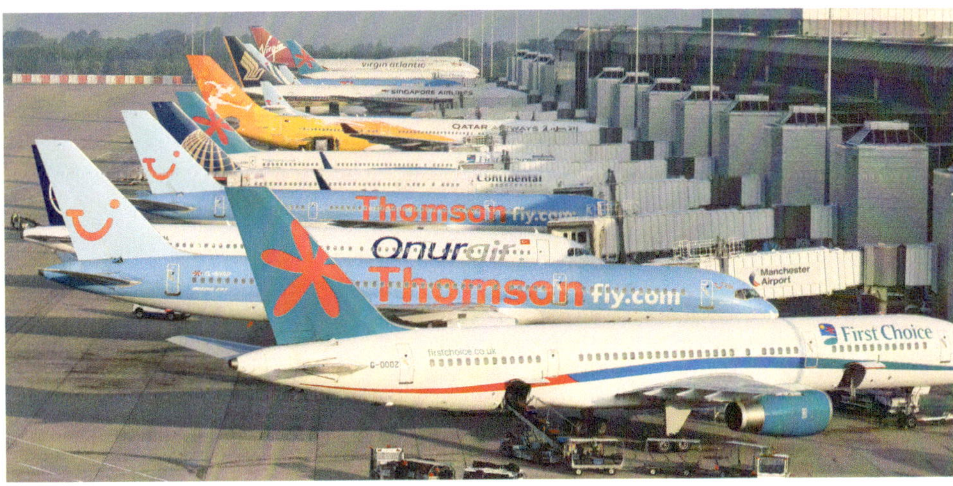

Early morning at Terminal 2 on 14 September 2008. (David Hinsley)

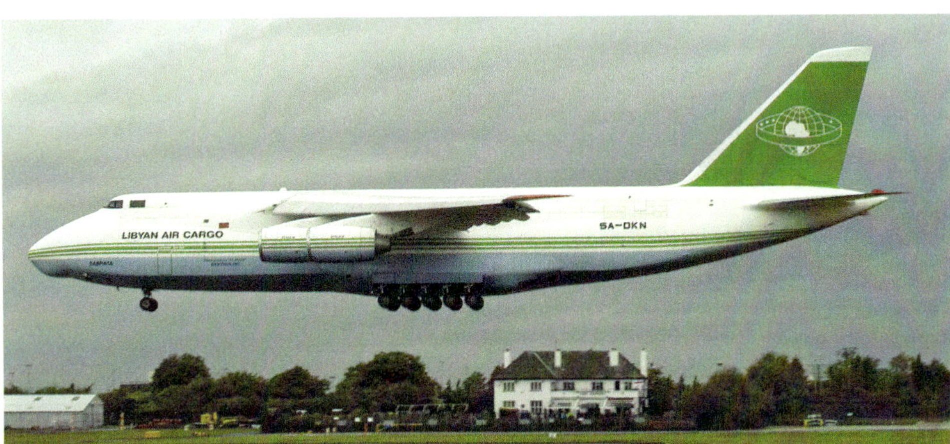

Libyan Air Cargo An-124-100 (5A-DKN) passes the airport hotel when about to touch down on runway 23R on 4 May 2009. (Alan Lord)

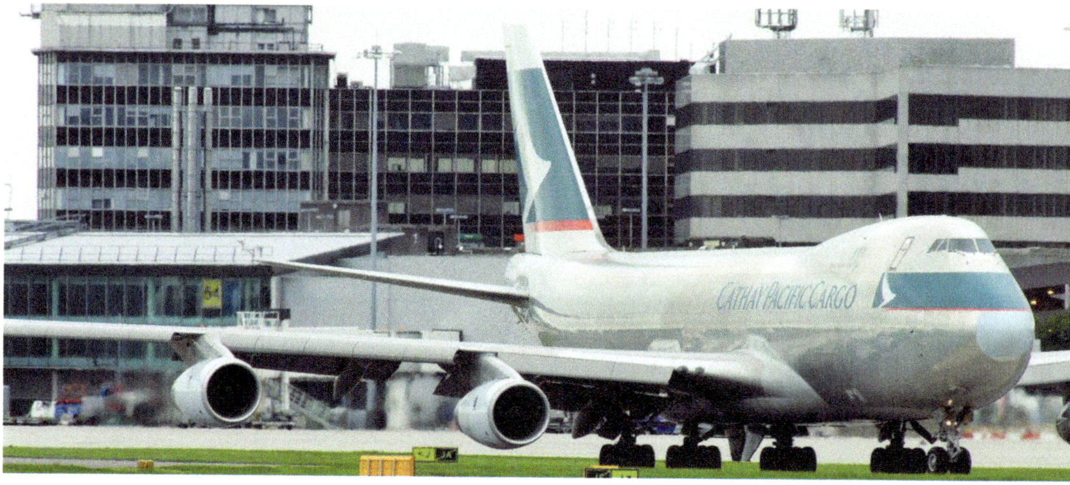

Cathay Pacific Cargo Boeing 747-467F (B-HUH), moving on taxiway Juliet on 4 April 2009. (Paul Atkinson)

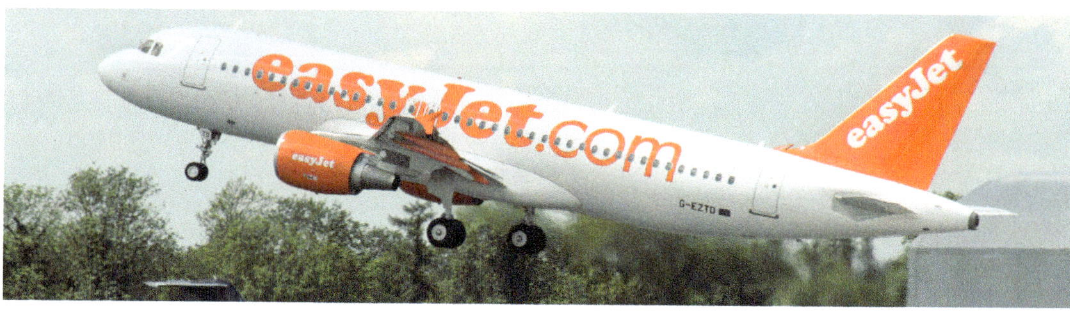

easyJet Airbus A320-214 (G-EZTD) on 21 May 2009. (David Hinsley)

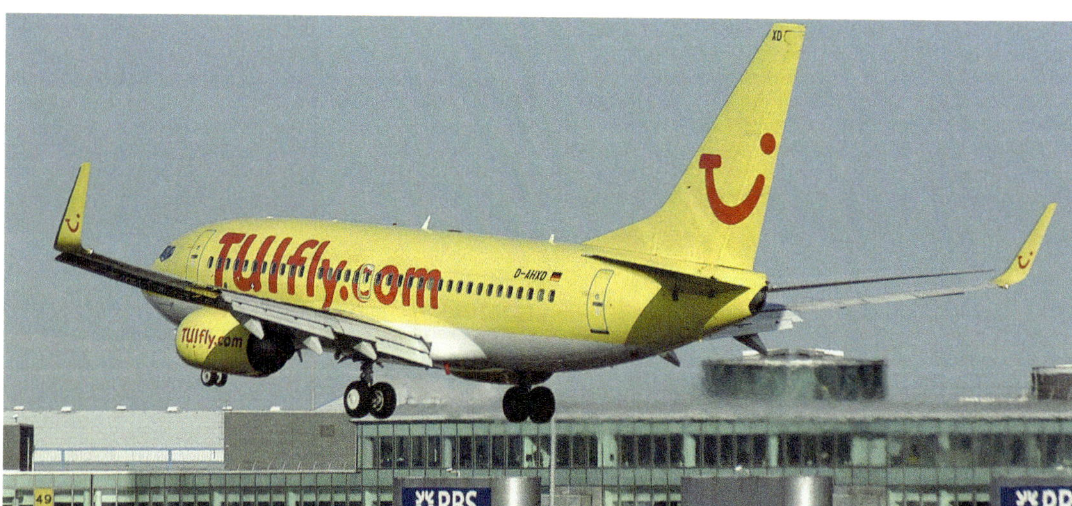

The German leisure airline TUIfly Boeing 737-700 (D-AHXD) on 13 July 2009. (Alan Lord)

A £21-million runway refurbishment project began, with upgrades that included the removal of the old Runway 1 surface (which hadn't had any major work carried out for thirty years) and a new asphalt surface laid. It was designed, produced, mixed and re-laid by specialist paving contractor Colas to the French BBA (Béton Bitumineux Aéronautique) specification, and pioneering LED runway lighting technology was also installed. Clough Bank Farm (a listed building situated between the aviation viewing area and the Ringway Chapel crossroads) was used as a work yard while the upgrading of the runway progressed, and strict night-time possession of the runway was observed between 9 p.m. and 6.30 a.m., during which all flights were switched to Runway 2, but positioning movements of aircraft were permitted across Runway 1 while the works were being carried out.

For the fourth year running, Manchester Airport was honoured at the annual Travel Weekly Globe Awards, where it was named 'Best UK Airport' in 2012 in one of the few award ceremonies where the winners are voted solely by the industry. By the time it celebrated its seventy-fifth birthday on 25 June 2013, it had acquired London Stansted for £1.5 billion, making MAG the third-busiest airport in the UK after Heathrow and Gatwick.

The new 196 ft (60 m) air traffic control tower, which was designed by CPMG Architects and the work carried out by contractor Morgan Sindall at a cost of £20 million, opened on 25 June 2013. The tower's reinforced concrete structure consists of an independent central internal square core, surrounded by a 29 ft (9 m) diameter round tower. Concrete was poured in shifts around the clock for 222 hours, from the morning of Tuesday 13 March to the early evening of Thursday 22 March. The steel-framed tower contains the control rooms, which are fitted with the latest ATC technology, and the transition from the old control tower, which had been operational since 1962, took place on 27 June.

Six new Oshkosh Striker vehicles that had been ordered from America were unveiled in October 2014 as part of £4.2-million investment in the capabilities of the airport fire operation. All eighty-four firefighters based at the airport have been fully trained on the 12-m-long, 70-mph-capable vehicles, which are equipped with the latest technology, including infrared cameras, high-reach extending turrets with a variable output nozzle (known as 'snozzles'), and a device resembling a spike that can pierce the fuselage of an aircraft and deliver large amounts of water and environmentally friendly foam inside it. The fire appliances are augmented by First Attack/Rapid Intervention vehicles.

Work was also started on building a terminus adjacent to the mainline railway at the airport for the Manchester Metrolink Light Rail Network, which, as part of Phase 3, saw the line extended from St Werburgh's Road into the airport site (with a major financial contribution by MAG). It opened over a year ahead of schedule on 3 November 2014, with the tram service operating with a 12-minute headway.

Construction of the fourth railway station platform was completed in May 2015 as part of the Northern Hub project, which is expected to increase passenger capacity by 44 million a year and create 20,000 jobs. As part of the project, direct services from Bradford, Halifax and Rochdale to Manchester Airport will be introduced.

Planning consent was granted by Manchester City Council on 3 March 2016 for a £1-billion transformation of Manchester Airport, which is said to be the biggest single construction project ever to take place in Greater Manchester. The ten-year scheme includes a 886,892 sq. ft (82,394.96 sq. m) extension to the north-west elevation of Terminal 2, which will provide expanded passenger facilities, an extension of both the upper and lower level Terminal 2 forecourts, reconfiguration of the Terminal 2 multistorey car park, the creation of a new access road to Terminal 2 from the elevated roundabout on the M56 spur road, and a link to an improved Terminal 3, along with sixty other significant airside and landside developments included in the scheme. Terminal 1, which was built in 1962, is set to be phased out by 2022.

The airport now serves more than seventy airlines and 210 destinations, and brings £1.8 billion to the regional economy every year, employing 20,000 people and supporting a further 25,000 jobs. With the £1-billion investment, Manchester will become one of the most modern and customer-focused airports in Europe, demonstrating the importance of Manchester as a global gateway.

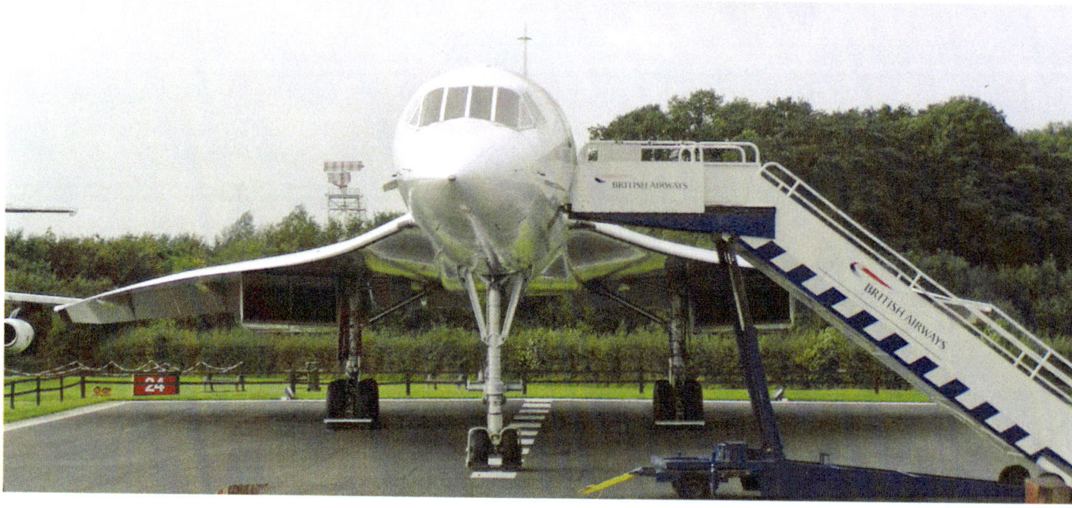

The legendary Concorde (G-BOAC), on static display at the Runway Visitor Park on 13 July 2010. (Martin Jones)

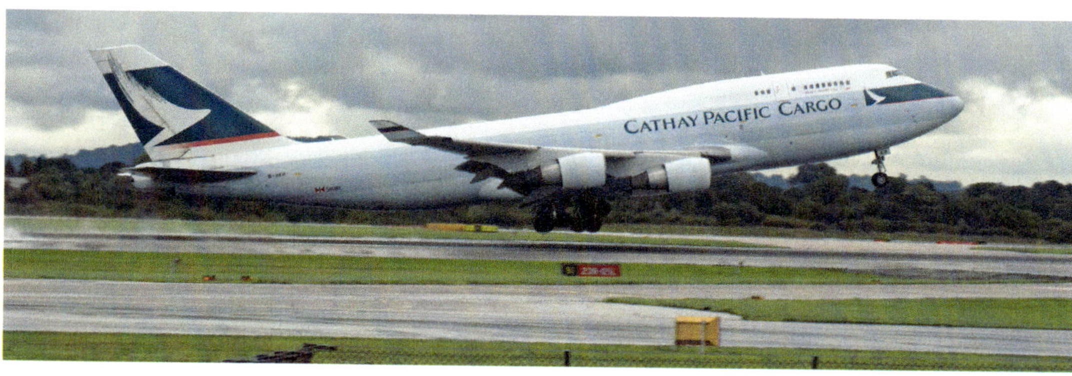

Cathay Pacific Cargo Boeing 747-400 (B-HKH) on 17 August 2010. (Martin Jones)

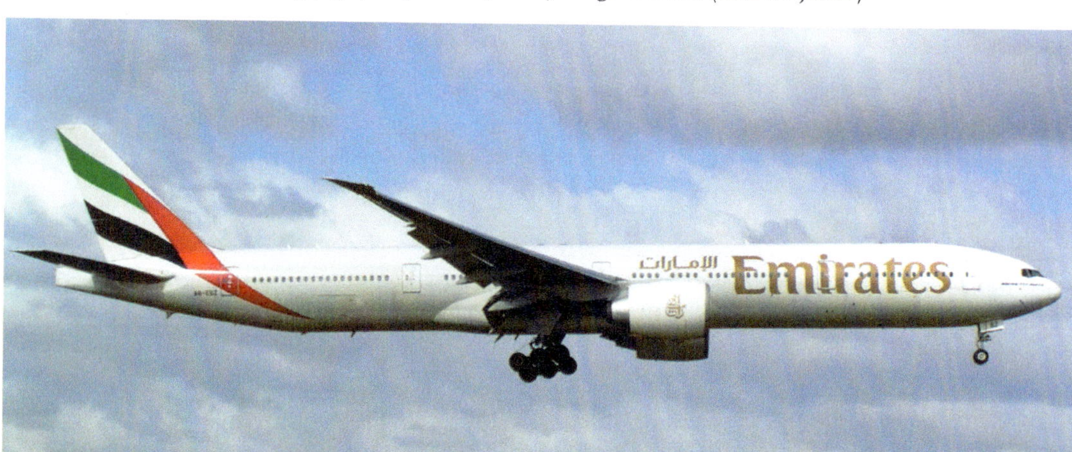

Emirates Boeing 777-31J(ER) (A6-EBZ), on approach in 2010. (Martin Jones)

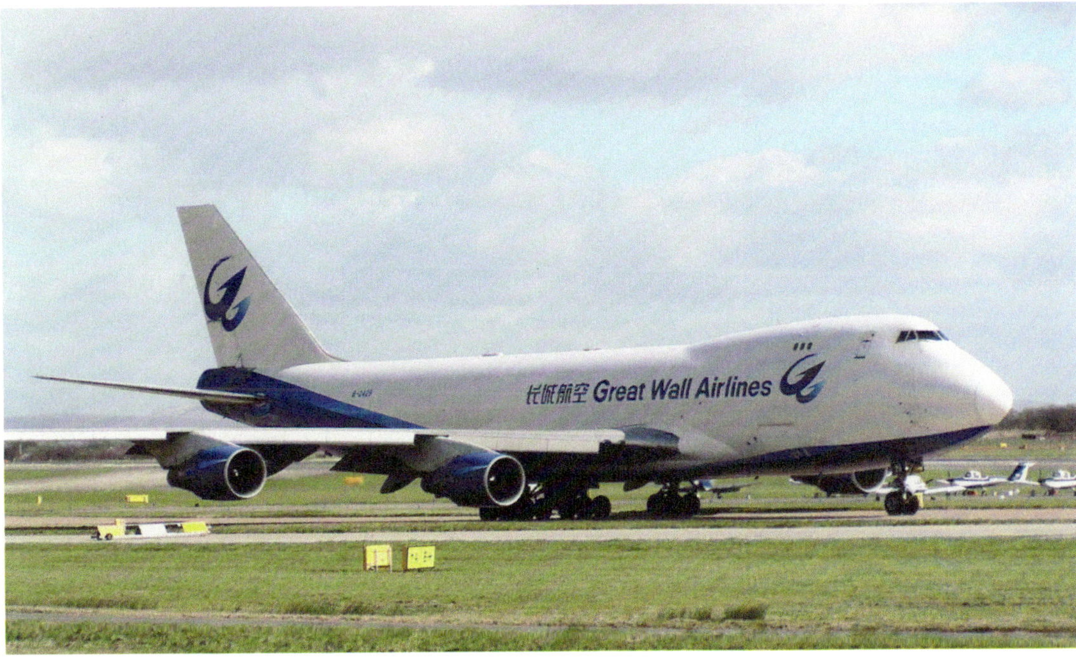

Great Wall Airlines Boeing 747-412F (B-2429) in 2010. The Shanghai-based company ceased operations a year later, following a merger with China Cargo Airlines. (Martin Jones)

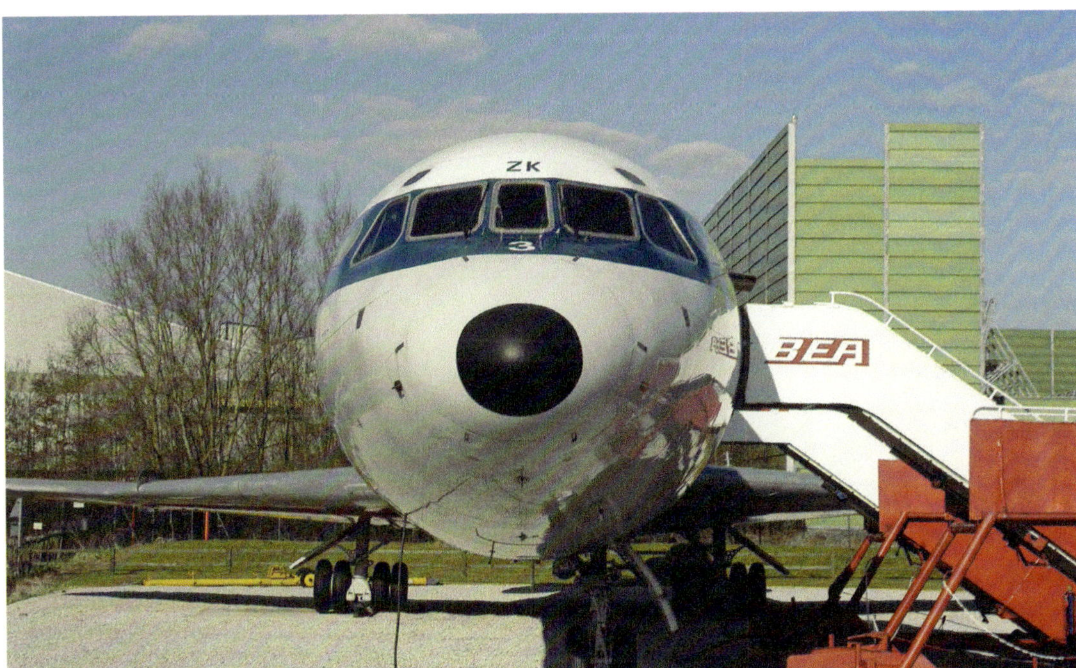

The fully restored BEA Hawker Siddeley HS121 Trident 3B (G-AWZK) is preserved at the Viewing Park at Manchester Airport. The Trident was a medium-range three-engine jet airliner and was the first aircraft to make a fully automated approach and landing. 8 March 2010. (Alan Lord)

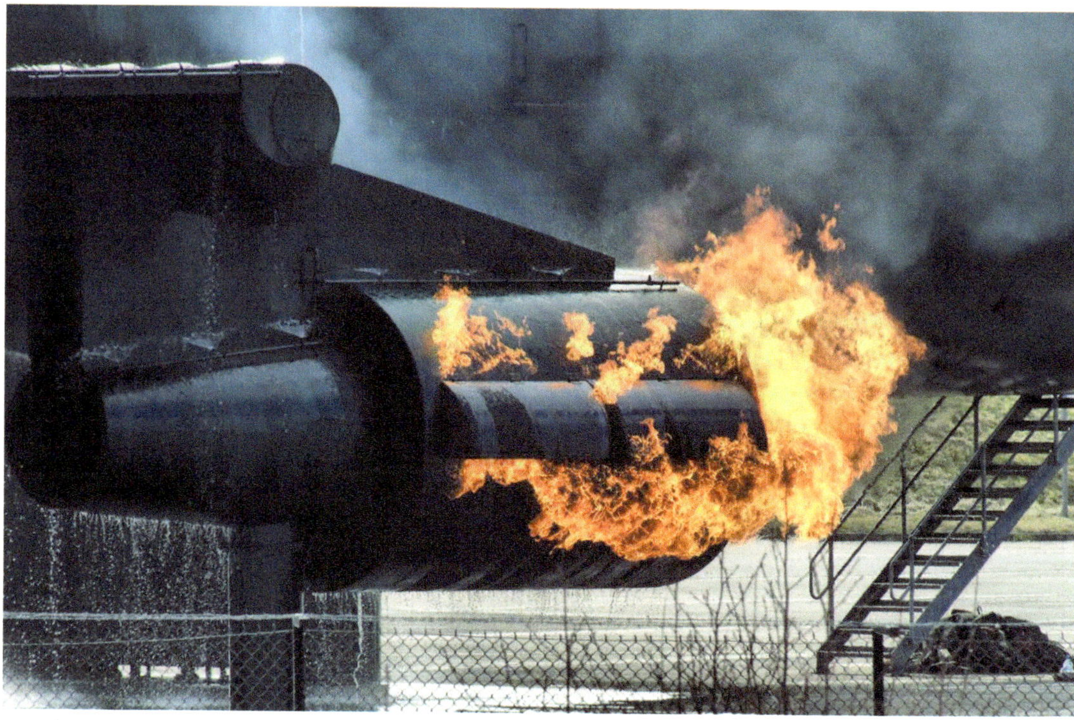

The advanced 747 MD11 Fire Service Training Simulator burning aviation fuel and gas at Manchester Airport on 11 March 2010. (Paul Atkinson)

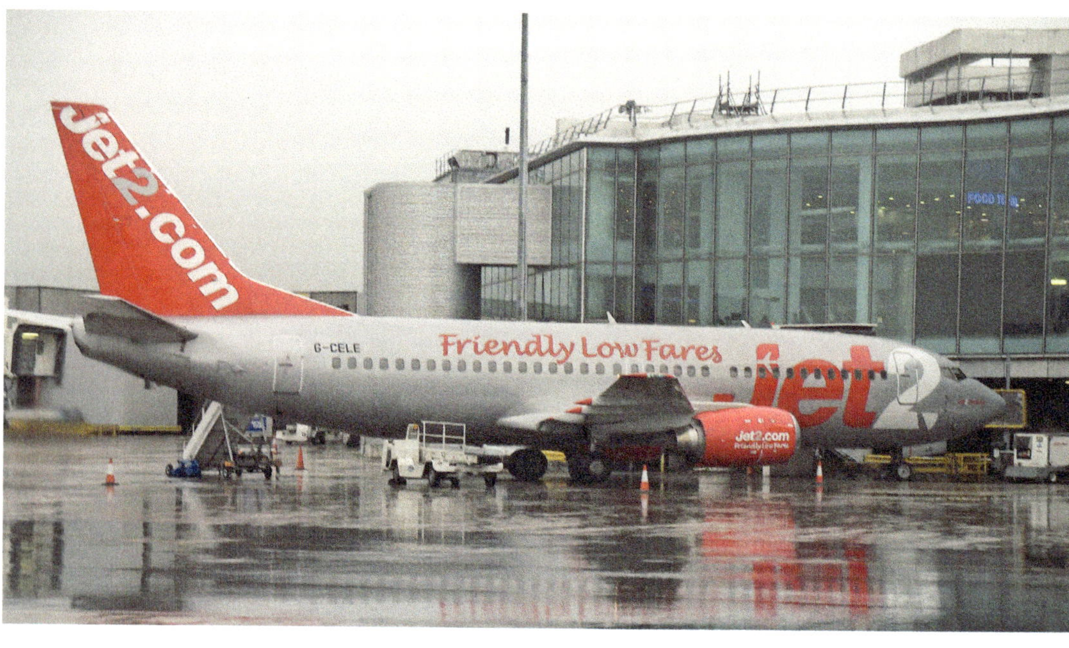

Jet 2 Boeing 737-33A (G-CELE) on stand 21 at Manchester on 21 July 2010, having just arrived from Nice. New to Monarch in 1988, G-CELE came to Jet 2 in 2006 via Euro Berlin, Ansett and Channel Express. (Mike Welsby)

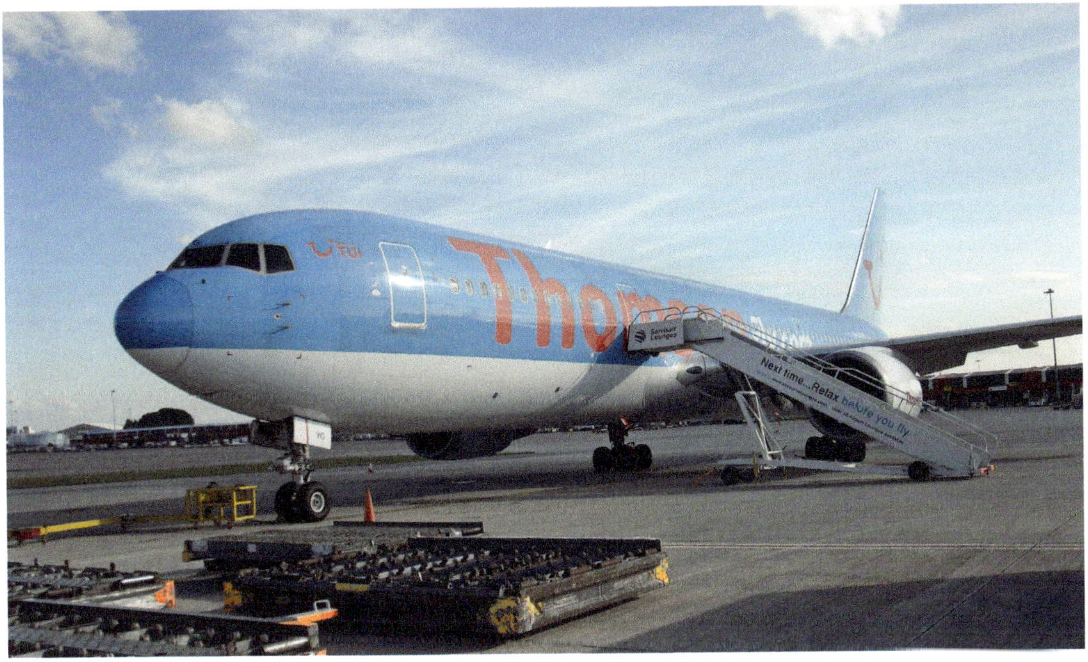

New to Britannia in 1999, Boeing 767-304 (G-OBYG) is parked on stand 85 at Manchester in TUI livery on 6 January 2010. (Mike Welsby)

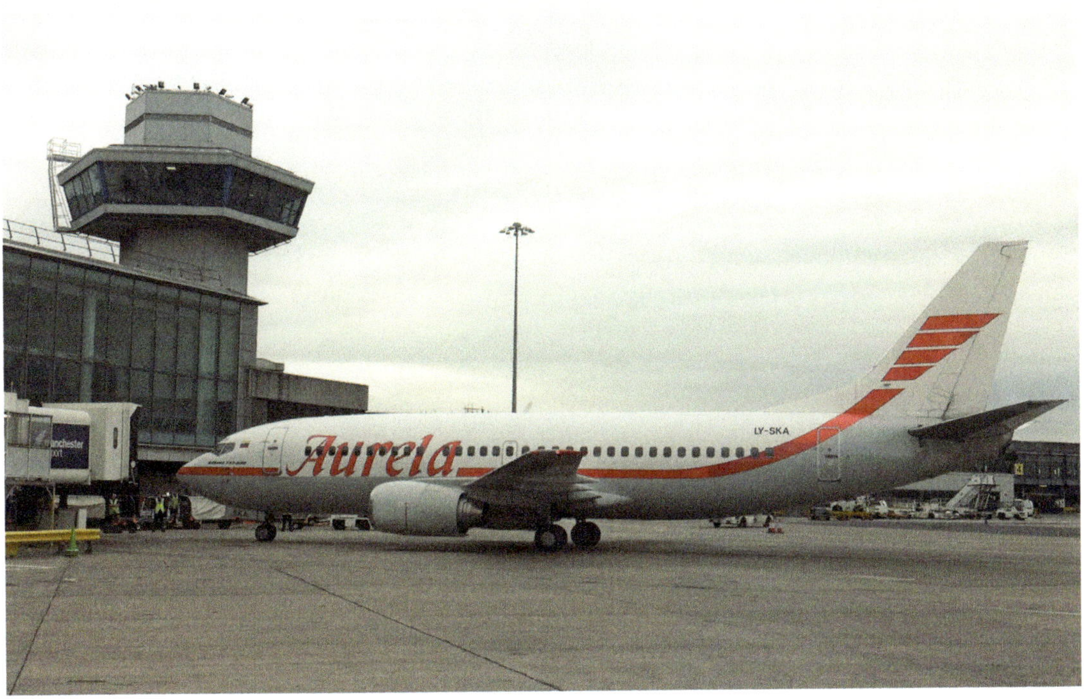

Air Aurela Boeing 737-35B (LY-SKA) working for Thomas Cook, arriving on stand 21 on Flight TCX523L from ACE (Lanzarote) on 26 August 2010. (Mike Welsby)

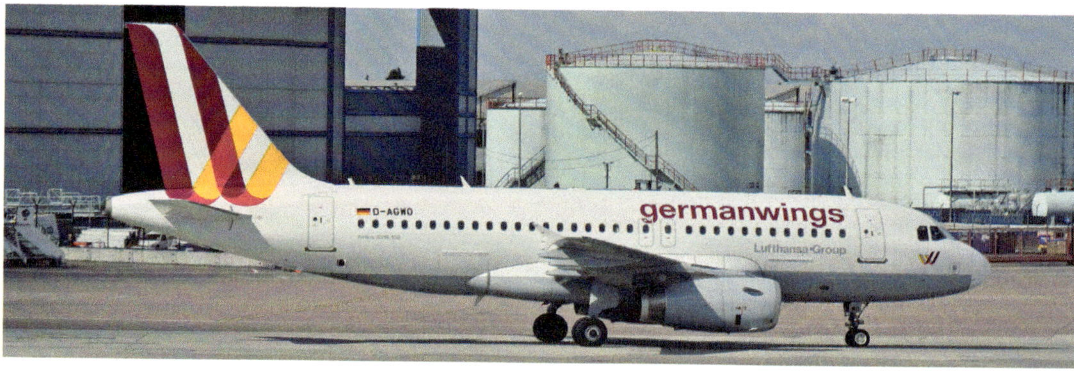

German low-cost airline Germanwings Airbus 319-132 (D-AGWO), in its new colours, arriving at Manchester on 30 April 2011. (Alan Lord)

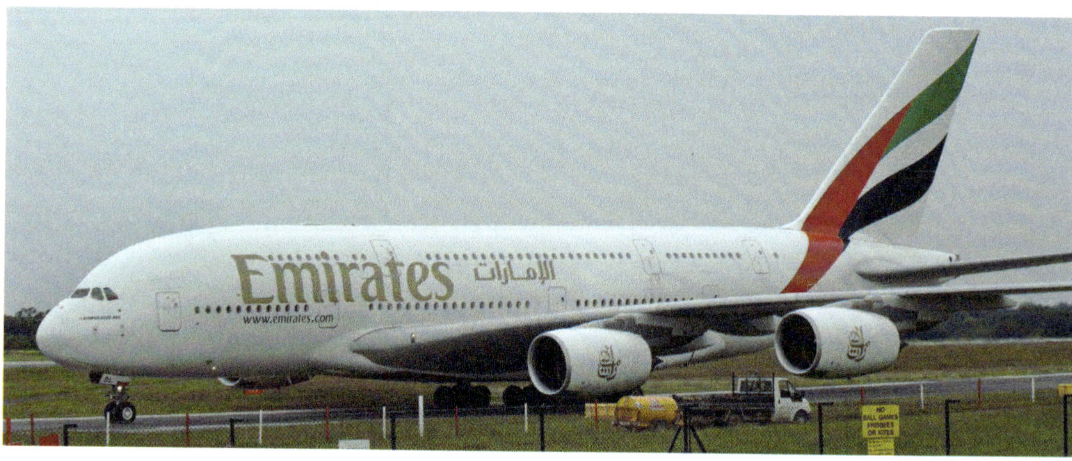

Emirates Airbus A380-800 (A6-EDL) on 5 July 2011. (Martin Jones)

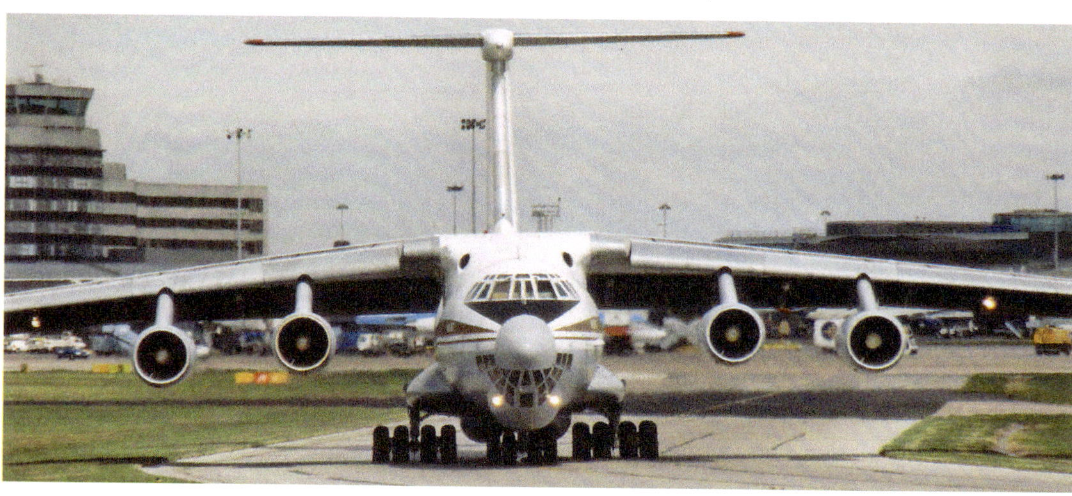

Riga (Latvia)-based Cargo Airline Inversija Ilyushin IL-76T (YL-LAJ) heads towards a 06 departure at Manchester Airport on 2 May 2011. (Alan Lord)

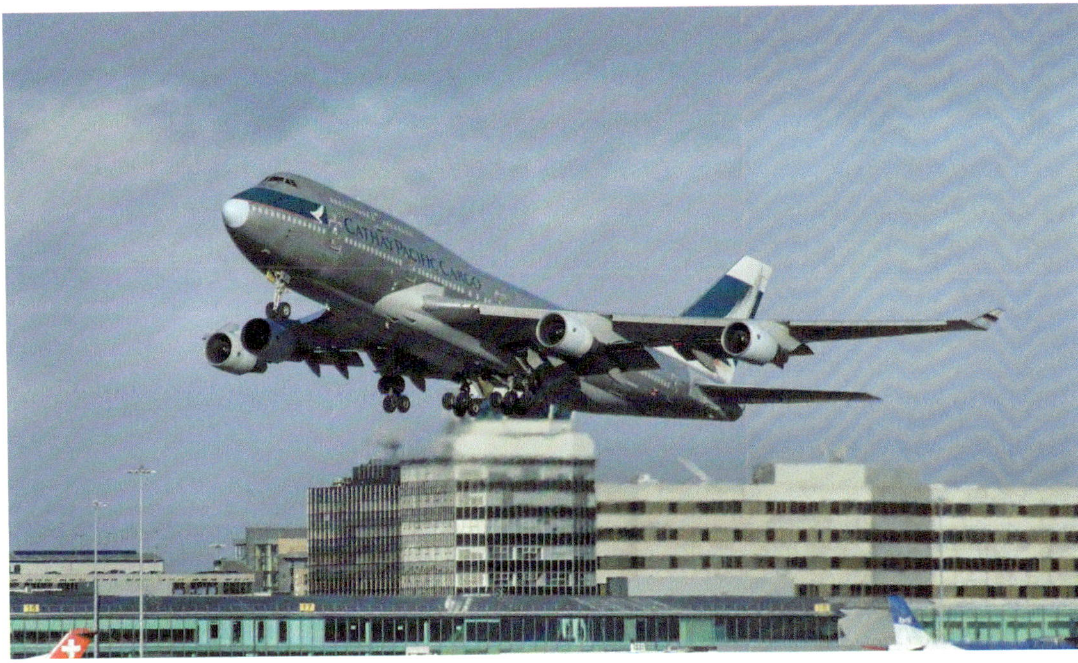

Cathay Pacific Cargo's Boeing 747-412(BCF) (B-HKJ) climbs away from runway 23R, with the airport control tower and terminal buildings in the background on 3 February 2011. (Paul Atkinson)

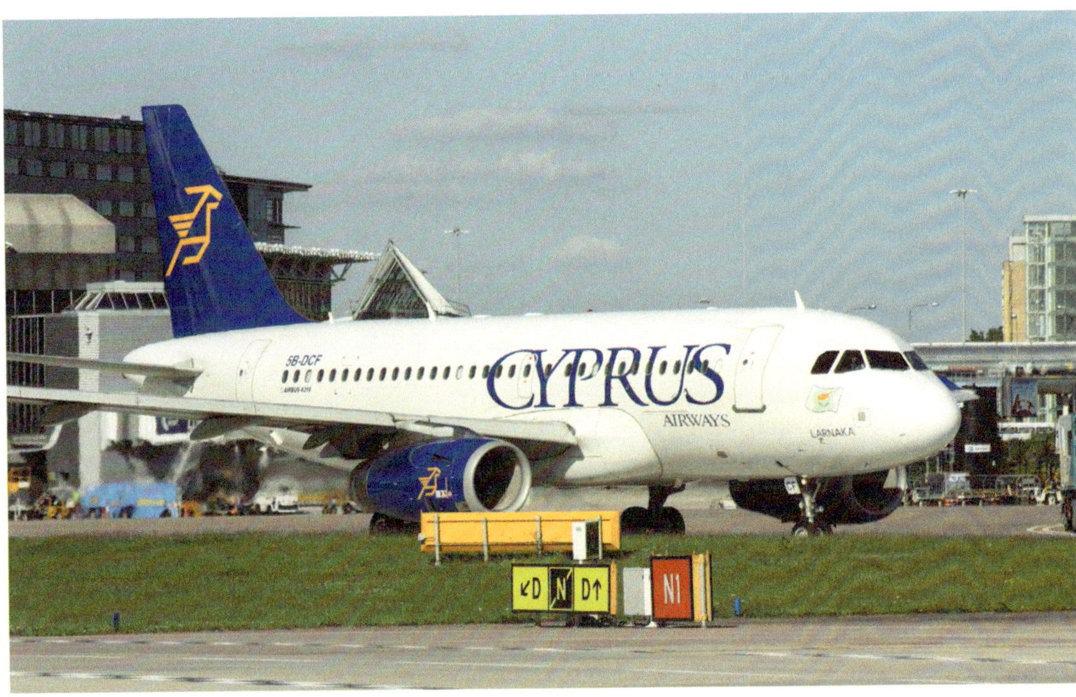

Cyprus Airways Airbus A319-132 (5B-DCF) heads along taxiway DELTA, having pushed from 'C' pier on Terminal 1, bound for Larnaca on 3 June 2011. (Mike Welsby)

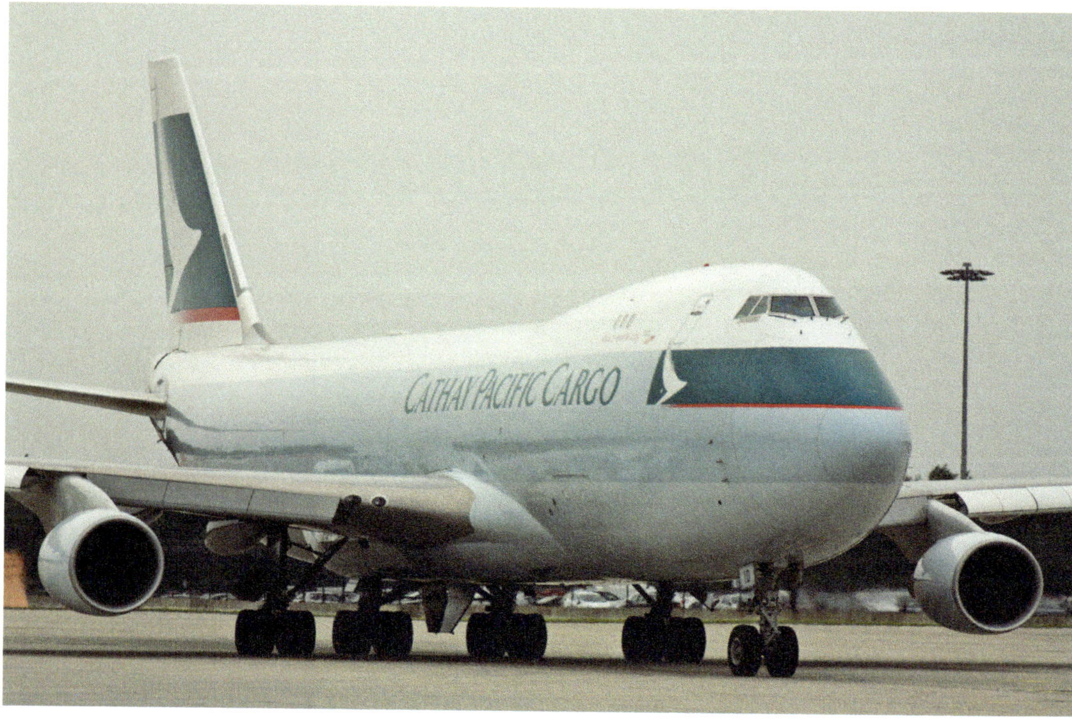

Cathay Pacific Cargo Boeing 747-467(ER) (B-LID) LID is bound for Hong Kong, following a turn round on the West Apron freight area on 27 June 2011. (Mike Welsby)

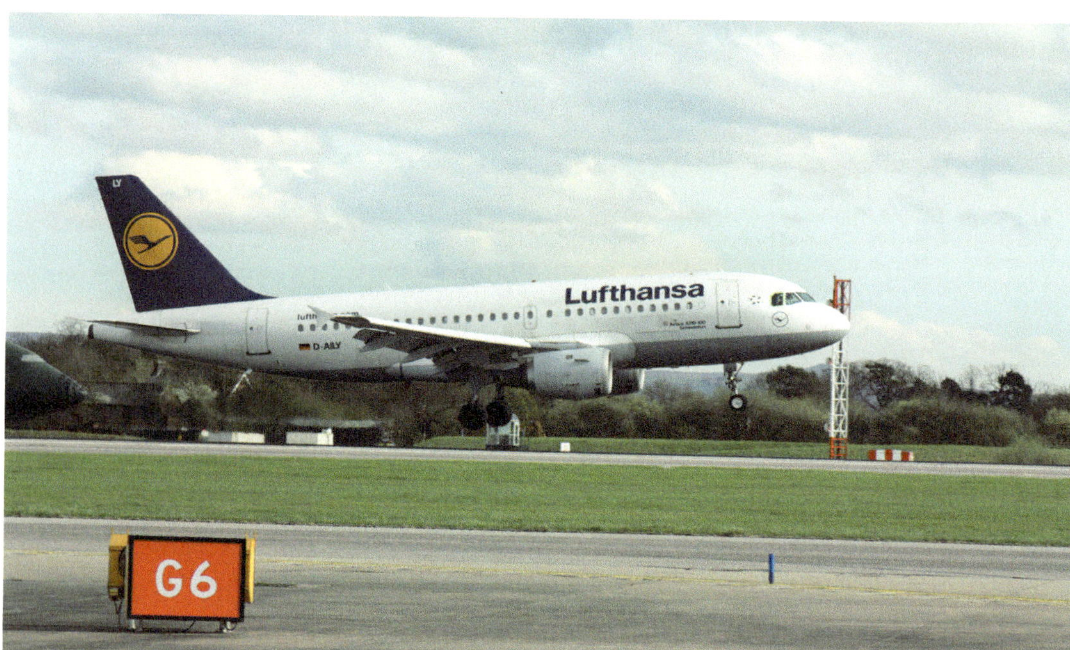

Lufthansa Airbus A319-100 (D-AILY) has just crossed the threshold of runway 23R on one of several daily scheduled flights from Germany on 2 April 2011. (Mike Welsby)

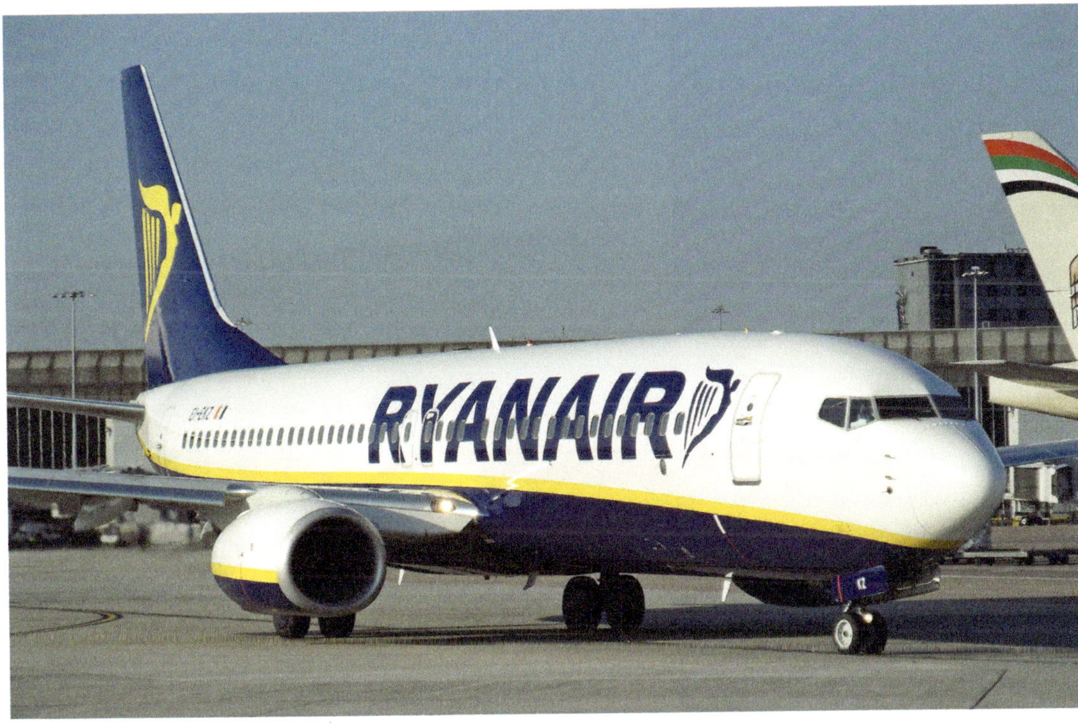

Ryanair Boeing 737-8AS (EI-EKZ), leaving Terminal 2 on 2 June 2011. (Mike Welsby)

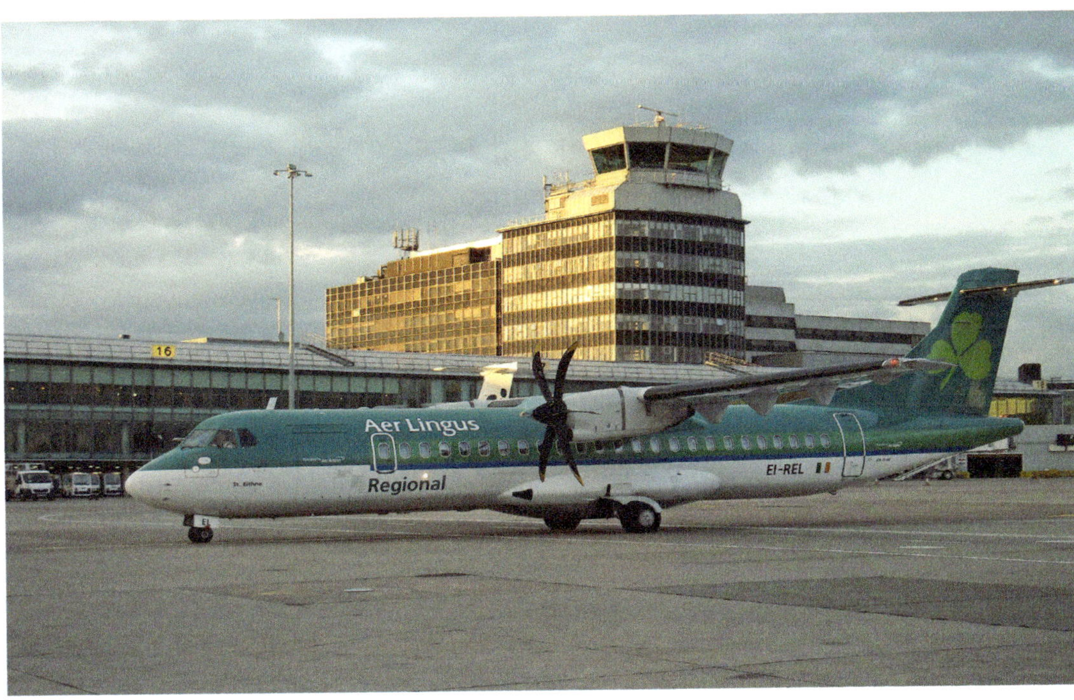

Aer Lingus Regional's twin-engine turboprop short-haul airliner ATR 72-500 *St Eithne* (EI-REL), holding short of stand 5 at MAN on 7 July 2011. (Mike Welsby)

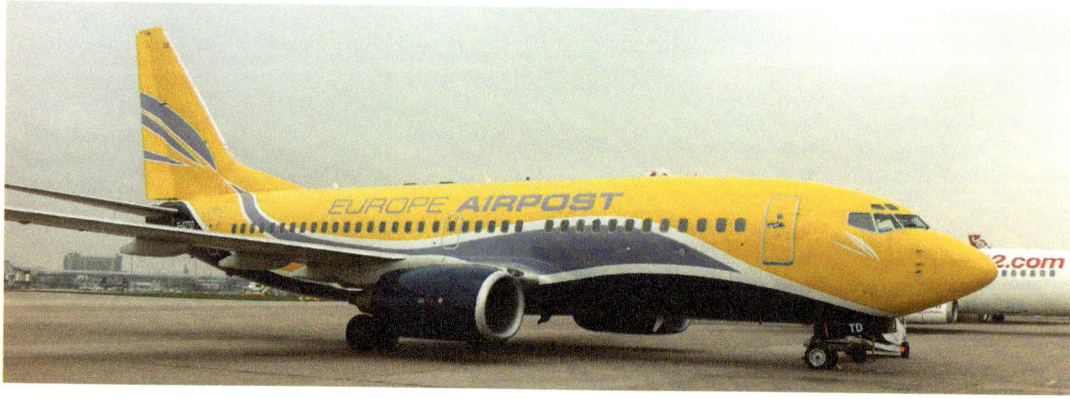

In its former livery of Europe Airpost, ASL Airlines Ireland's Boeing 737-73V (F-GZTD) is pictured at Manchester Airport on the occasion of the football match between Manchester United and Marseille on 15 March 2011. Europe Airpost was rebranded as ASL Airlines France in 2015. (Mike Welsby)

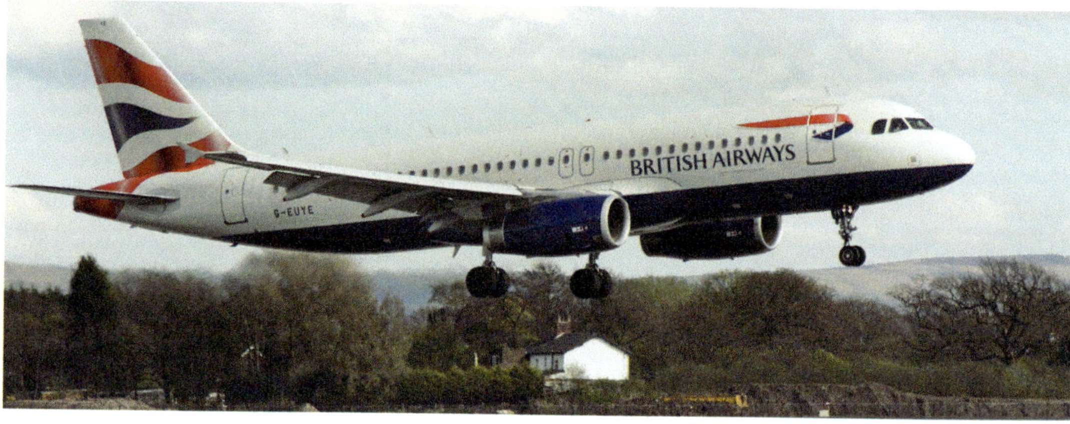

British Airways Airbus A320-232 (G-EUYE) from Heathrow, about to touch down on 23R on 2 April 2011. (Mike Welsby)

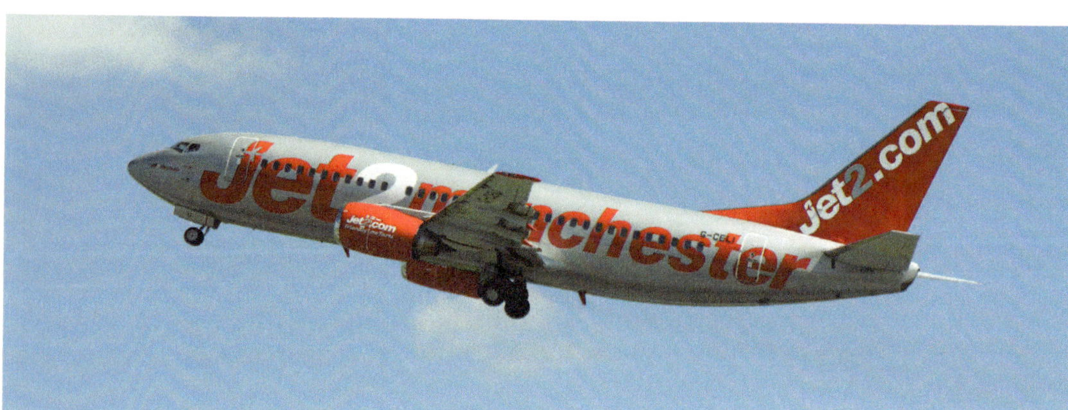

Jet2 Manchester Boeing 737-330 (G-CELI), climbing into the sky on 3 June 2011. (Mike Welsby)

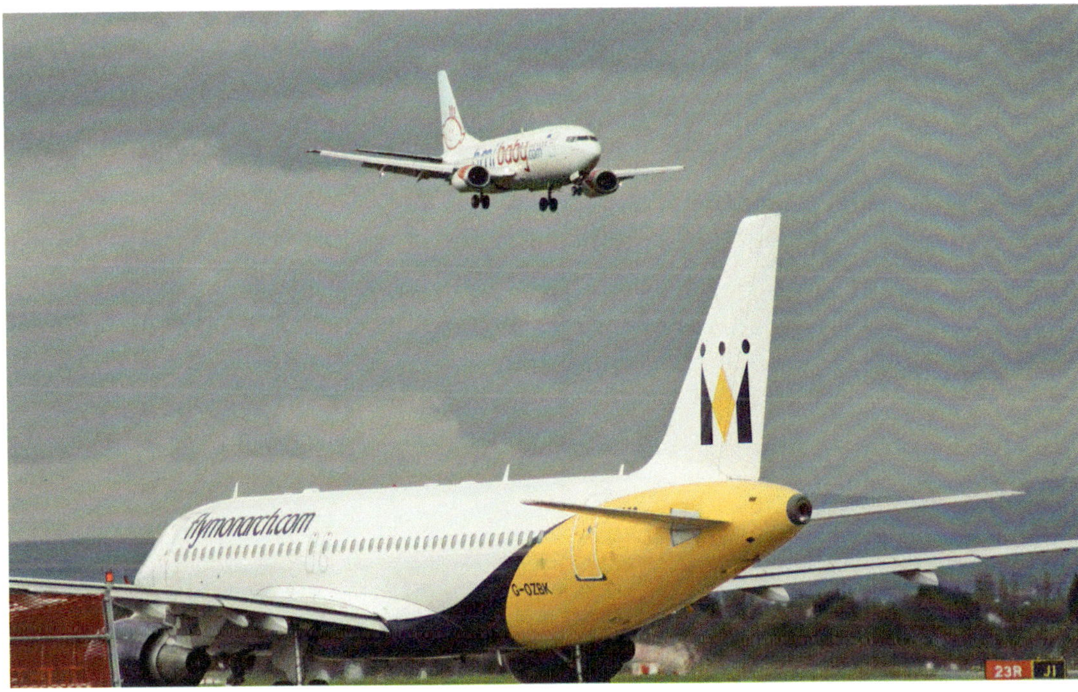

Monarch Airlines Airbus A320-214 (G-OZBK), heading along Juliet for runway 23R with the now-defunct bmibaby Boeing 737-37Q (G-ODSK) on short finals on 3 April 2011. Monarch would soon end its association with Airbus by becoming an all Boeing 737 fleet. (Mike Welsby)

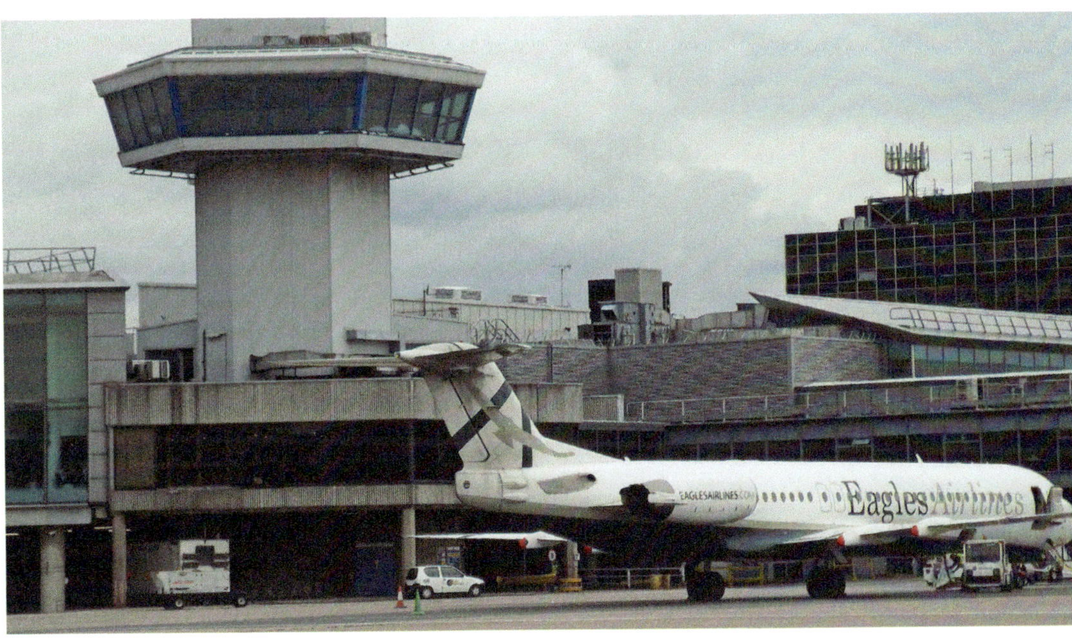

In its former Eagles Airlines livery, PRiMA Aero Trasporti Italiani Fokker F100 (I-GIOI) is pictured on 1 August 2011. (Eagle was formerly Alpi Eagles, which had its licence to operate suspended in 2007.) (Mike Welsby)

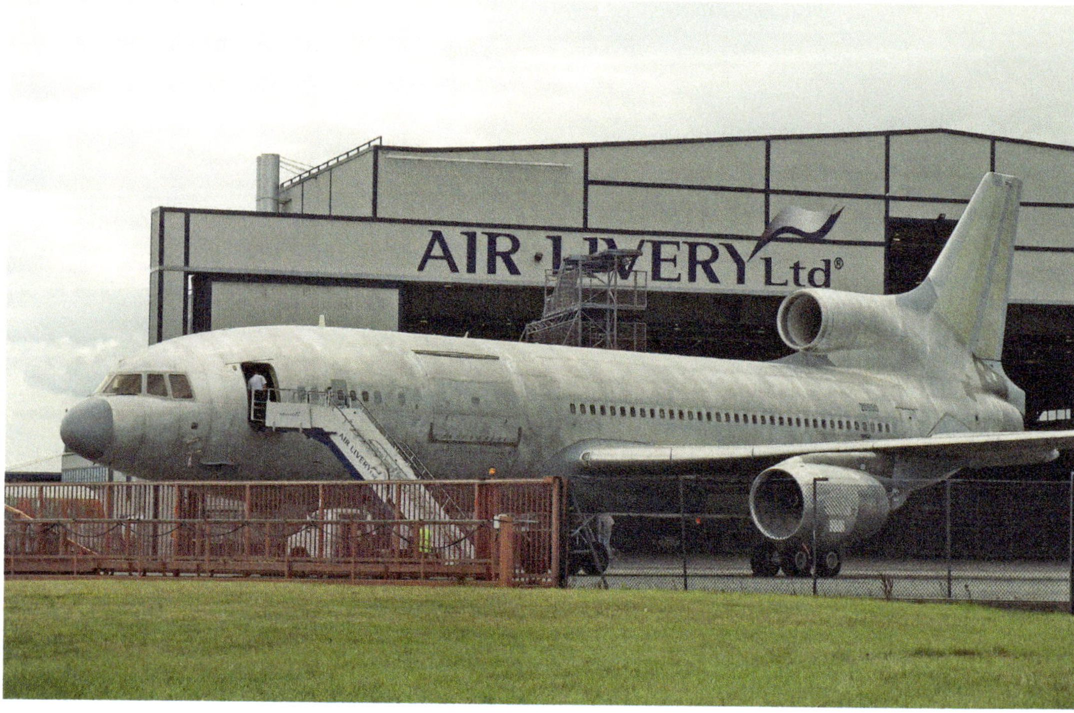

Ex-216 Squadron (RAF) Lockheed L1011 Tristar KC 1 (ZD950), which had been converted from a L-1011-500 to a tanker/cargo role. It is seen here outside the Air Livery hanger on 1 August 2011. (Mike Welsby)

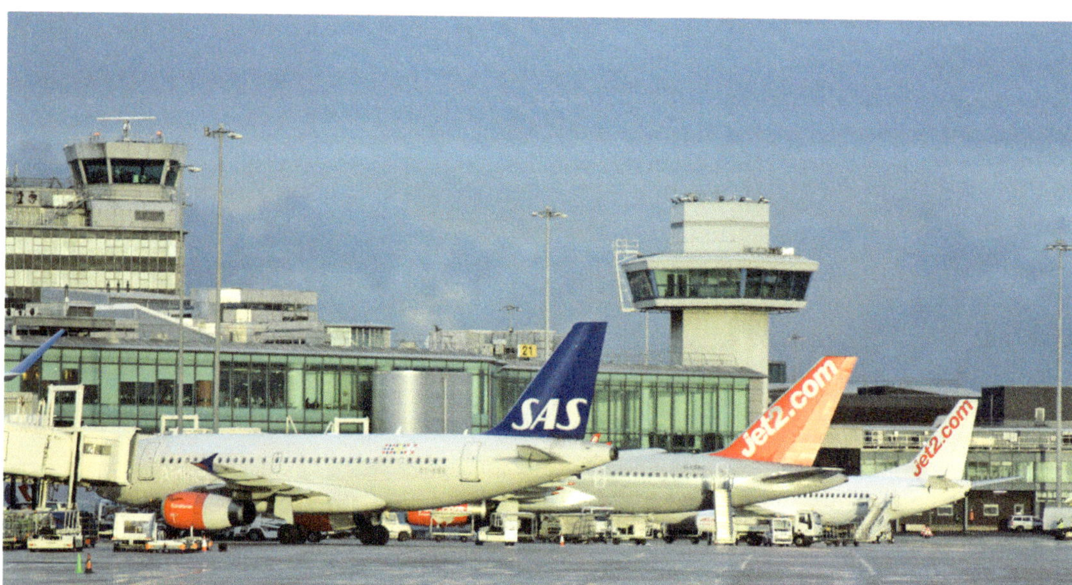

Scandinavian Airlines (SAS) Airbus A319-131 (OY-KBR), Jet2 Boeing 757-23A (G-LSAC) and Jet2 Boeing 737-3Q8 (G-GDFE), pictured between the redundant ATC tower on the left and the former Apron Control Tower on the right. 3 April 2011. (Mike Welsby)

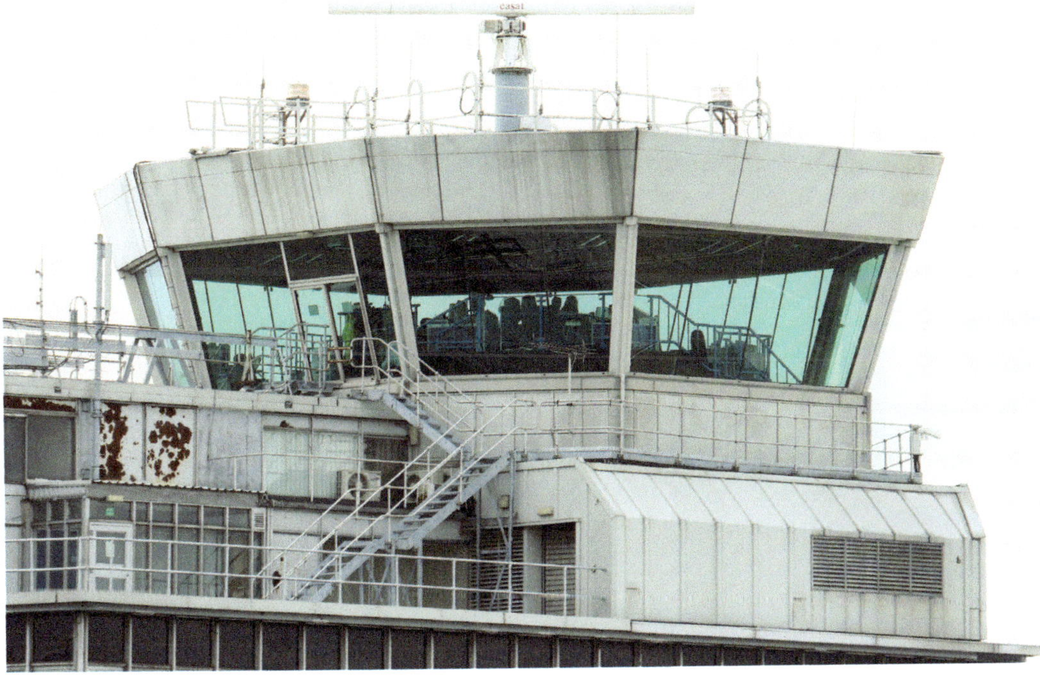

The former control tower (which had been operational since 1962), already looking like a relic on top of Terminal 1 on 8 May 2011. (David Hinsley)

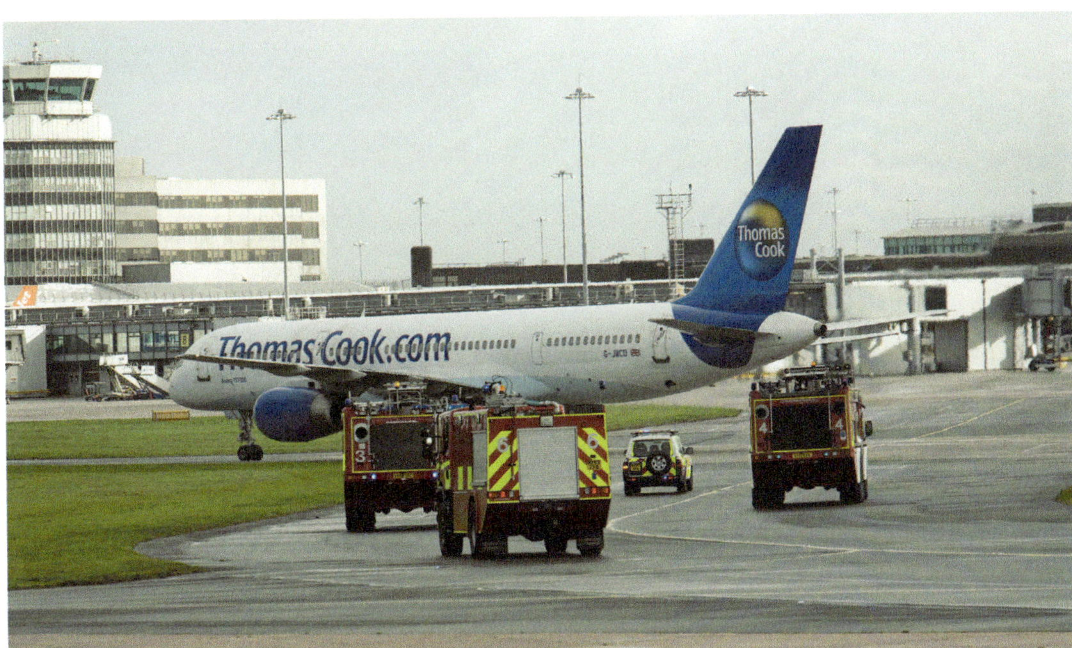

Thomas Cook Boeing 757-200 (G-JMCD) on a quick escorted return, following 'smoke in the cockpit', on 29 September 2012. (Mike Illien)

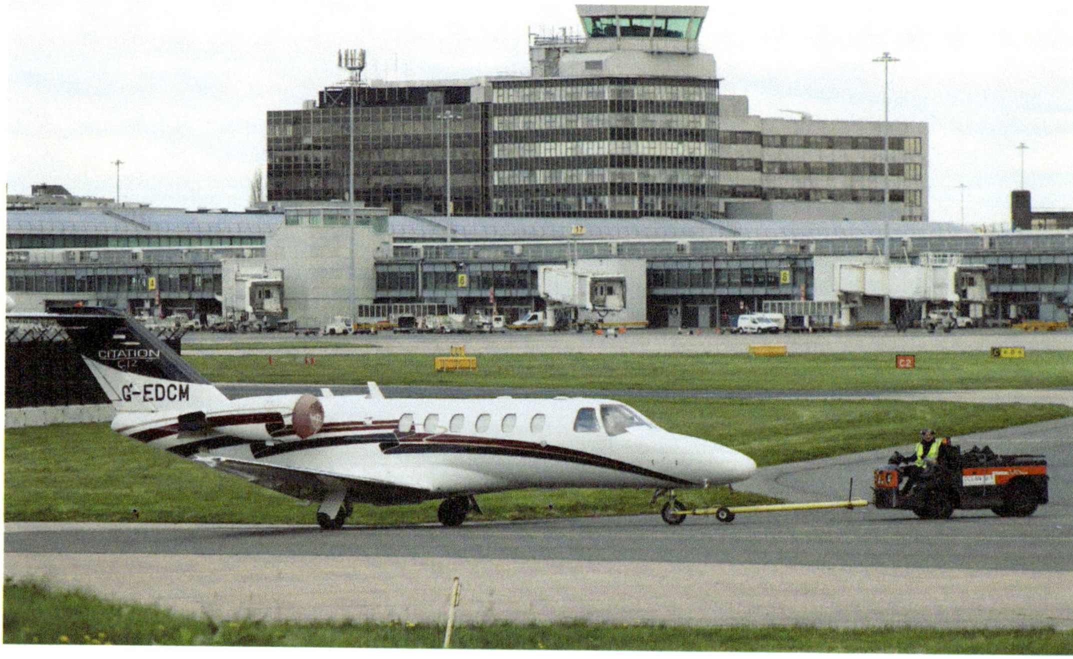

Cessna Citation CJ2 (G-EDCM), being pushed back on 10 April 2012. (Ben Weaver)

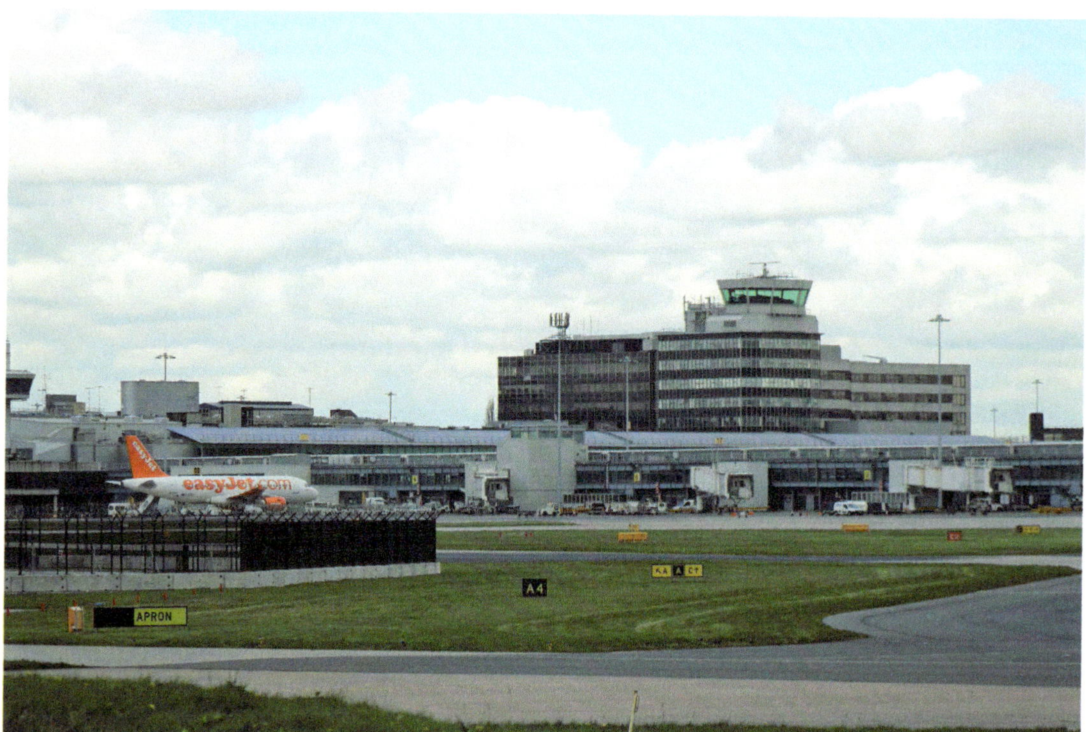

Manchester International Airport with easyJet Airbus A319-111 (G-EZDJ) parked during turnaround at Terminal 1 on 10 April 2012. (Ben Weaver)

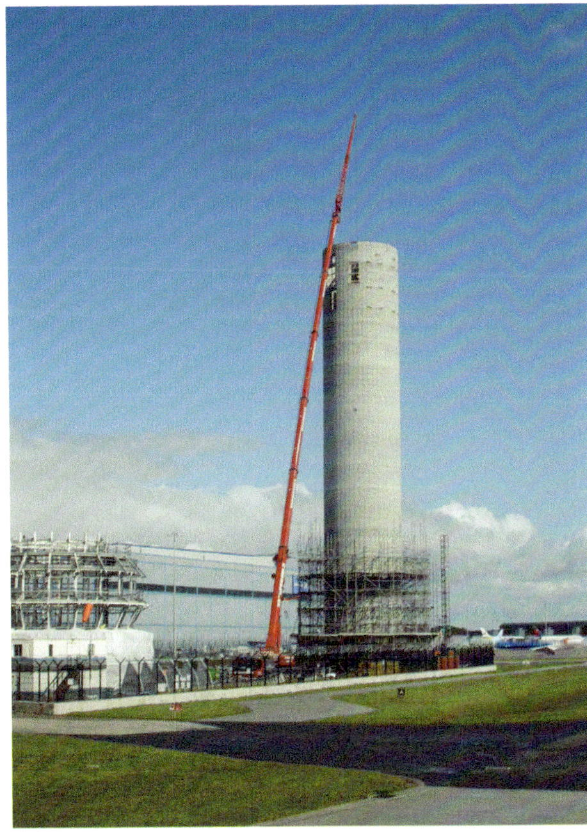

Right: The progress on the new control tower was slow but steady on 16 May 2012. (Alan Lord)

Below: Monarch Airbus A320-212 (G-MPCD) (Ex-C-FTDU G-GZCD), touching down on 23 April 2012. (Martin Jones)

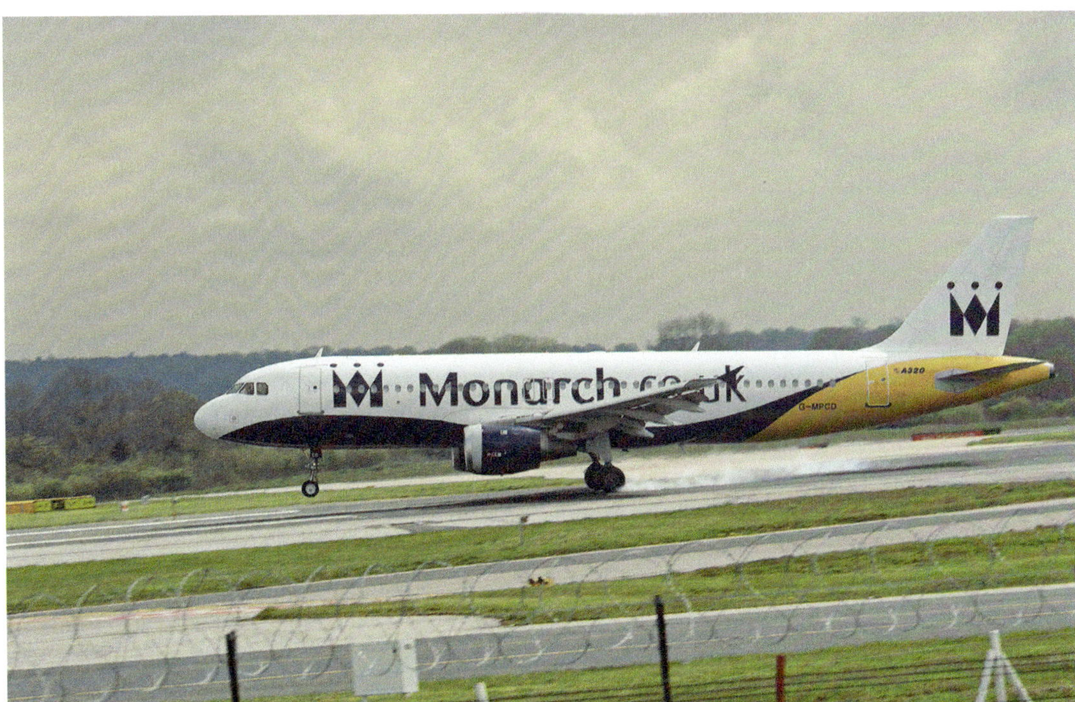

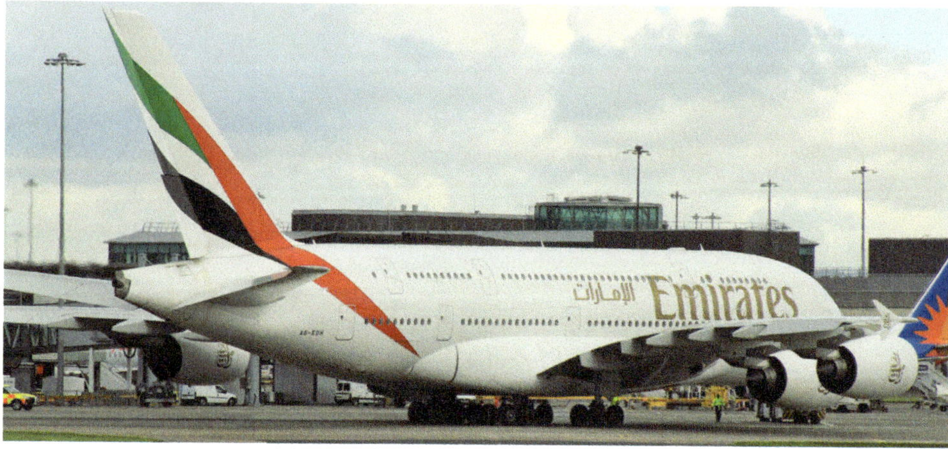

Emirates Airbus A380-861 (A6-EDH), taxiing on 10 April 2012. (Ben Weaver)

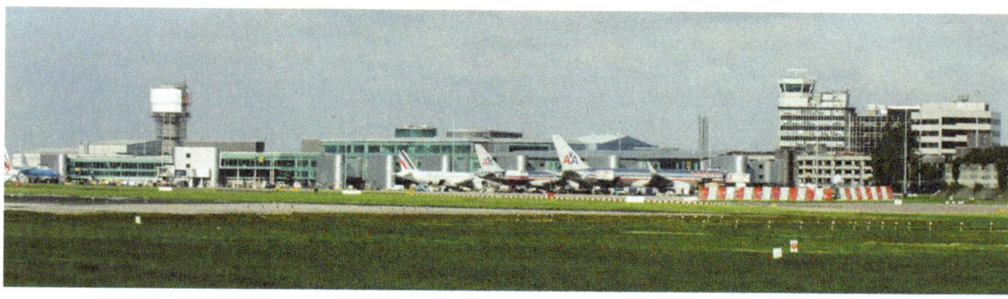

View of Manchester Airport with the runway 23R threshold in the foreground; Terminal 3 with aircraft on the gates; the old ATC tower on the right; and the new ATC tower under construction on the left on 28 July 2012. (Paul Atkinson)

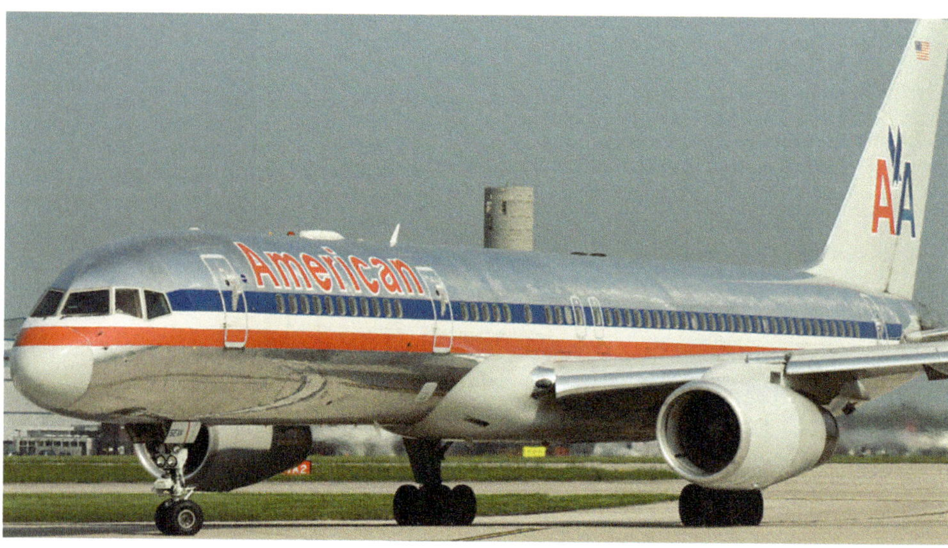

American Airlines Boeing B757-223 (N188AN), with the new ATC tower column nearing completion in the background on 24 May 2012. (NTG)

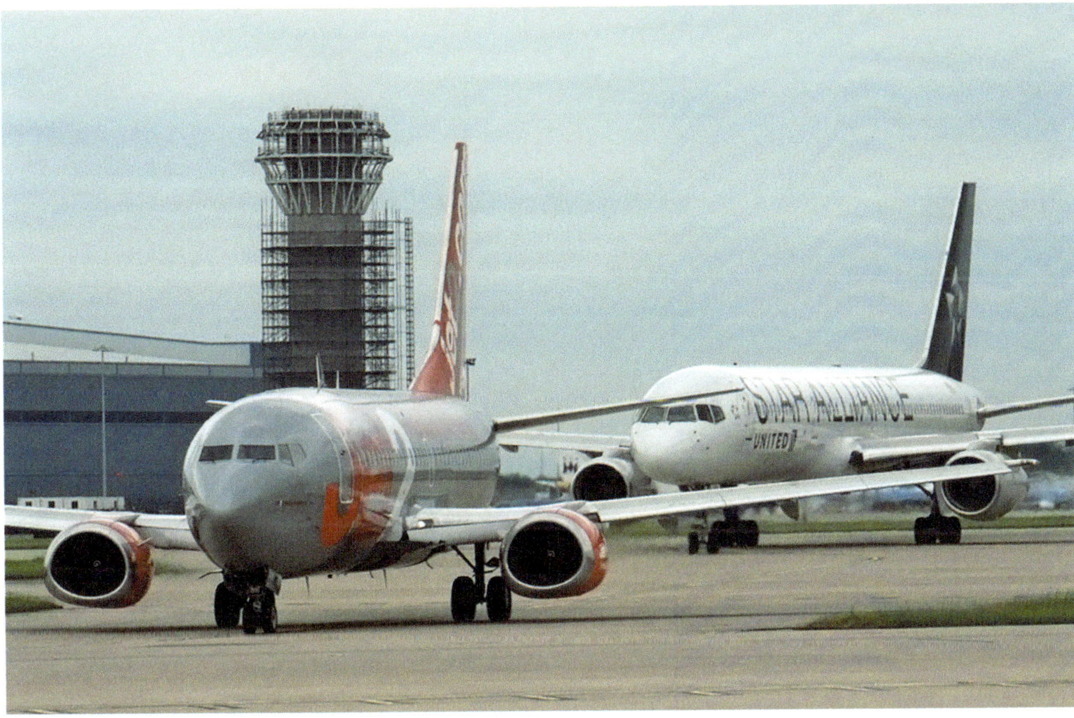

Jet2 Boeing B737-377 (G-CELS) leads United Airlines Boeing B757-224 (N14120) to runway 23R in front of the rapidly growing new ATC tower on 5 June 2012. (NTG)

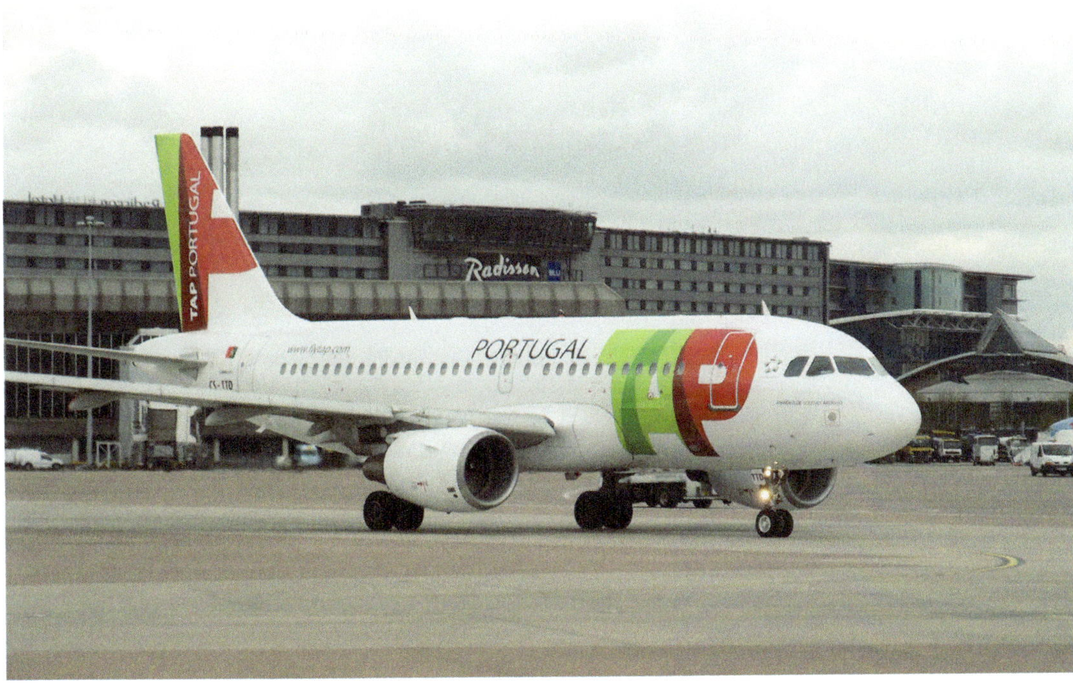

TAP Portugal Airbus 319-111 (CS-TTD) on 21 April 2012. (Mike Welsby)

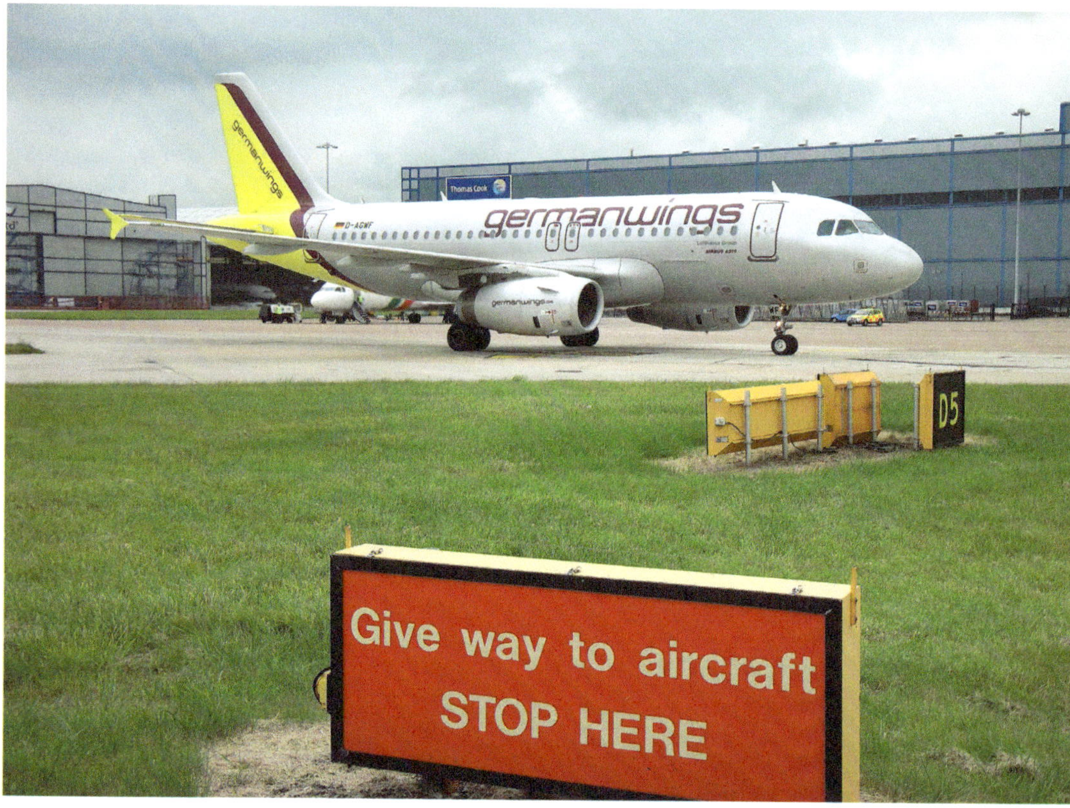

Germanwings Airbus 319-132 (D-AGWF), heading for Terminal 1 on 21 June 2012. (Mike Welsby)

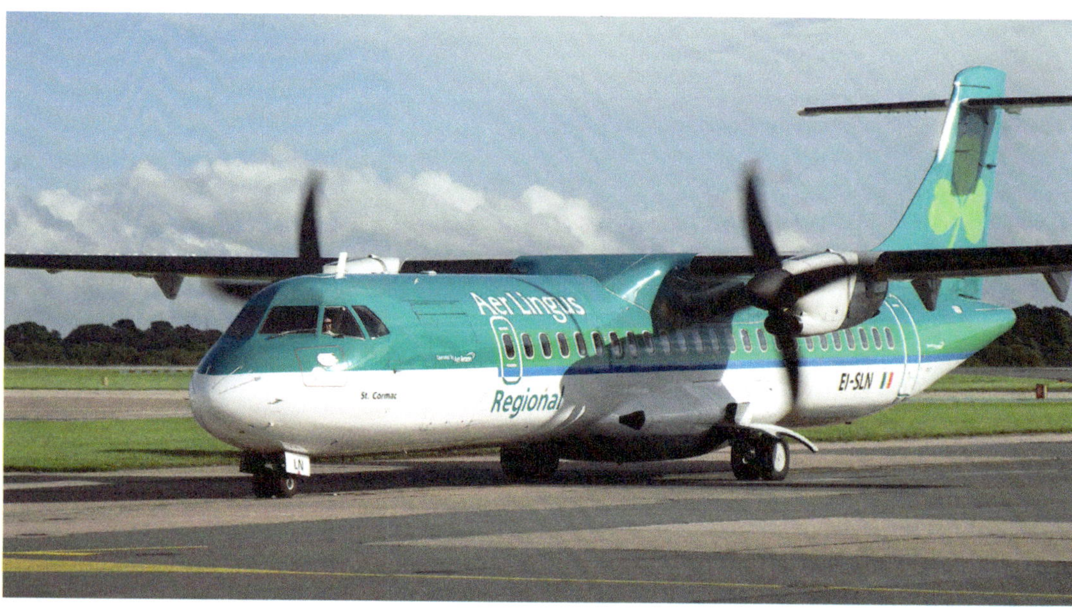

Aer Lingus Regional ATR 72-212 (EI-SLN) *St Cormac*, approaching stand 7 on 29 August 2012. (Mike Welsby)

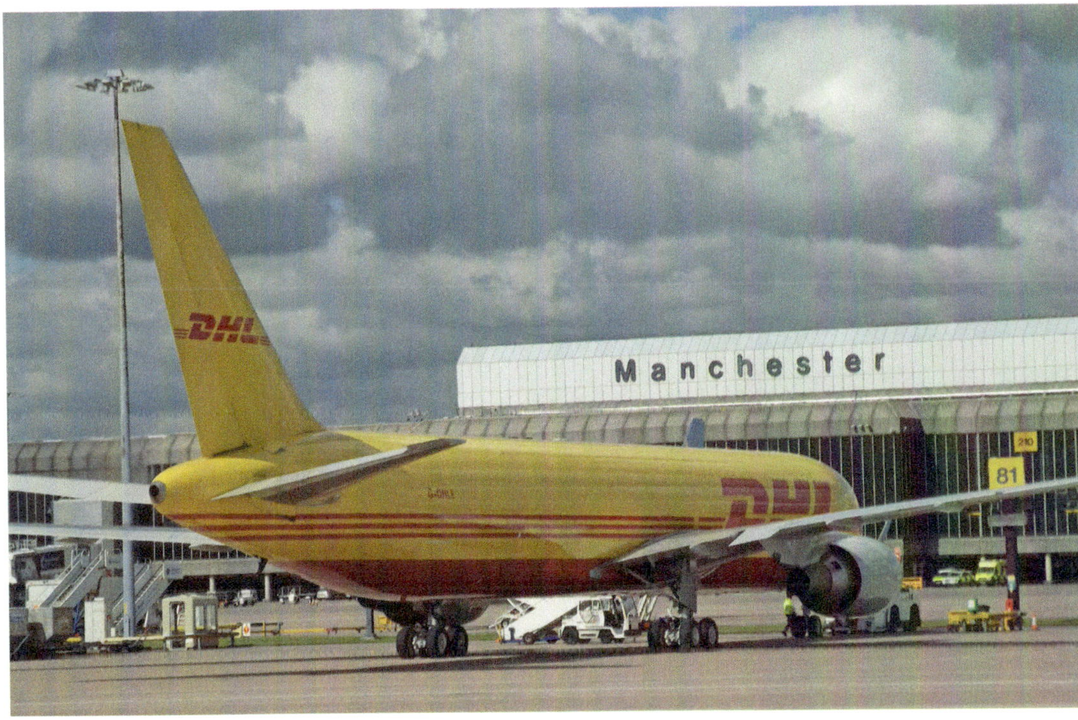

DHL Boeing 767-3JHF(ER) (G-DHLE) on 16 May 2012. (Mike Welsby)

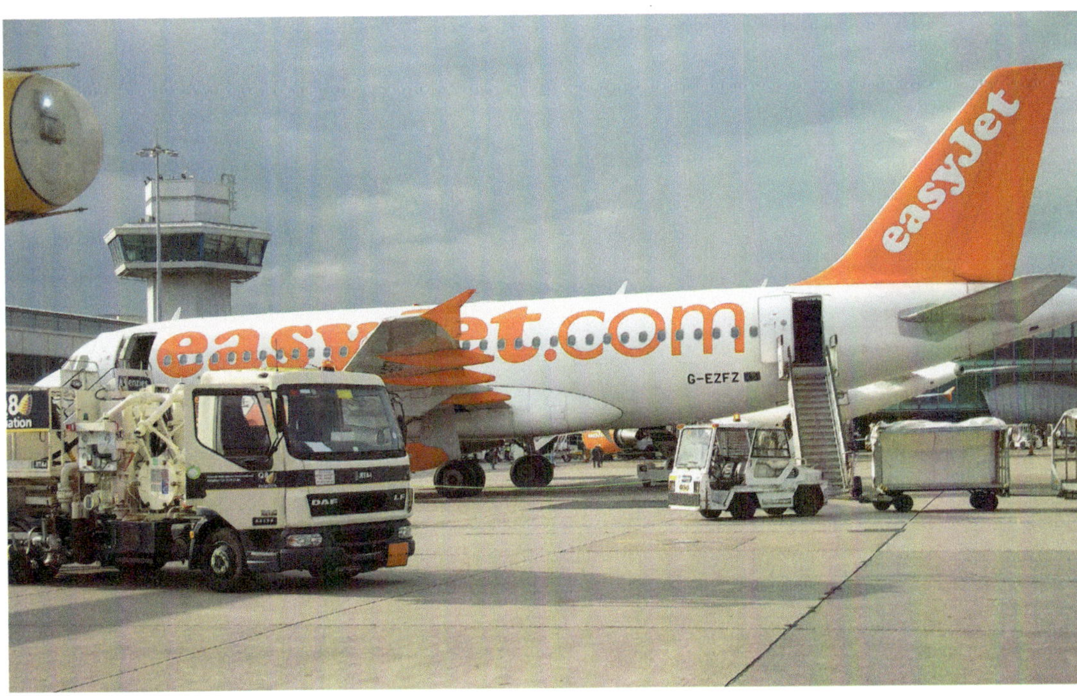

EasyJet A319-111 (G-EZFZ), amid the clutter of an aircraft turnaround at stand 1, on 10 June 2012. (Mike Welsby)

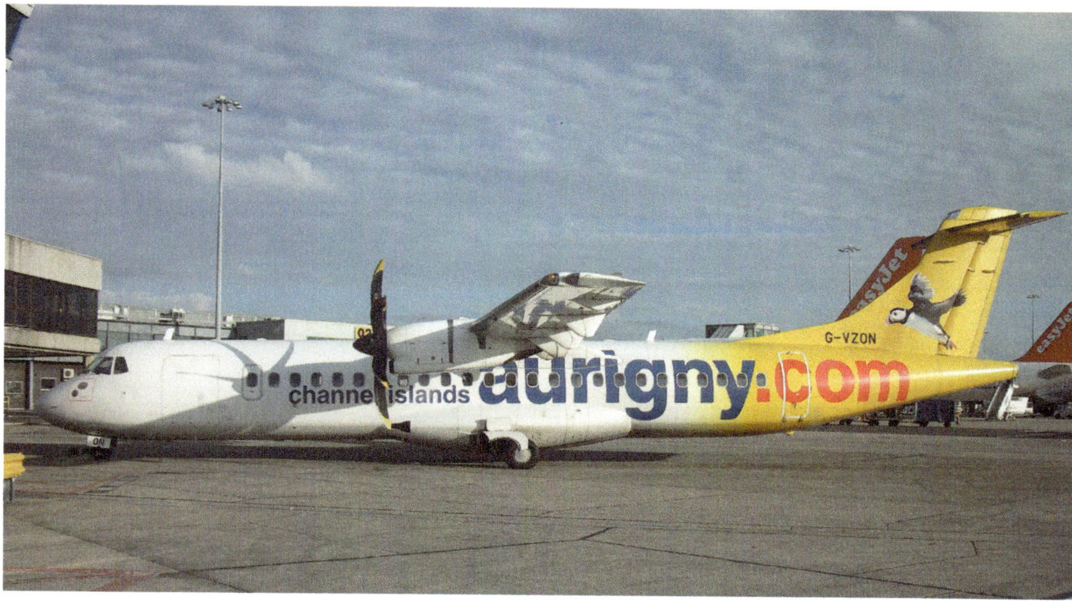

Aurigny Air Services ATR 72-212A (G-VZON), arriving at stand 21 on 28 August 2012. (Mike Welsby)

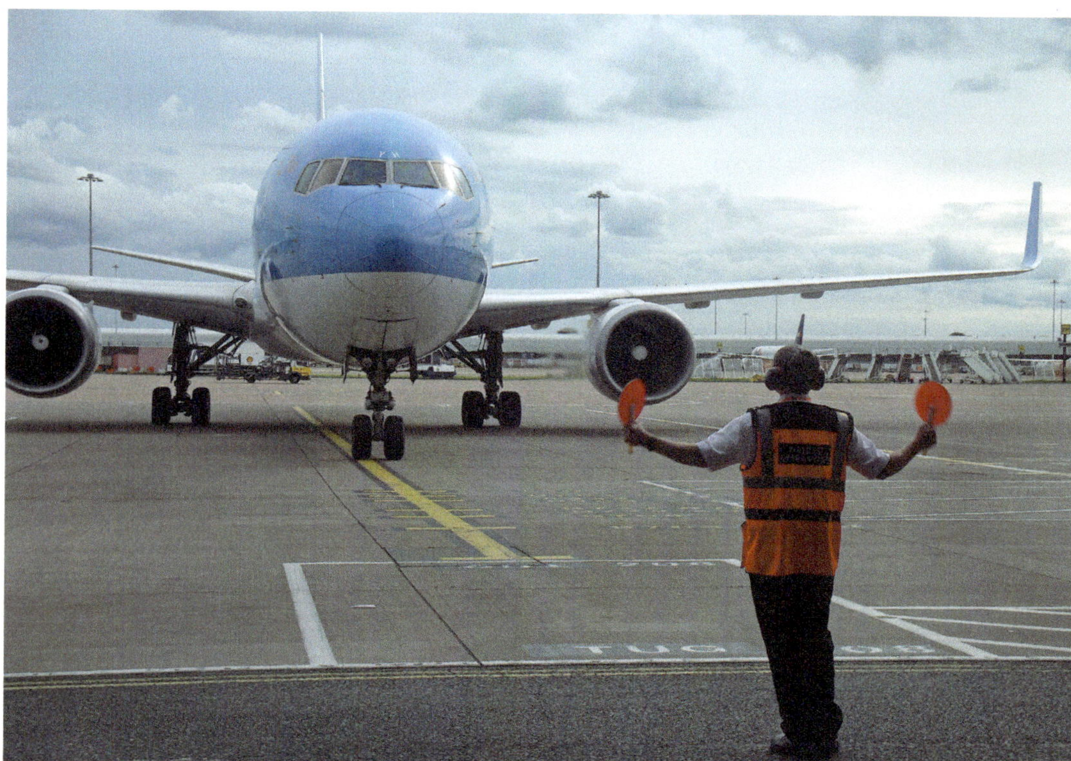

Marshalling – soon to be discontinued at Terminal 2, with the advent of an automated docking system. Thomson Airways 767-300 (G-OBYH) is being 'waved-on' to stand 208 on 12 July 2012. (Mike Welsby)

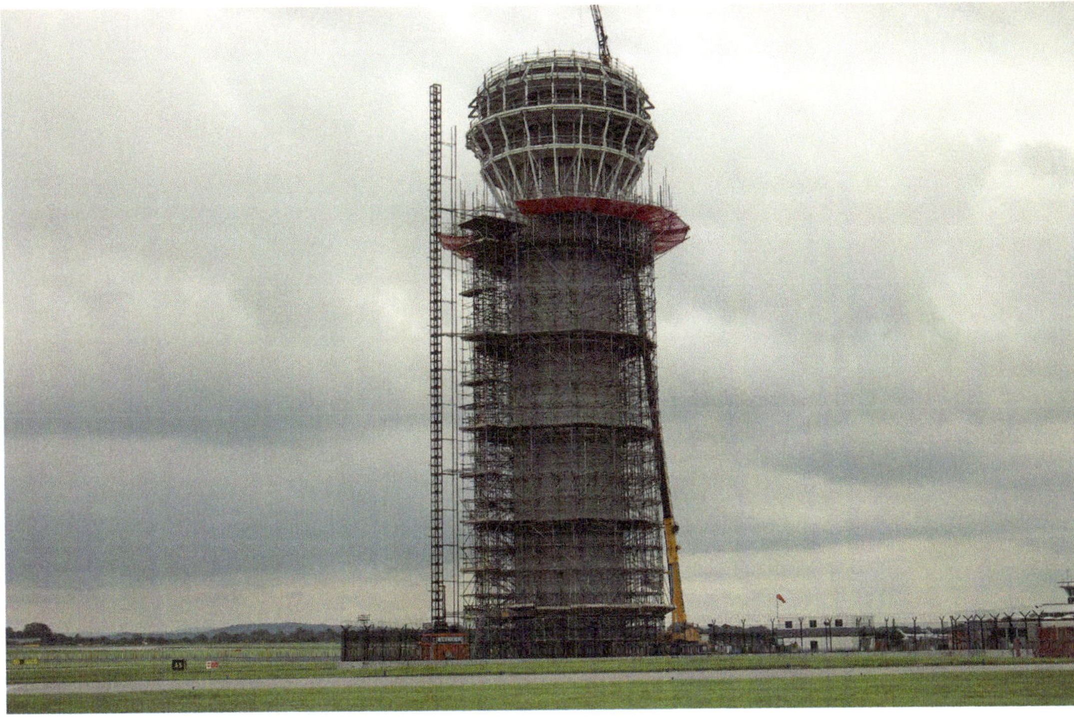

Progress on the new air traffic control tower on 11 June 2012. The central shaft took just nine days to rise from the ground to its current height of 60 metres. (Mike Welsby)

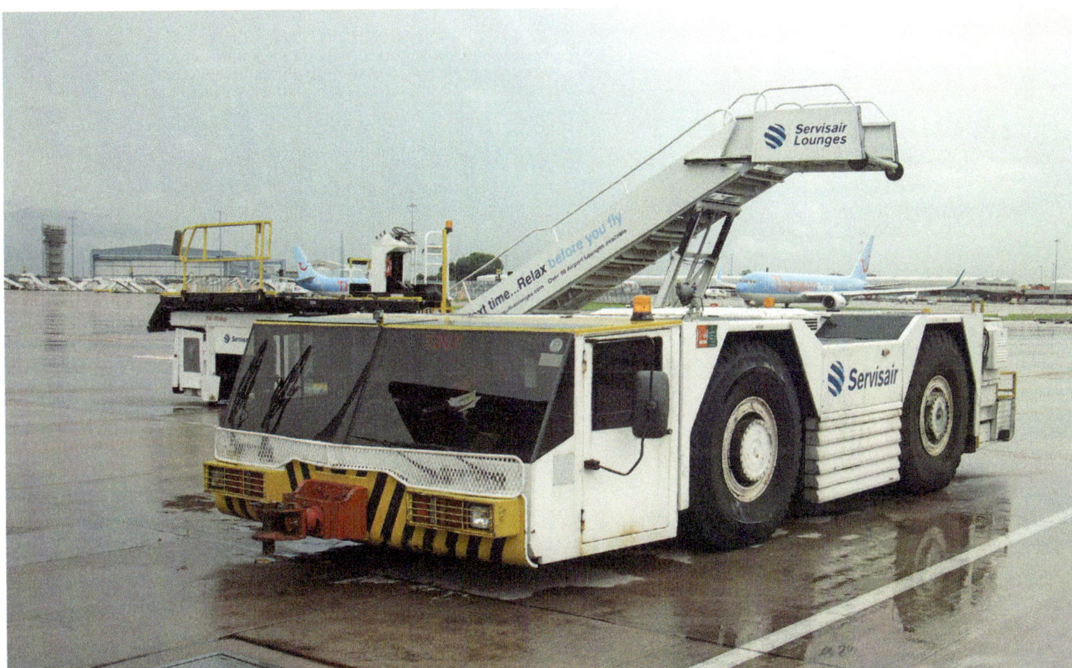

Servisair airside Pushback Tug No. 7, pictured on 2 July 2012. (Mike Welsby)

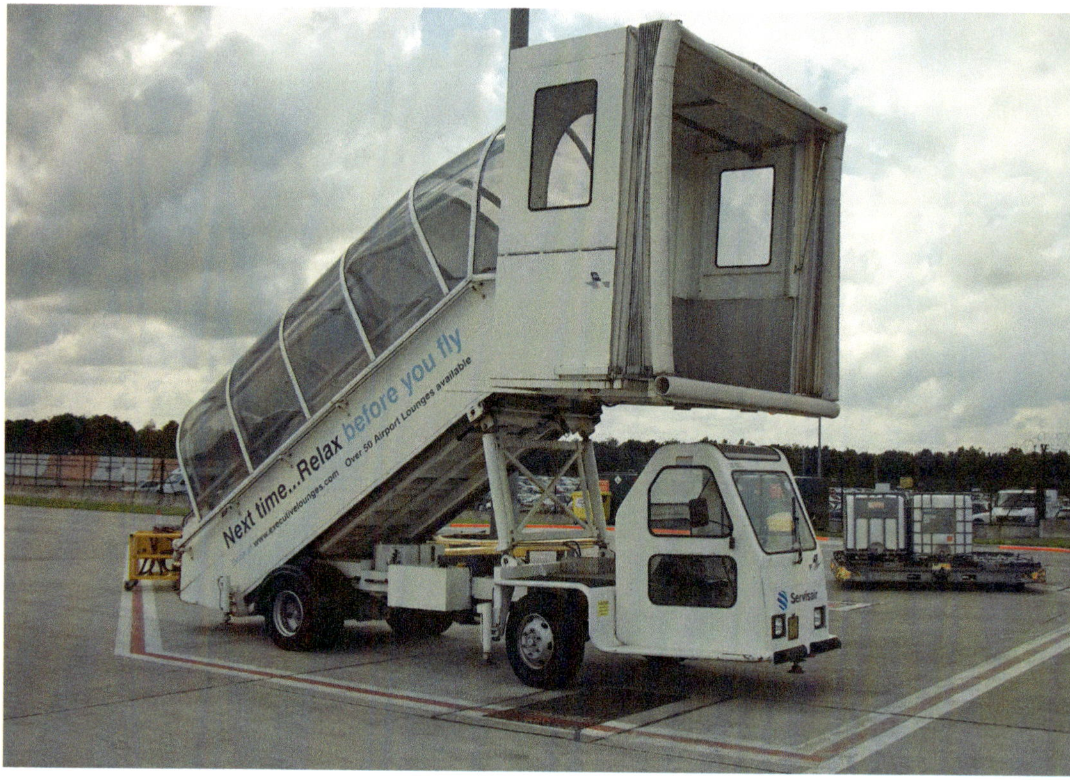

Servisair tug and steps on 8 July 2012. The aviation handling services of Servisair, which was owned by the Derichebourg Group, were acquired by Swissport in December 2013.

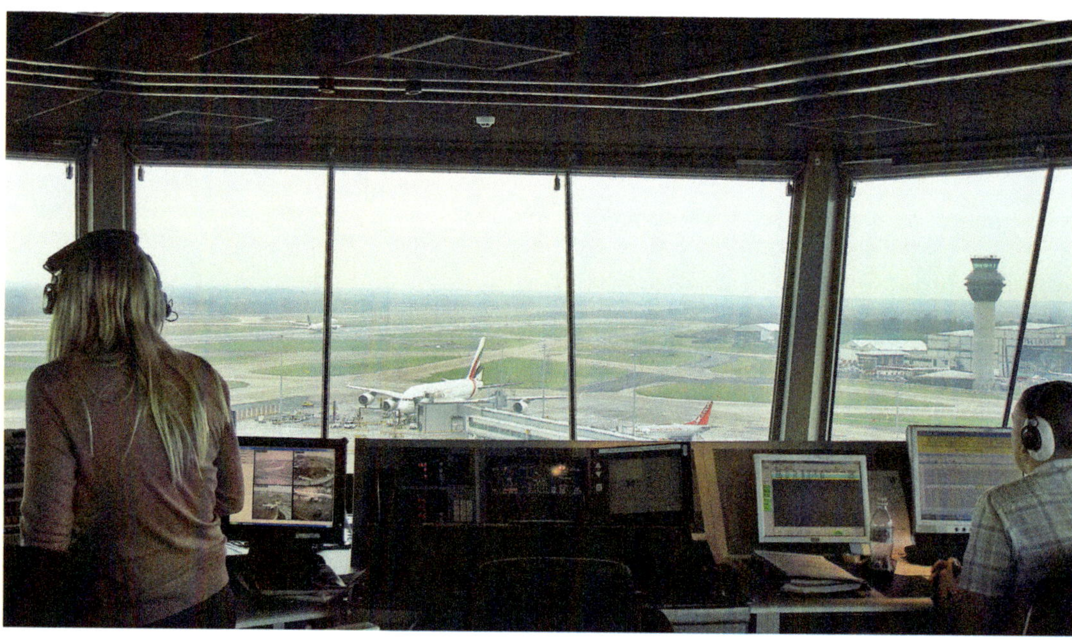

Controllers in the Visual Control Room on 17 January 2013. (David Vickers)

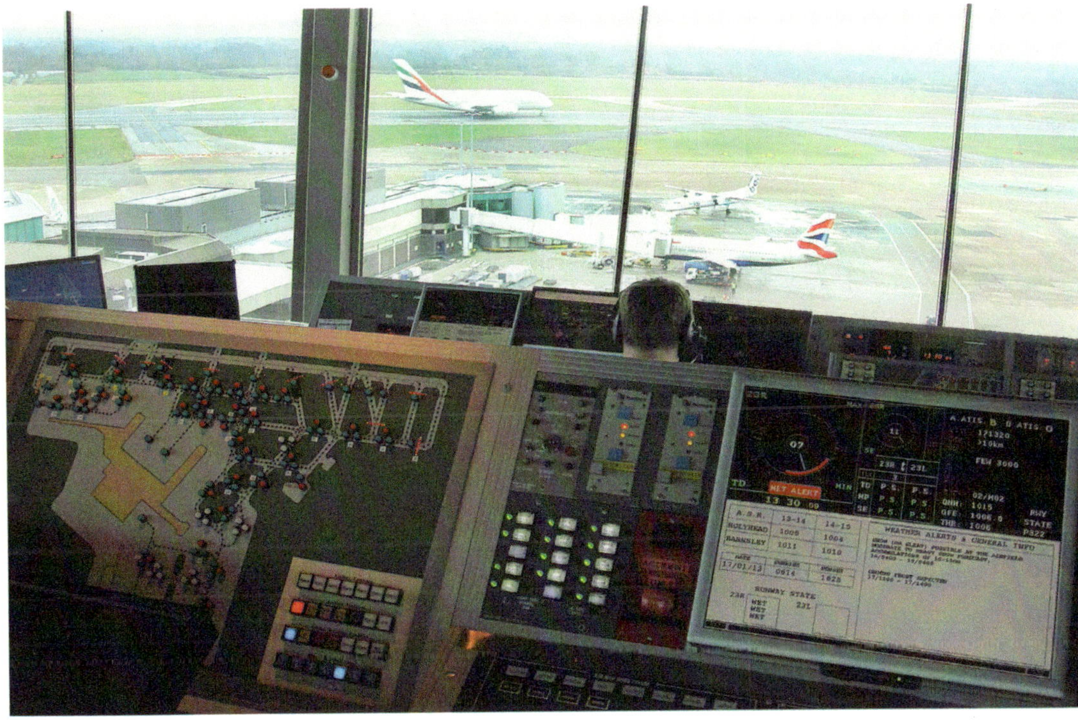

United Arab Emirates Flight UAE17 to Dubai observed from the old 1962 ATC tower on 17 Jan 2013. (David Vickers)

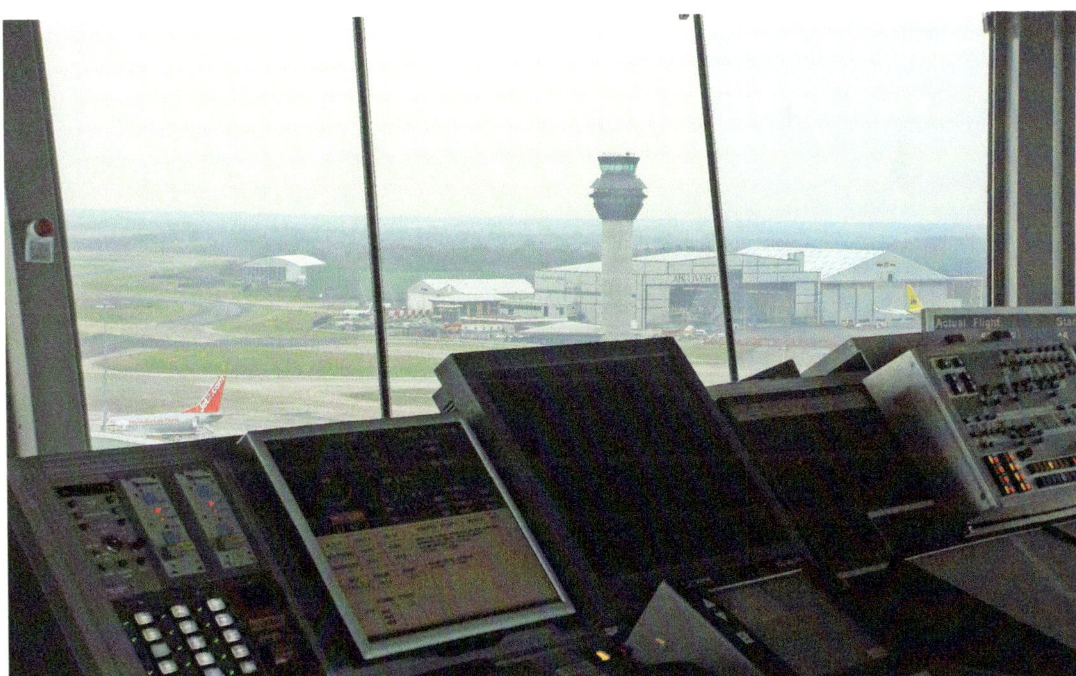

View of the new 60-m tall air traffic control tower on 17 January 2013. (David Vickers)

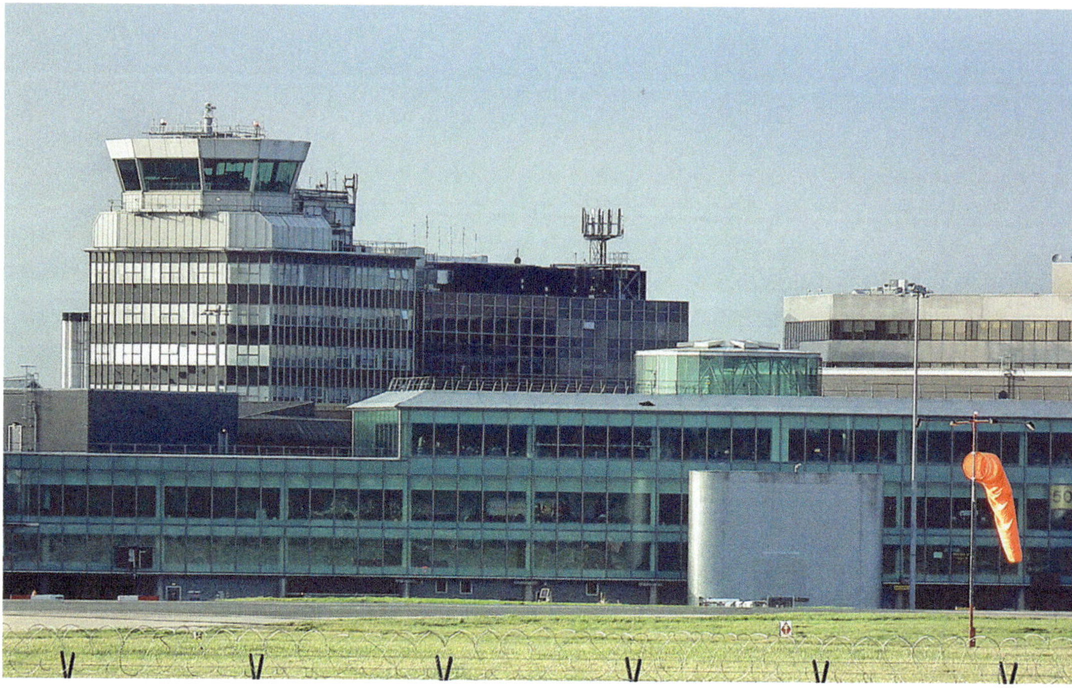

The old air traffic control tower and Terminal 3 on 17 January 2013. (David Vickers)

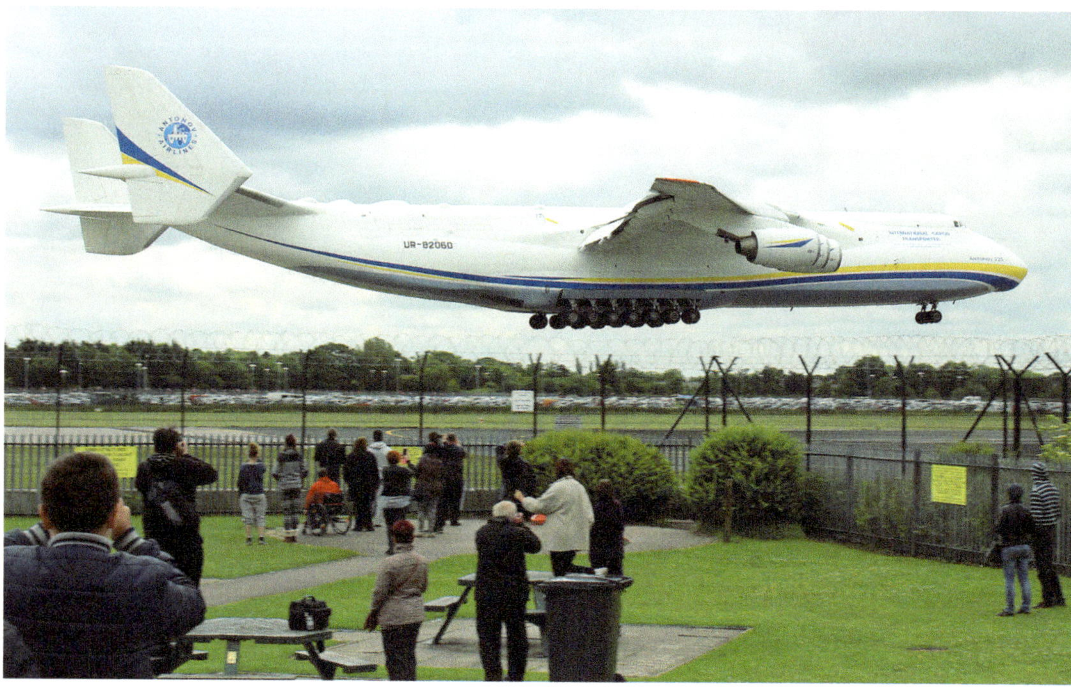

Antonov AN-225 (UR-82060) Mriya, landing on 24 June 2013. The world's largest aircraft at 84 m long, with twice the wing surface area of a Boeing 747; it has an utmost take-off weight of 640 tonnes, and thirty-two wheels. (Enda Burke)

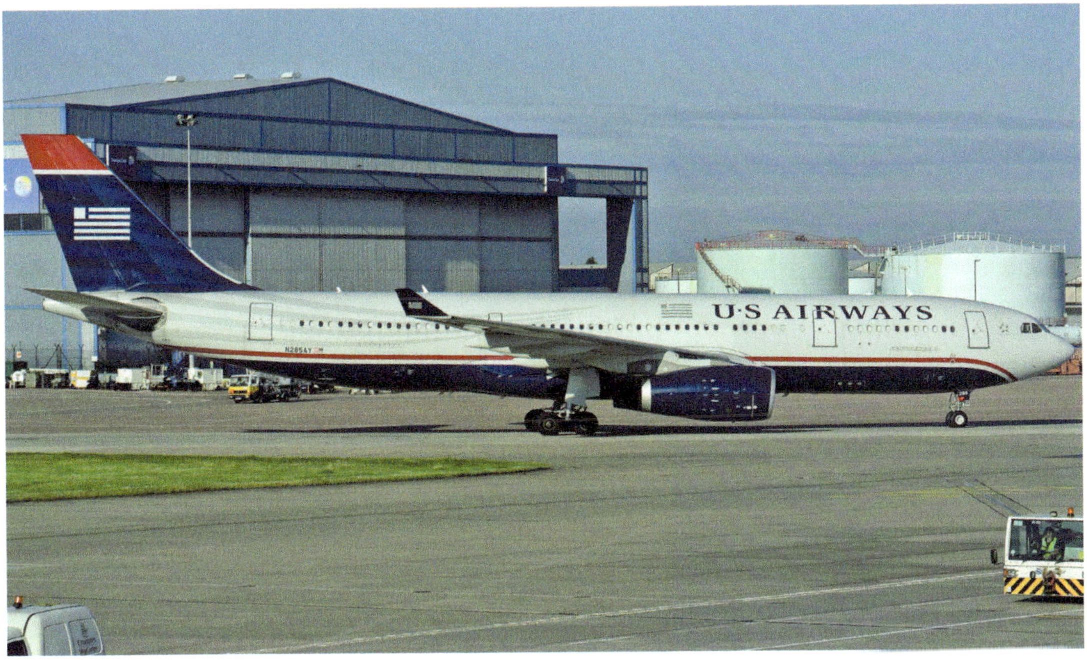

US Airways Airbus A330-243 (N285AY), arriving into Manchester from Philadelphia on its daily service on 14 August 2013. (Alan Lord)

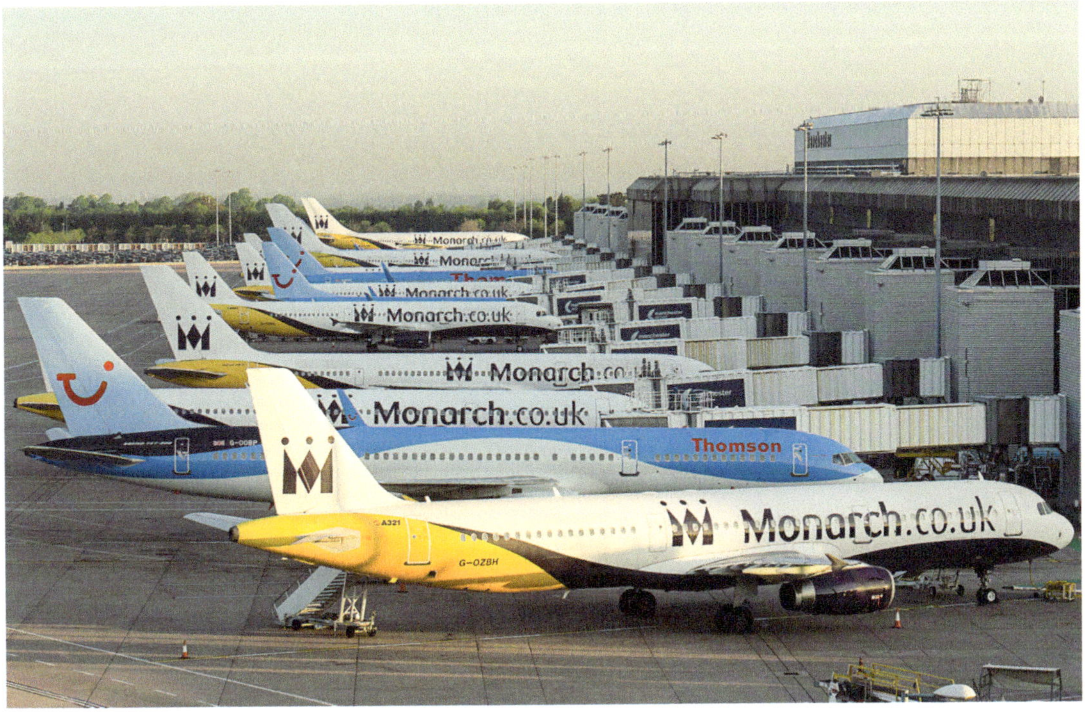

Early morning at Manchester's Terminal 2. A variety of aircraft from both Monarch Airlines and Thomson Airways has the monopoly on the stands on 26 May 2013. (Paul Atkinson)

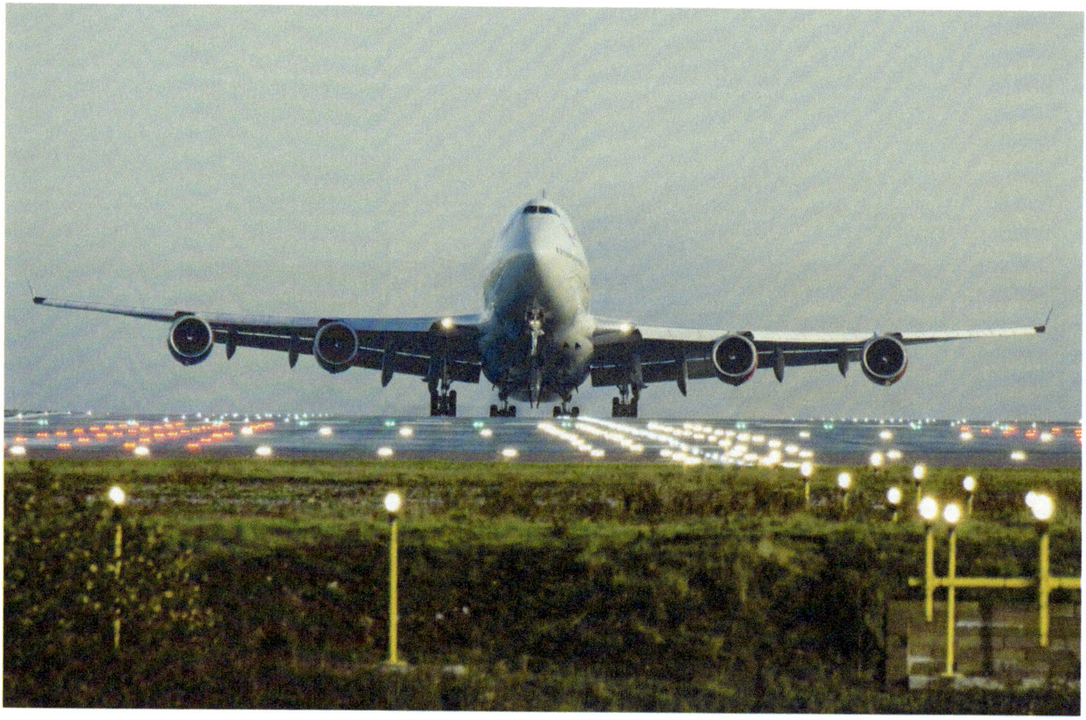

Taking off from runway 23R is Virgin Atlantic Airways Boeing 747-443 (G-VROY) *Pretty Woman* on 12 November 2013. (Paul Atkinson)

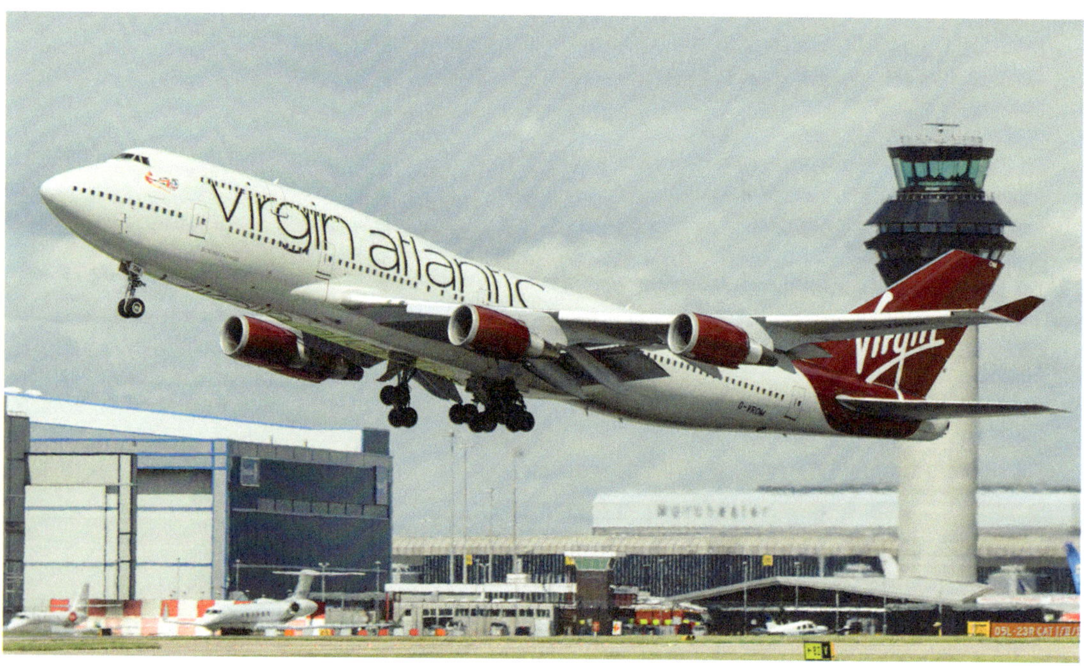

Seen on departure from Manchester's runway 23R, bound for Orlando, is Virgin Atlantic Airways Boeing 747-443 (G-VROM) *Barbarella* on 3 August 2013. (Paul Atkinson)

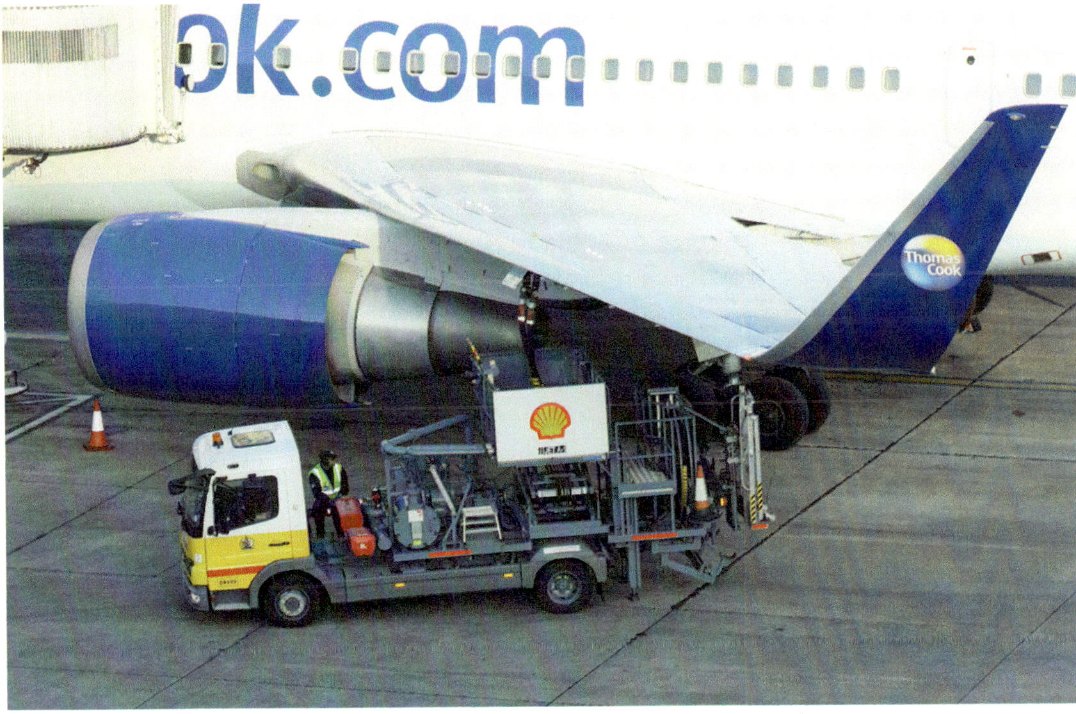

A Mercedes fuel bowser, pictured with Thomas Cook Boeing 767-31K (G-TCCB) on 19 May 2013. (NTG)

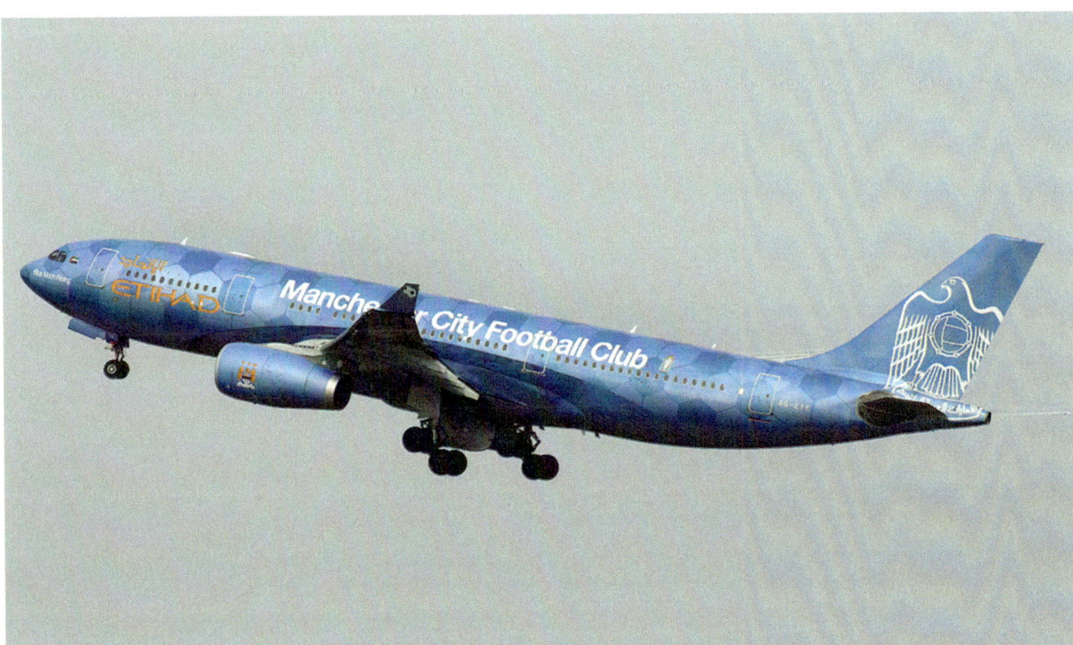

Etihad Airways Airbus A330-243 (A6-EYE) on 7 April 2013. Painted in the colours of Manchester City FC and named *Blue Moon Rising*, the football club and airline are owned by the same sheikh. (NTG)

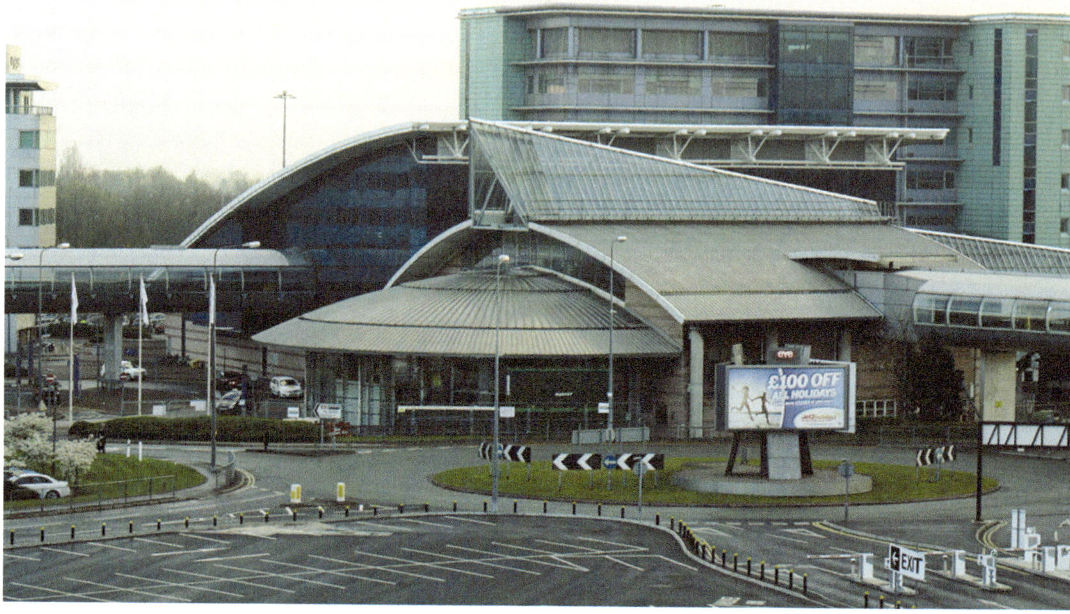

Manchester Airport railway station, which opened together with Terminal 2 in 1993. The Skylink moving walkway system links terminals 1, 2 and 3. 20 November 2013. (NTG)

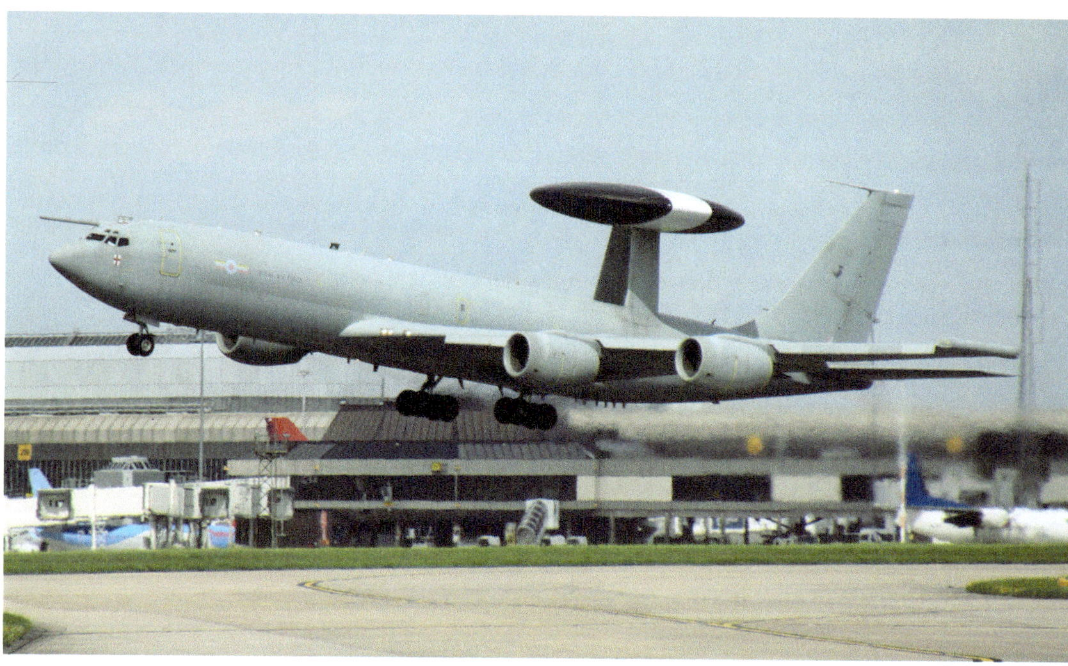

RAF Boeing Sentry AEW.1 (E-3D) (ZH101) departs on 26 April 2014 as NATO35, having diverted to MAN the night before due to bad weather at RAF Waddington. (NTG)

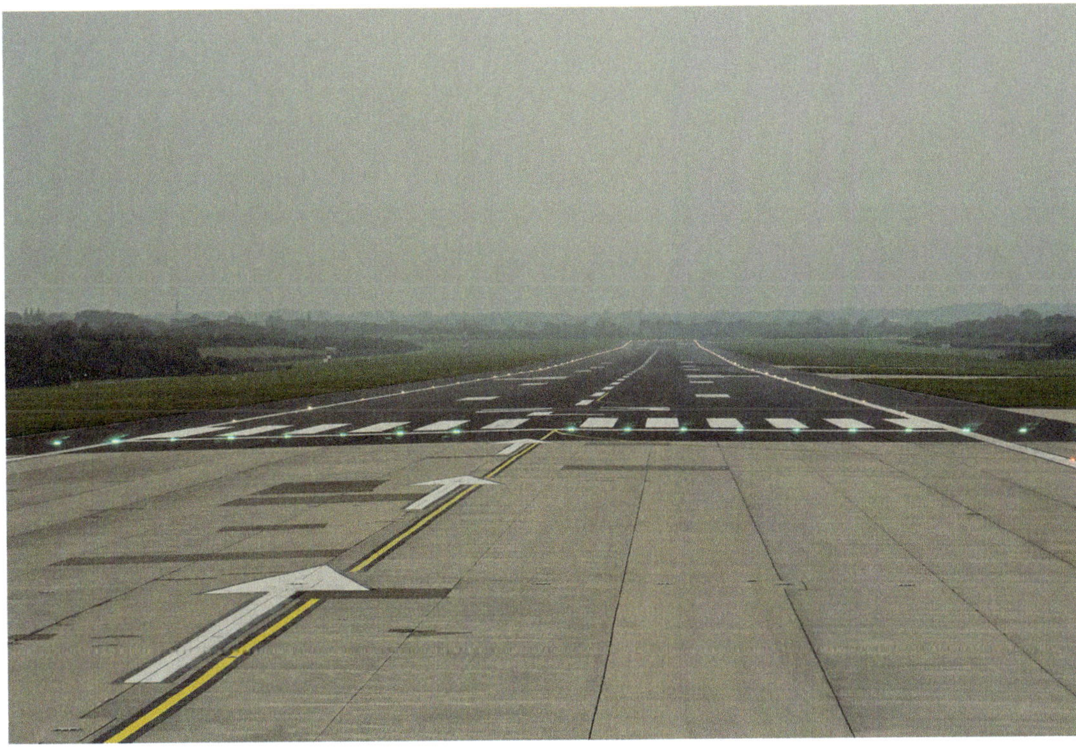

A clear runway 23L on 12 September 2014. (Paul Atkinson)

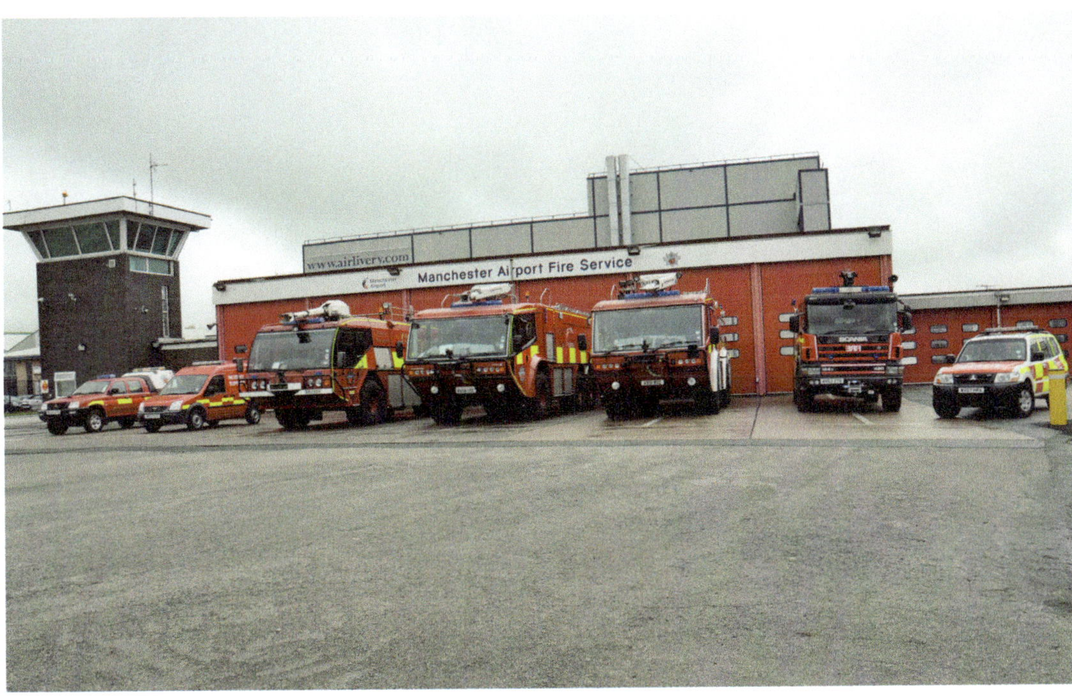

Manchester Airport Fire & Rescue Service main station line-up. (Shane Casey)

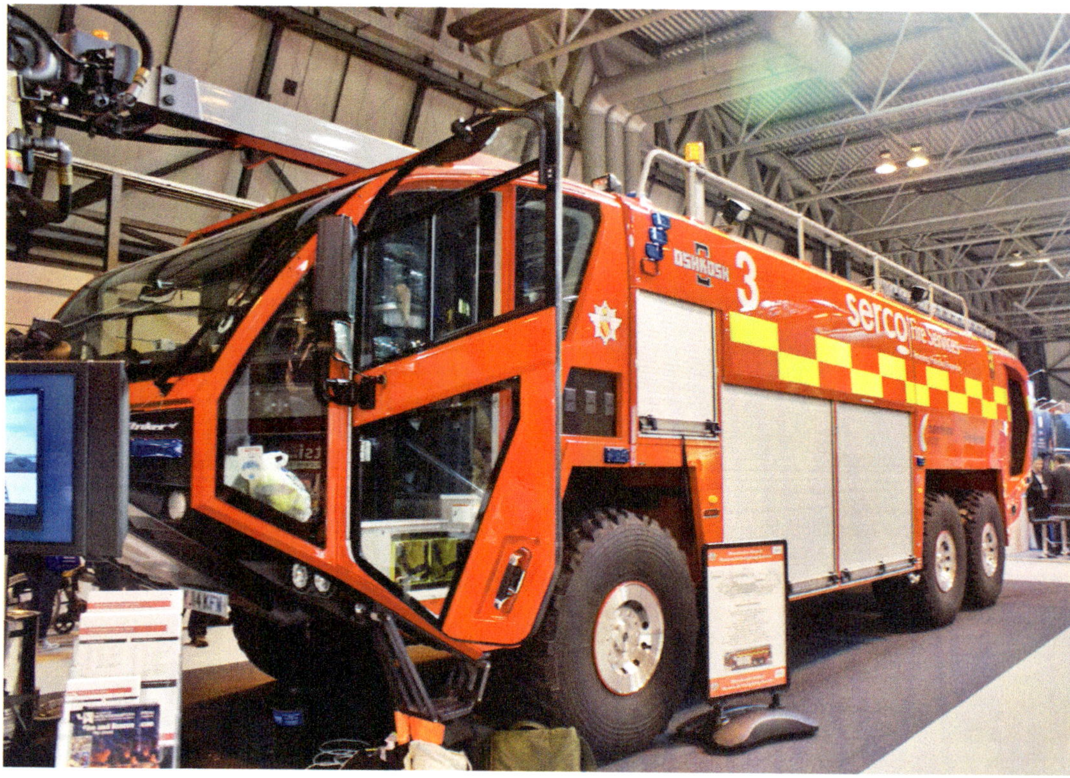

Manchester Airport Fire Service Oshkosh Striker crash tender at the NEC Emergency Services Show on 24 September 2015. (Martin Jones)

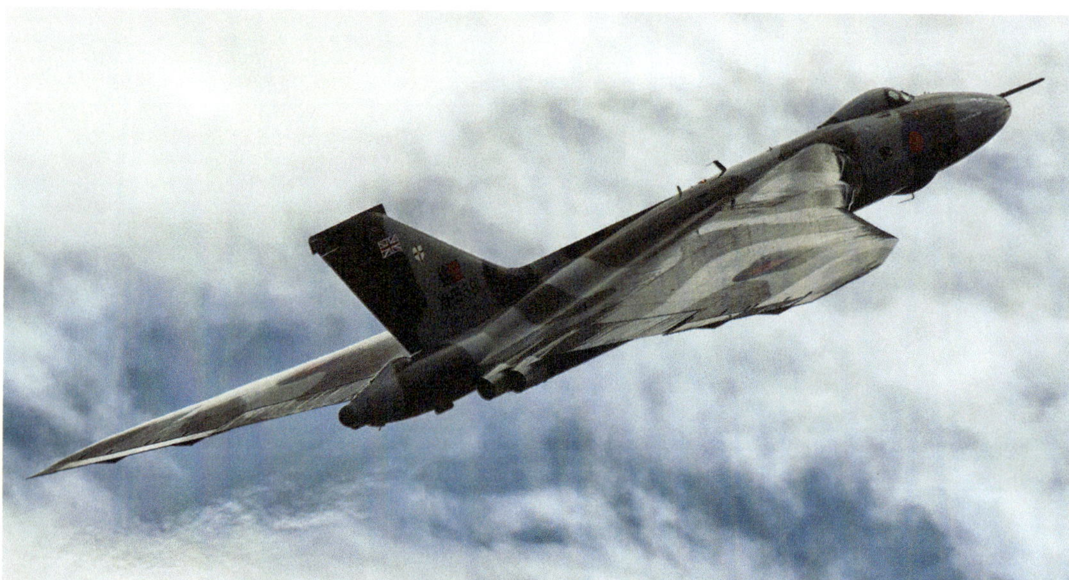

Avro Vulcan B2 (G-VLCN) (ex-XH558) *The Spirit of Great Britain* on a Manchester Airport fly-past on 27 June 2015. XH558's final ever flight occurred on 28 October 2015. (Enda Burke)

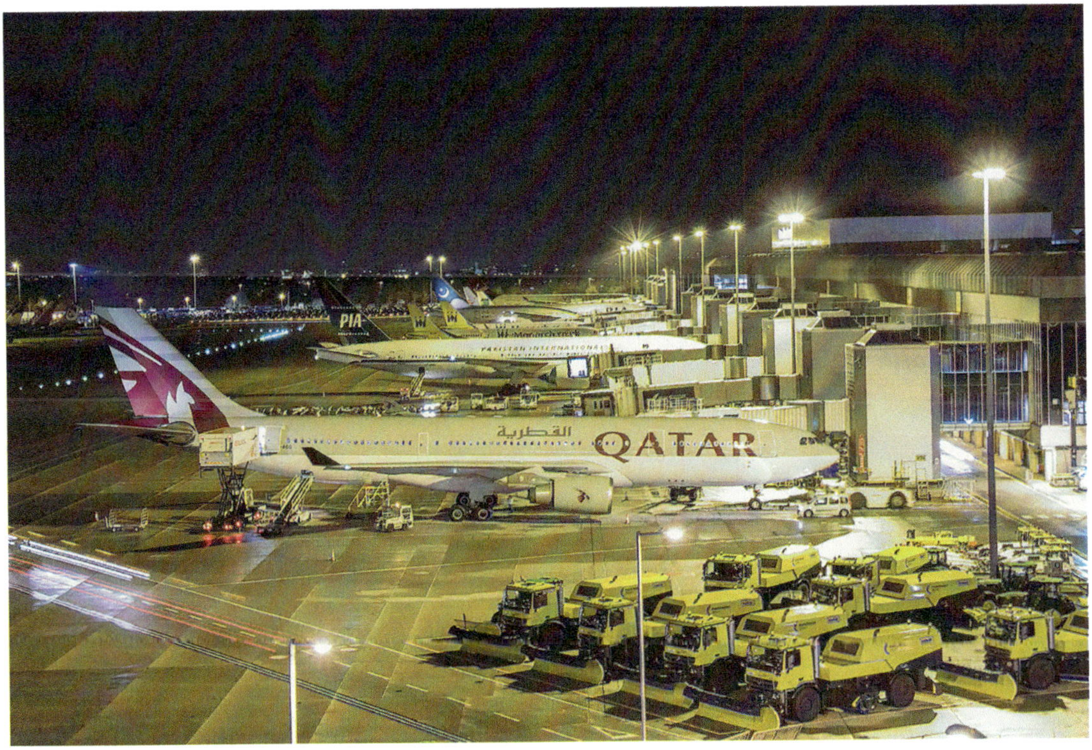

Qatar Airways Airbus A330-202 (A7-ACG) heads a line-up at Terminal 2 on the night of 8 December 2015. (Enda Burke)

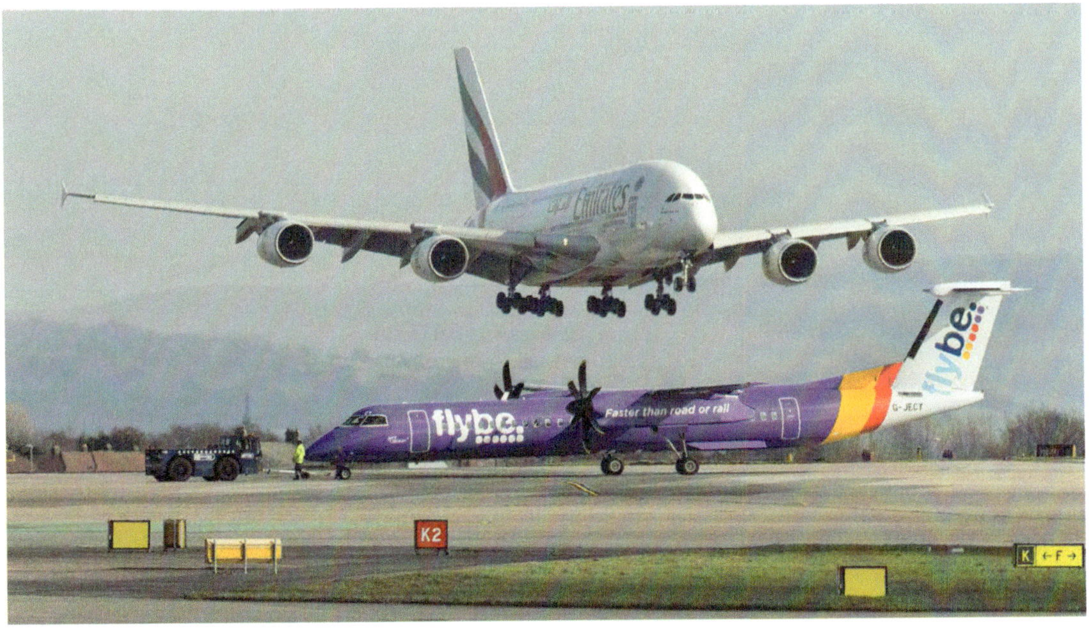

View from Manchester's Runway Visitor Park, as Flybe Bombardier DHC-8-402Q (G-JECY) is pushed back and Emirates Airbus A380-861 (A6-EED) prepares to land on 6 March 2015. (Paul Atkinson)

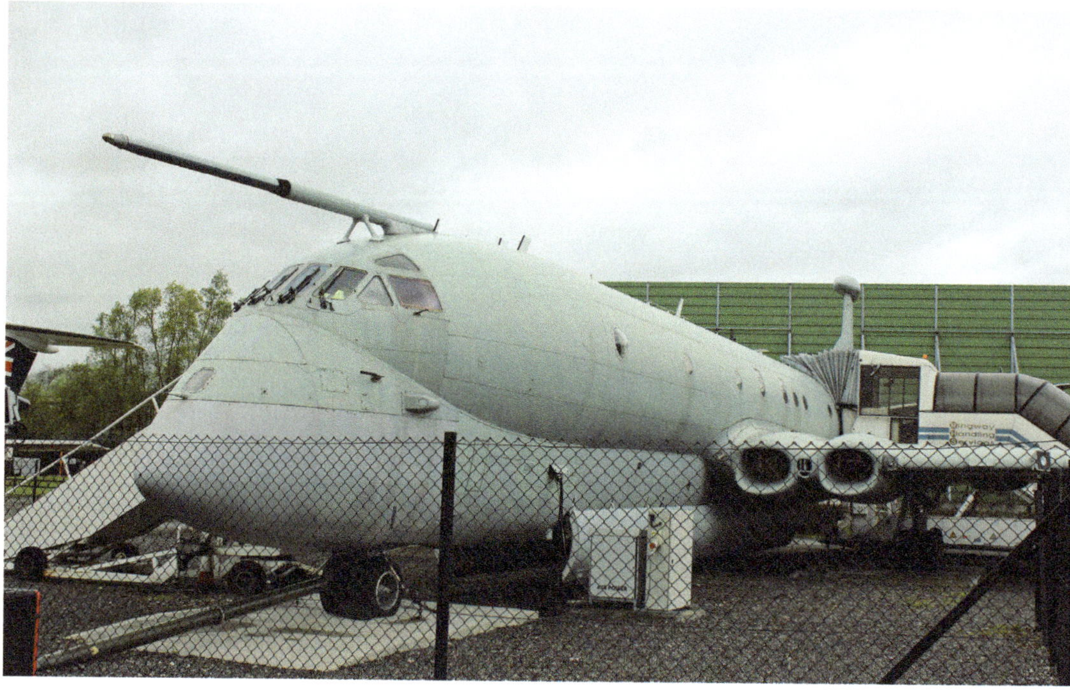

Preserved ex-RAF Hawker Siddeley Nimrod MR.2 (XV231) on display in the Runway Visitor Park on 6 May 2015. (Trevor Hall)

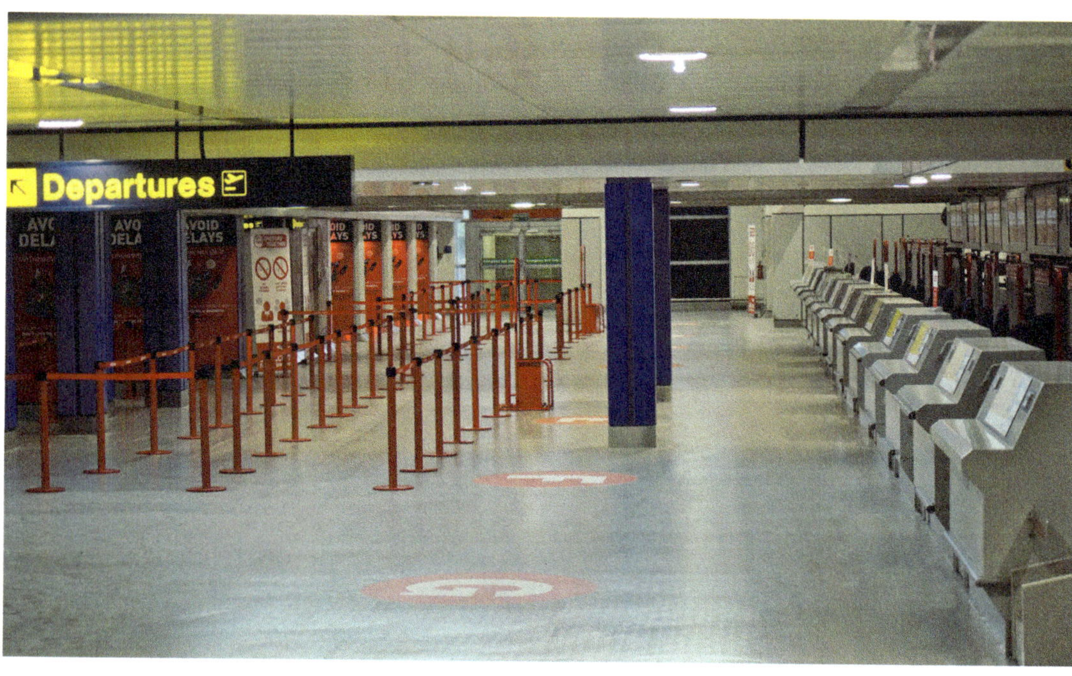

Terminal 1 ground-level Check-in B, which is now only used by Jet2. It was used by Air Canada during 2013 before they moved to Terminal 2. Terminal 1 is due to be demolished during 2024, once Terminal 2 has been completed. (Cameron Gaines)

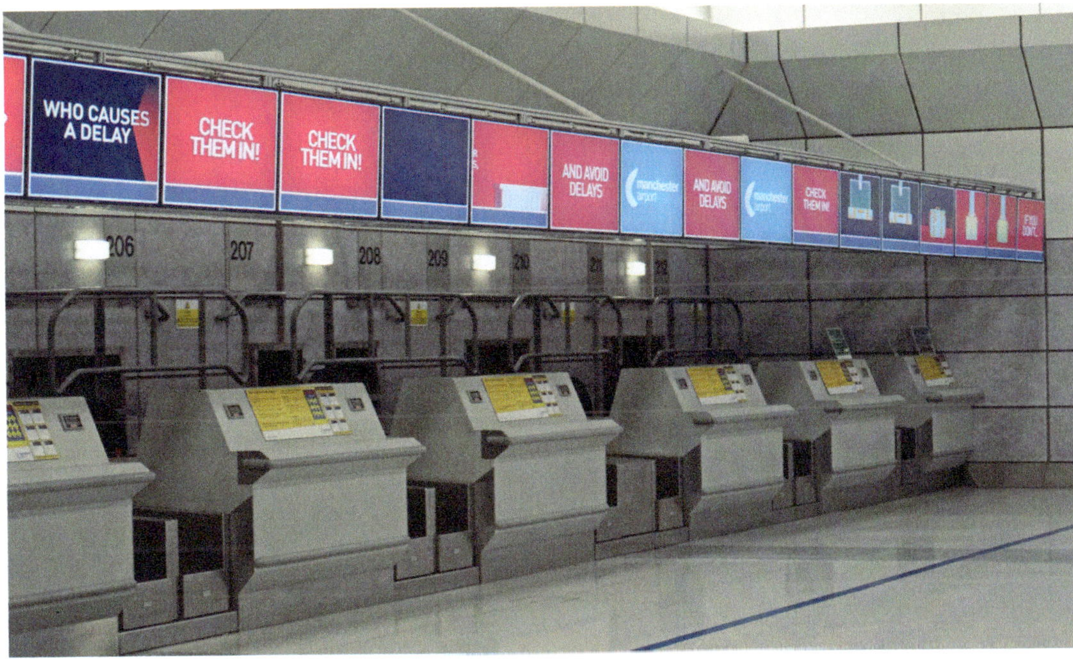

Terminal 2 lower-level check-in, which is used by Air Canada, Germania and other charter airlines. Under the £1-billion Manchester Airport Transformation Programme, the terminal is to be expanded by 140 per cent, with construction due to begin in the autumn of 2016. (Cameron Gaines)

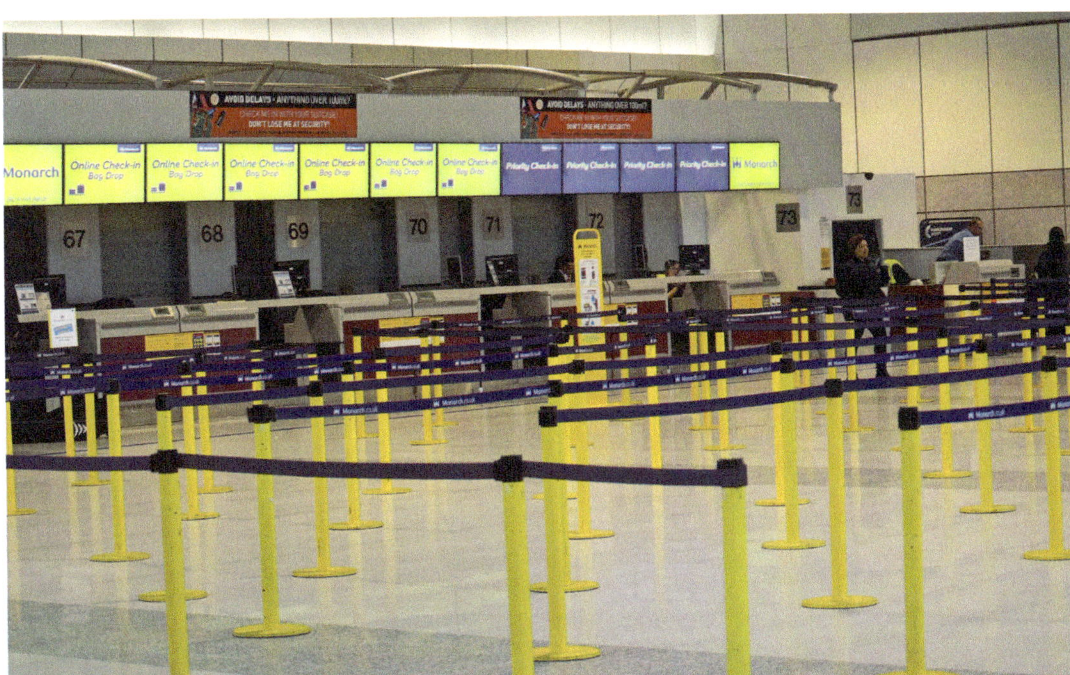

Monarch's check-in desks on the main level on the far right of the check-in hall in Terminal 2. (Cameron Gaines)

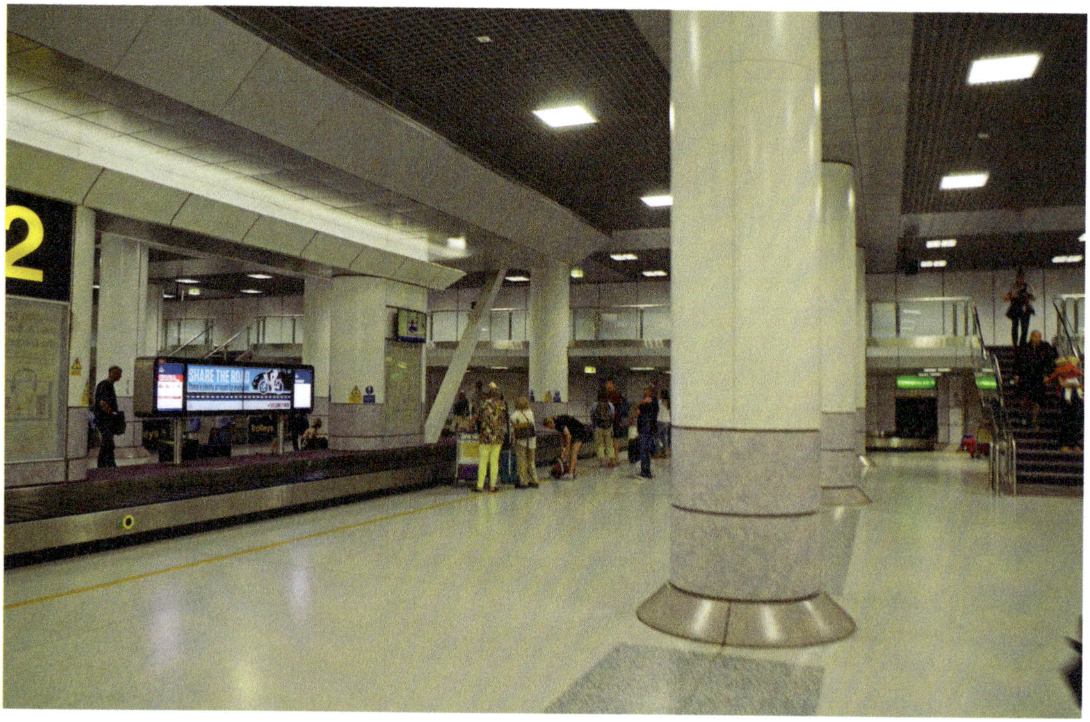

The baggage hall in Terminal 2 on 30 March 2016. (Michael Humphries)

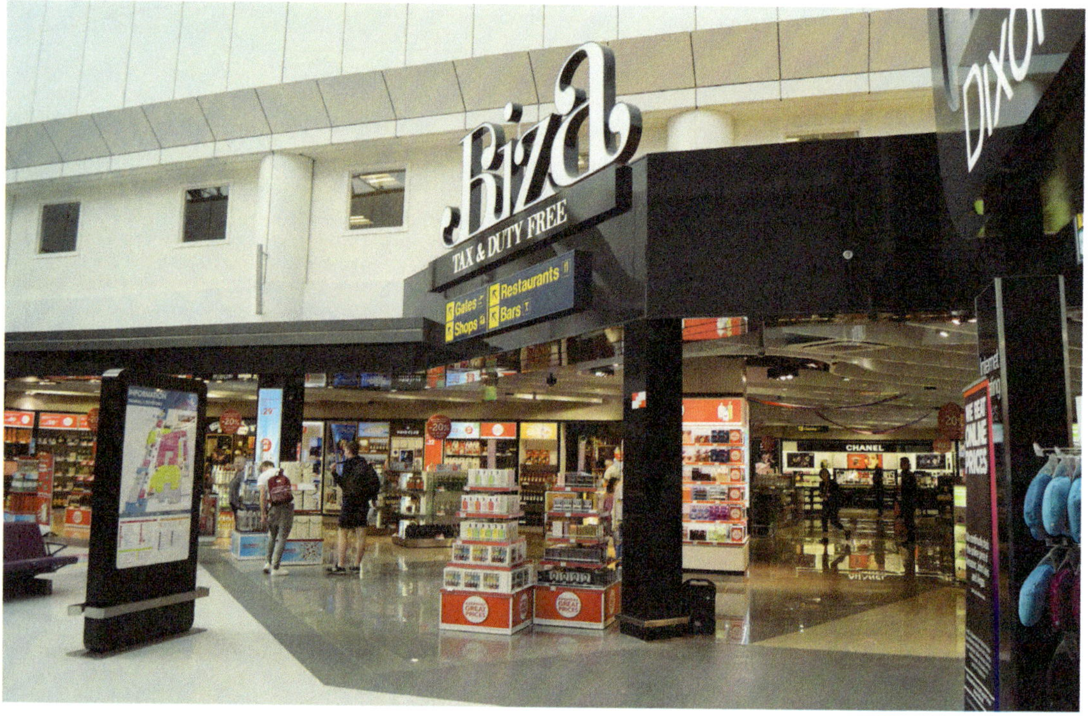

Terminal 2 shopping concourse and the Biza tax and duty free shop. (Cameron Gaines)

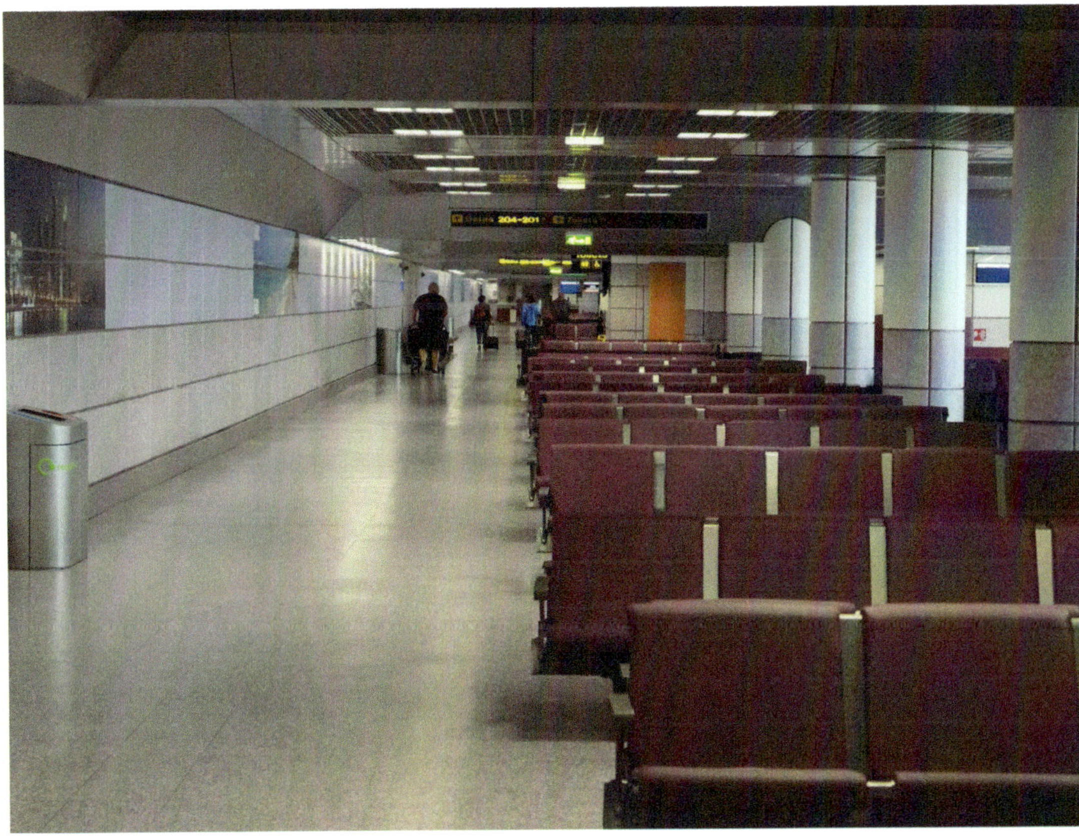

Terminal 2 waiting area for Gate 204–201. (Cameron Gaines)

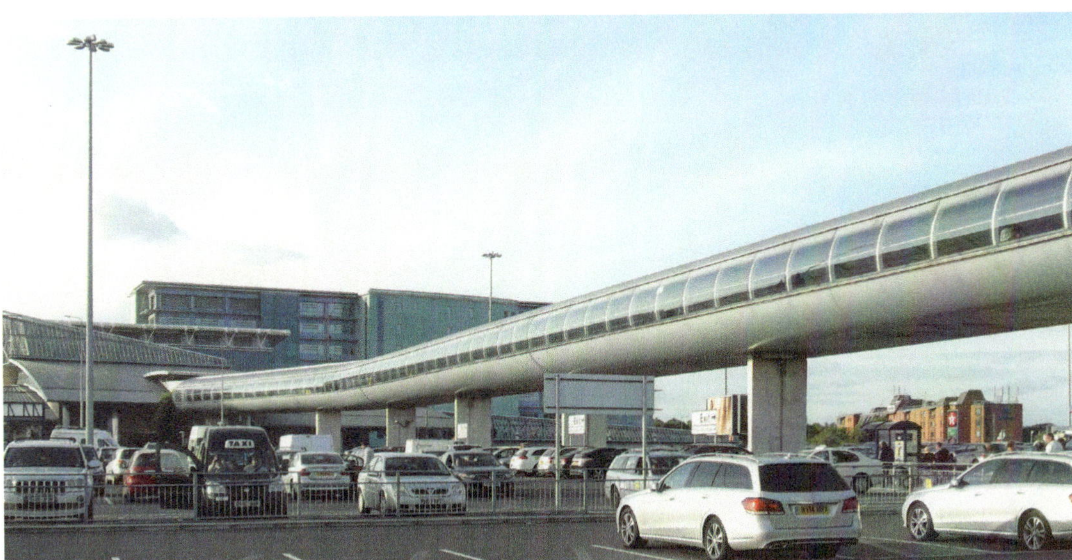

The 'Skyway' pedestrian link from Terminal 3 to Manchester railway station on 17 June 2014. (Robert Wade)

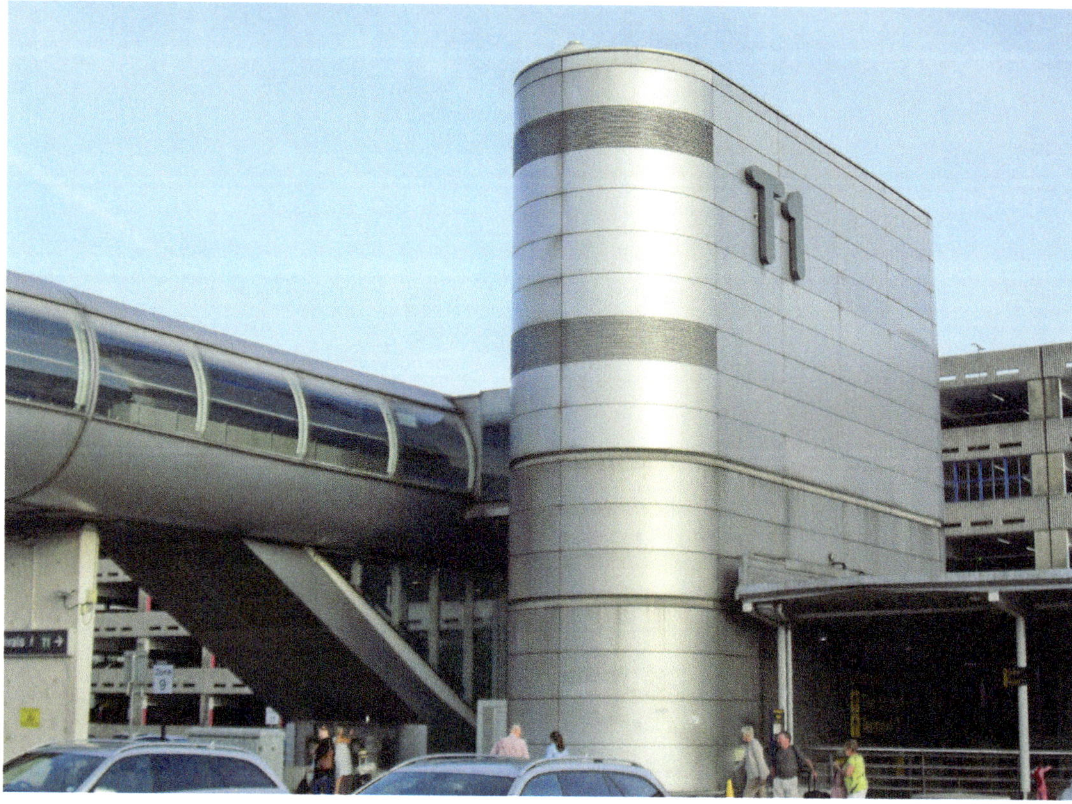

Terminal 1 on 17 June 2014. Originally built in 1962, it is set to be phased out by 2022. (Robert Wade)

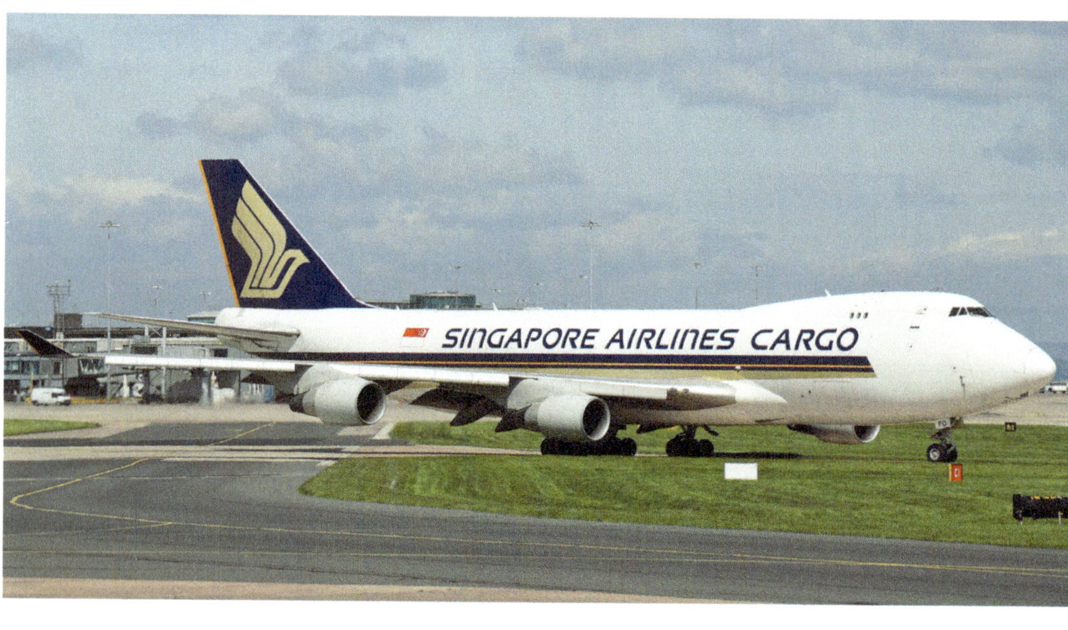

Singapore Airlines Cargo Boeing 747-412F (9V-SFO), taxiing to 05L for a flight to Amsterdam (AMS) on 30 May 2016. (Cameron Gaines)

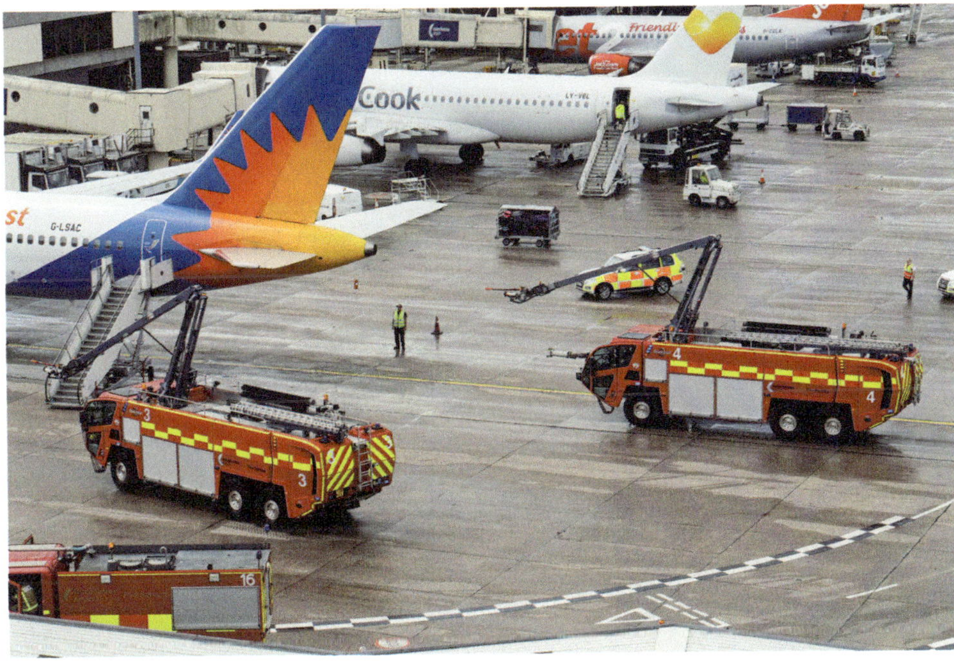

Jet2 Boeing 757-23A(WL) (G-LSAC), parked at stand 22 (Terminal 1) and surrounded by four fire engines after smoke was seen coming from the aircraft's undercarriage. The airport fire service remained at the aircraft until it had been reduced to a safe temperature. 24 June 2016. (Cameron Gaines)

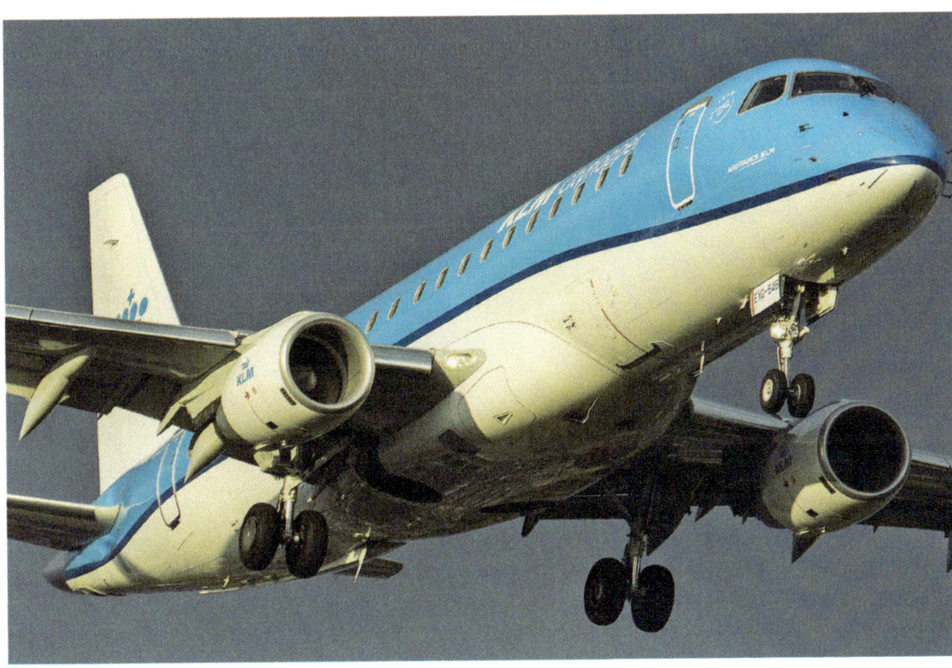

KLM Cityhopper Embraer ERJ-175STD (PH-EXG), taking off from MAN on 23 May 2016. (Enda Burke)

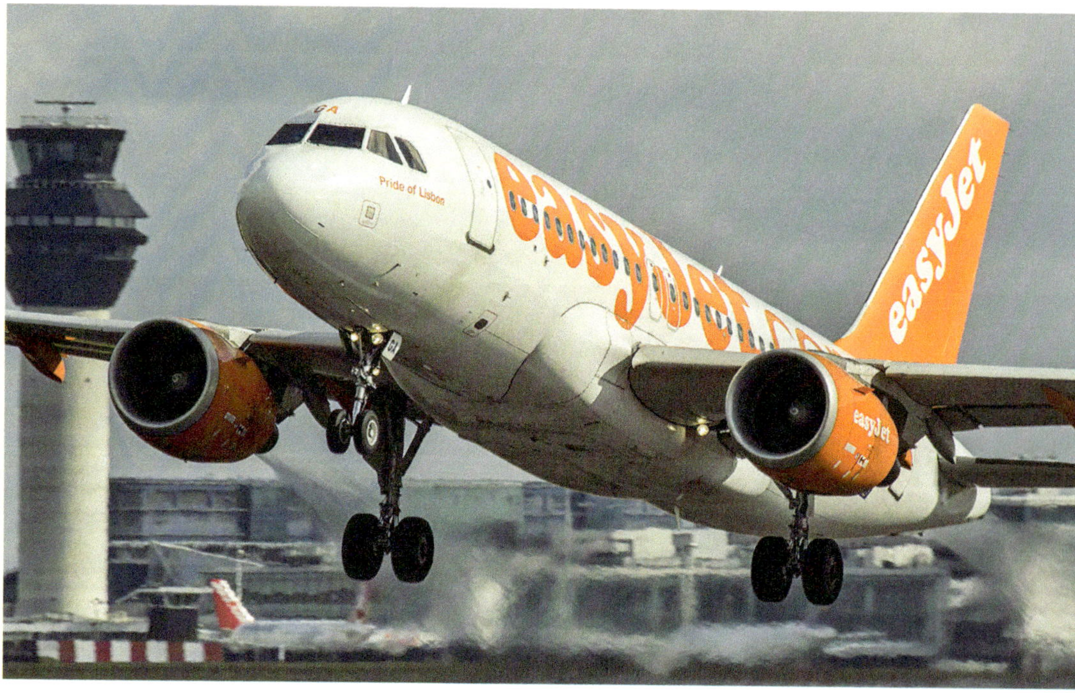

easyJet Airbus 319-111 (G-EZGA) *Pride of Lisbon,* taking off from MAN on 9 April 2016. (Enda Burke)

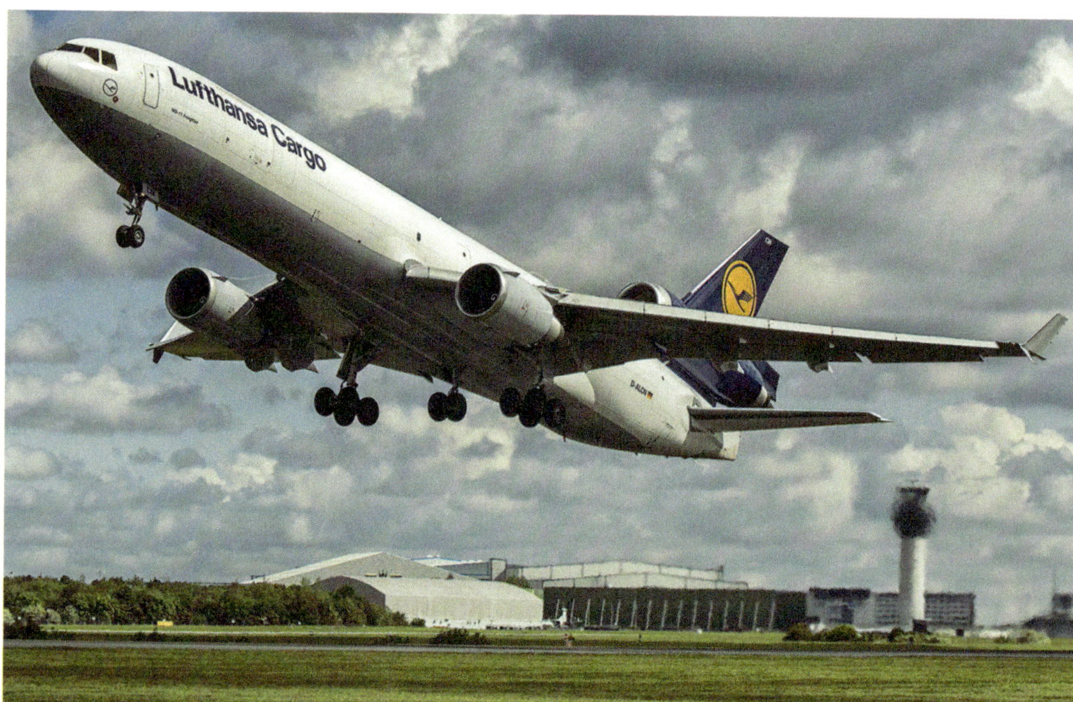

Lufthansa Cargo McDonnell Douglas MD-11F (D-ALCN) takes to the skies on 23 May 2016. (Enda Burke)

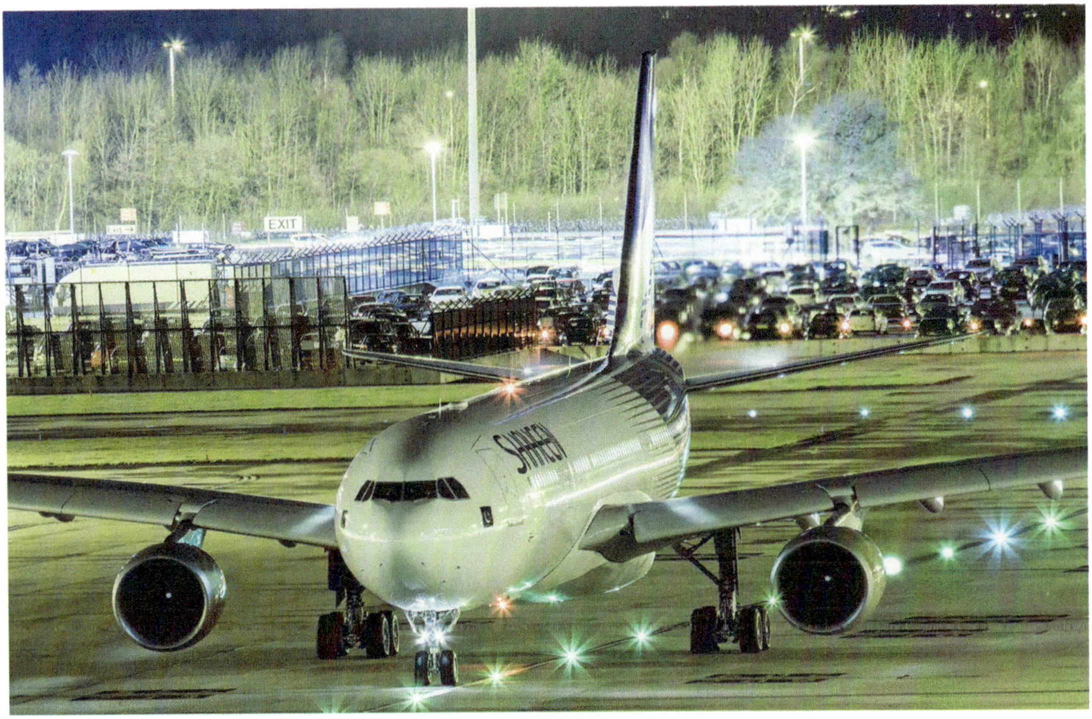

Karachi-based Shaheen Air International Airbus A330-203 (AP-BMI) on 27 March 2016. (Enda Burke)

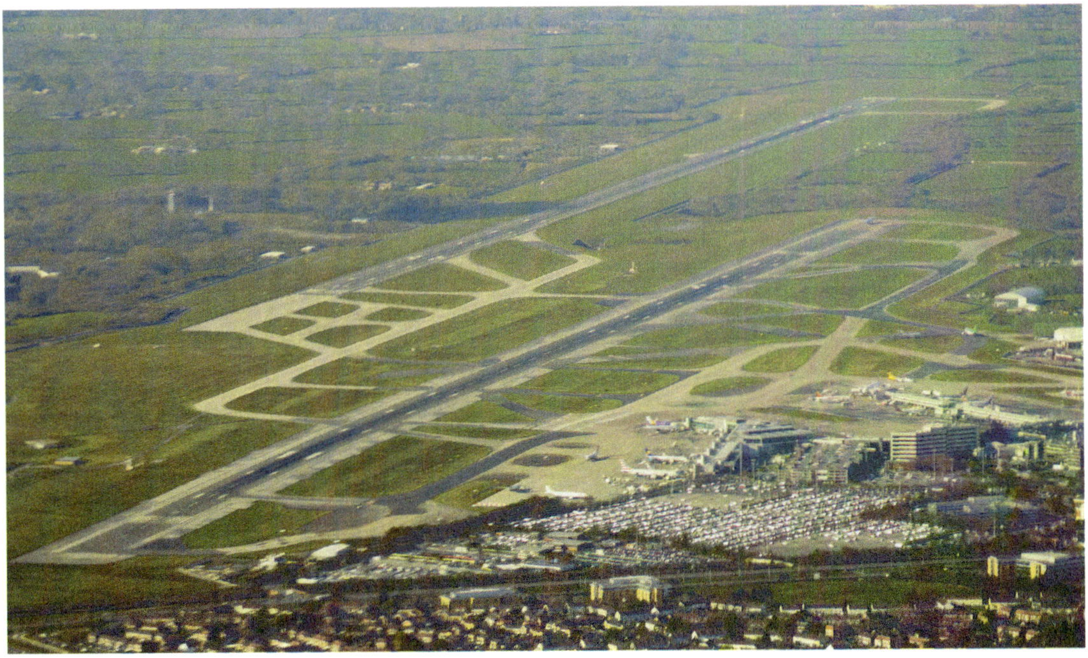

Aerial view of Manchester Airport in 2016. Terminal 2 is on the left, with Pier 'C' of Terminal 1 at the top of the photograph. (Cameron Gaines)

Air Accidents at Manchester Airport

An Armstrong Whitworth Whitley bomber, converted for carrying paratroopers, collided with another during an exercise on 23 February 1944, and crashed in flames 200 yards from a hangar. The other Whitley had a wing torn off. Miraculously, all personnel escaped relatively unharmed.

On 19 August 1949, a BEA Douglas DC-3 (G-AHCY), en route from Belfast, crashed into the side of a cloud-covered hill at about 1,400 ft, 15 miles short of Manchester Airport. All three crew members were killed and there were only eight survivors out of the twenty-nine passengers.

A Douglas C-47 Skytrain cargo aircraft (G-AJVZ), operated by Air Transport Charter, left Runway 6 on 27 March 1951 in freezing conditions for Nutts Corner Airport, Antrim, Northern Ireland. However, it failed to climb and clipped the top of a tree in Woodhouse Lane, close to the hamlet of Heyhead, half a mile from the end of the runway. It crashed in to an adjacent field, killing the crew of two.

BEA Vickers Viscount 701 *RMA Discovery* (G-ALWE), the first Viscount 701 type to be manufactured by Vickers in 1952, hit a house in Wythenshawe on approach to Manchester Airport after a flight from Amsterdam Schiphol International Airport on 14 March 1957. Twenty passengers and crew died in the crash, as did two people in the house. The cause of the crash was metal fatigue in flaps, causing loss of control.

A Meridian Air Maps Miles Aerovan 4 (G-AISF) crashed on take-off from Manchester. It hit the metal perimeter fence, which flipped it over. It then slid on its back across the B road and into a field. At least three people survived, but pilot Jean Lennox Bird, the first woman to receive RAF wings, and two passengers were killed.

What is referred to as the Stockport air disaster occurred on 4 June 1967. A Canadair C-4 Argonaut (G-ALHG) was carrying holidaymakers back from the Balearic Islands to Manchester Airport when its Nos 3 and 4 engines suddenly cut out. The aircraft crashed in an open area between buildings close to the town centre of Stockport. A plaque was unveiled at the site by two survivors of the crash in 1998, in memory of the seventy-two passengers and crew who were killed.

On 22 August 1985, a British Airtours Boeing 737-236 (G-BGJL), full of holidaymakers on Flight KT 328 bound for Corfu, was forced to abort its take-off because of an engine fire. A turbine blade in the port engine had broken from its cowling and punctured the fuel tank, severing the main fuel line. Hundreds of gallons of fuel was ignited and created an inferno as it sprayed along the fuselage. Only the flight deck remained intact, and fifty-three of the 131 passengers and two crew members were killed, in the biggest disaster in Manchester's history. Most of the deaths were due to smoke inhalation. It was announced on 6 August 1987 that purser Arthur Bradbury, stewardess Joanna Toff and two firemen of the Manchester Airport Fire Brigade had been awarded the Queen's Gallantry Medal for their bravery and professionalism in evacuating passengers from the smoke-filled aircraft. The award was also given posthumously to the two stewardesses in the aft section of the aircraft, who died in the fire: Jacqueline Urbanski and Sharon Ford.

The last airworthy de Havilland DH98 Mosquito T3 (G-ASKH) crashed near Barton airfield during an air show on 21 July 1996. Its aerial display was nearing its conclusion, with a fly past along the display axis from east to west that was followed by a steep climb into a 'wingover' to the right. During this, it was observed to have made a number of uncontrolled manoeuvres. Control appeared to have been regained, but at too low a height to prevent impact with the ground in front of hundreds of spectators. Pilot Kevin Moorhouse and his engineer Steve Watson were killed.